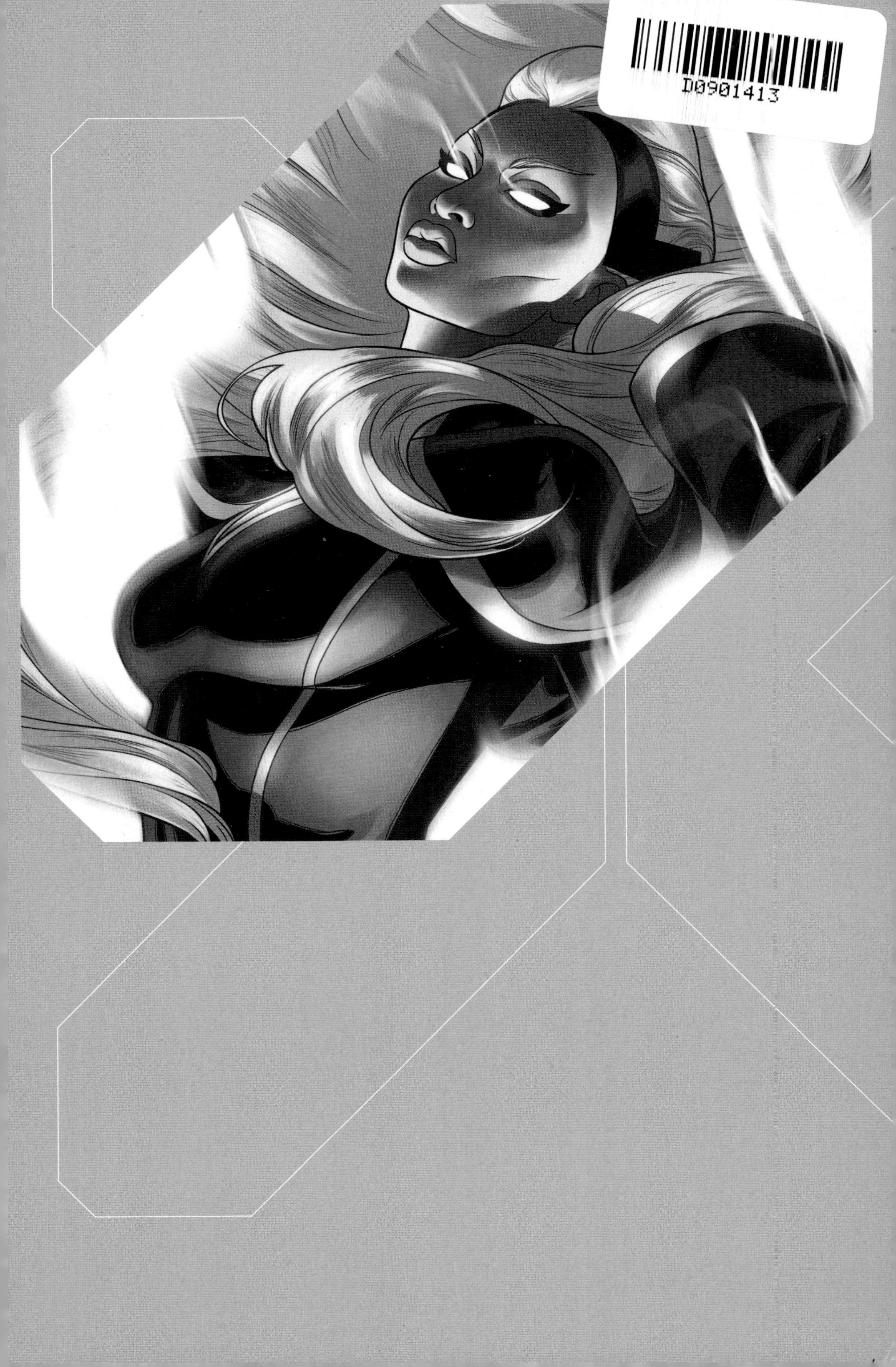

DAWN OF X VOL. 16. Contains material originally published in magazine form as GIANT-SIZE X-MEN: STORM (2020) 1, X-FORCE
(2019) 11-12, EXCALIBUR (2019) 11-12 and X-MEN (2019) 12. First printing 2021. ISBN 978-1-302-92773-8. Published by MARVEL
WORLDWIDE, INC., a subsidiary of MARVEL ENTERTAINMENT, LLC. OFFICE OF PUBLICATION: 1290 Avenue of the Americas,
New York, NY 10104. © 2021 MARVEL No similarity between any of the names, characters, persons, and/or institutions
in this magazine with those of any living or dead person or institution is intended, and any such similarity which may
exist is purely coincidental. **Printed in the U.S.A.** KEVIN FEIGE, Chief Creative Officer; DAN BUCKLEY, President,
Marvel Entertainment; JOE QUESADA, EVP & Creative Director; DAVID BOGART, Associate Publisher & SVP of
Talent Affairs; TOM BREVOORT, VP, Executive Editor; NICK LOWE, Executive Editor, VP of Content, Digital
Publishing; DAVID GABRIEL, VP of Print & Digital Publishing; JEFF YOUNGQUIST, VP of Production &
Special Projects; ALEX MORALES, Director of Publishing Operations; DAN EDINGTON, Managing
Editor; RICKEY PURDIN, Director of Talent Relations; JENNIFER GRÜNWALD, Senior Editor, Special
Projects; SUSAN CRESPI, Production Manager; STAN LEE, Chairman Emeritus. For information
regarding advertising in Marvel Comics or on Marvel.com, please contact Vit DeBellis,
Custom Solutions & Integrated Advertising Manager, at vdebellis@marvel.com. For Marvel
subscription inquiries, please call 888-511-5480. **Manufactured between 4/2/2021
and 5/3/2021 by FRY COMMUNICATIONS, MECHANICSBURG, PA, USA.**

10 9 8 7 6 5 4 3 2 1

DAWN OF X

Volume 16

X-Men created by Stan Lee & Jack Kirby

Writers:	**Jonathan Hickman, Benjamin Percy & Tini Howard**
Artists:	**Russell Dauterman, Jan Bazaldua & Marcus To**
Color Artists:	**Matthew Wilson, Guru-eFX & Erick Arciniega**
Letterers:	**VC's Ariana Maher & Joe Caramagna**
Cover Art:	**Russell Dauterman & Matthew Wilson; Dustin Weaver & Edgar Delgado; and Mahmud Asrar & Matthew Wilson**
Head of X:	**Jonathan Hickman**
Design:	**Tom Muller**
Assistant Editors:	**Annalise Bissa, Chris Robinson & Lauren Amaro**
Editor:	**Jordan D. White**
Collection Cover Art:	**Russell Dauterman & Matthew Wilson**
Collection Editor:	**Jennifer Grünwald**
Assistant Editor:	**Daniel Kirchhoffer**
Assistant Managing Editor:	**Maia Loy**
Assistant Managing Editor:	**Lisa Montalbano**
VP Production & Special Projects:	**Jeff Youngquist**
SVP Print, Sales & Marketing:	**David Gabriel**
Editor in Chief:	**C.B. Cebulski**

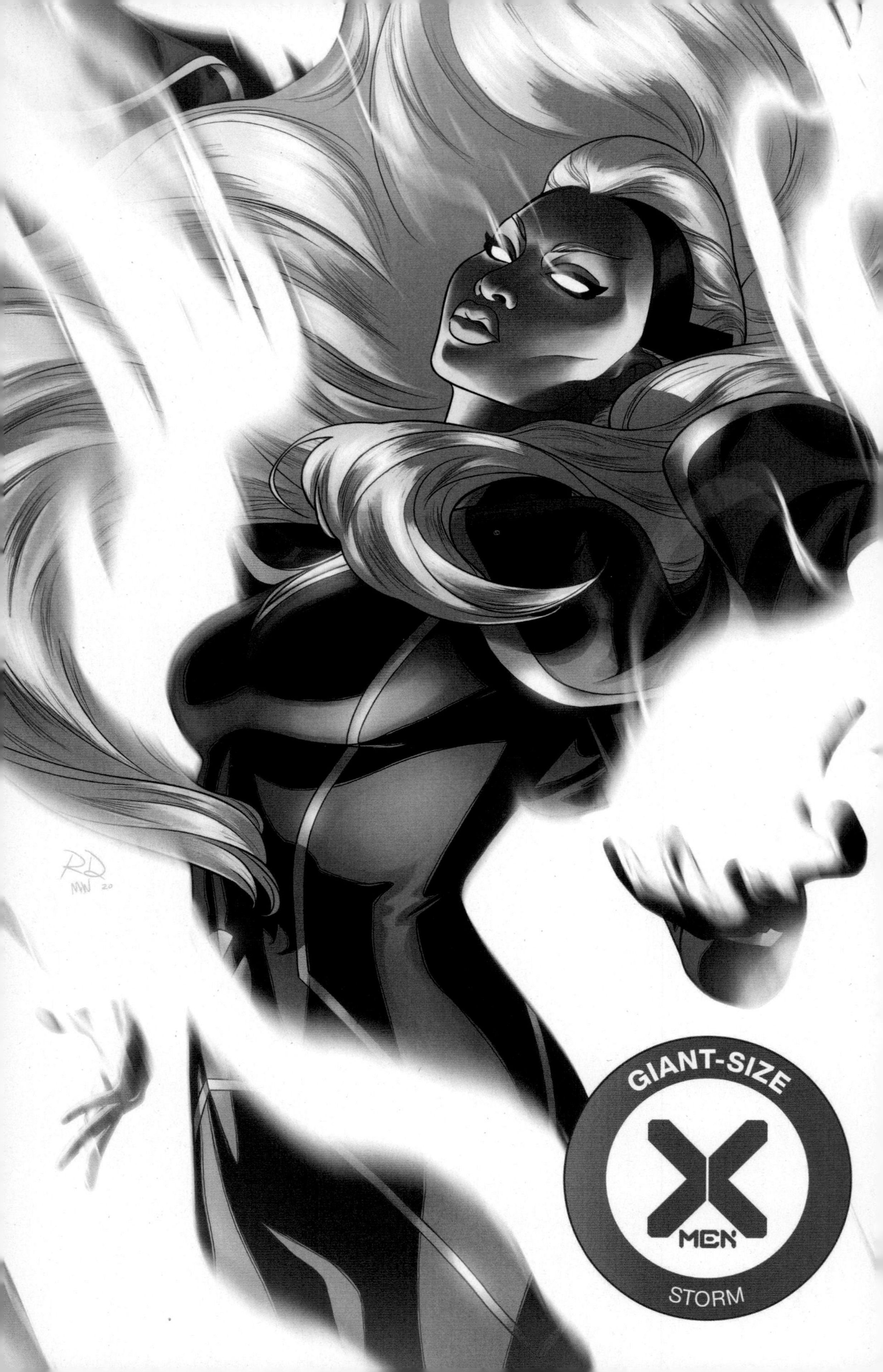
GIANT-SIZE
X
MEN
STORM

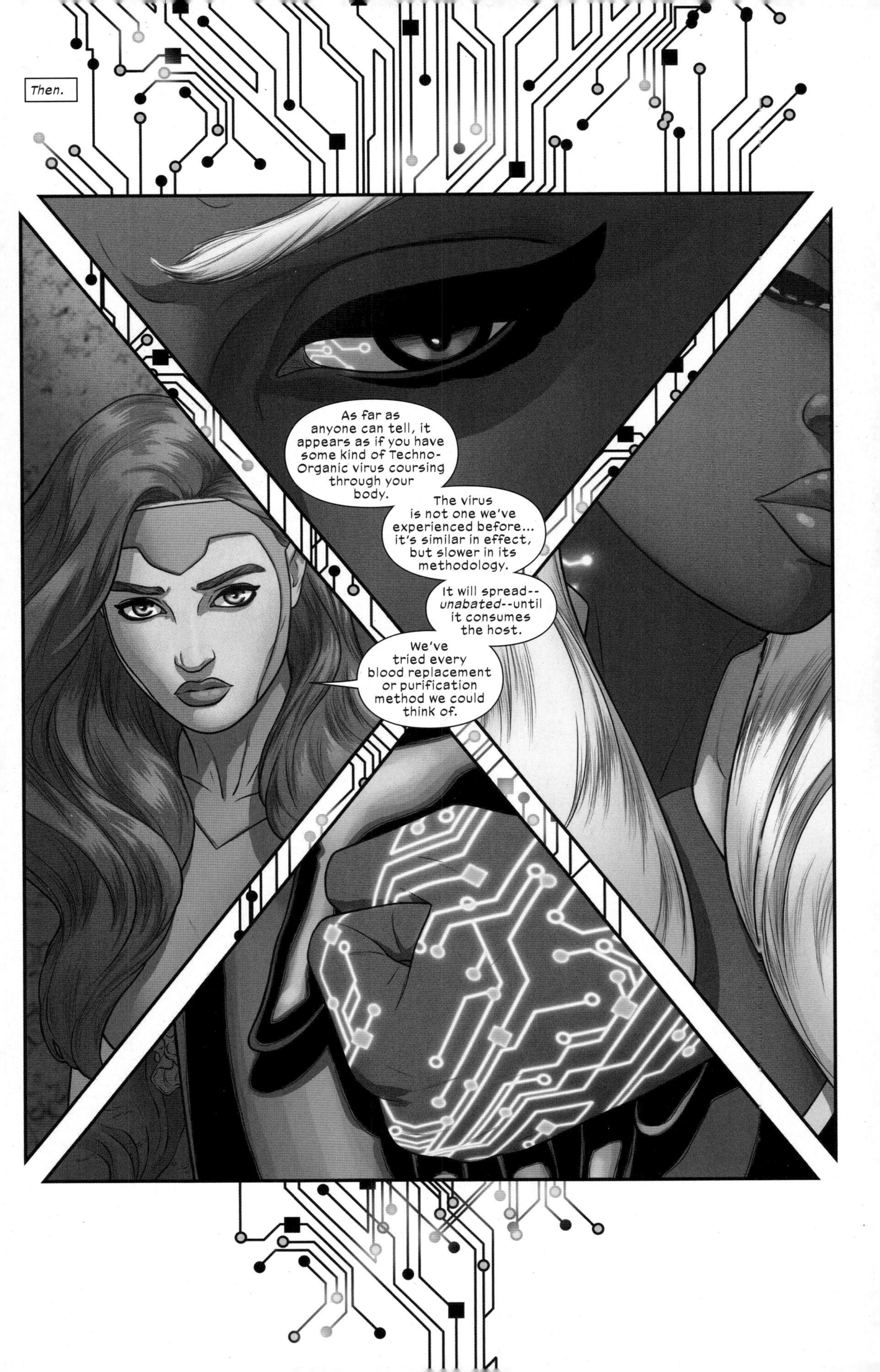
Then.
As far as anyone can tell, it appears as if you have some kind of Techno-Organic virus coursing through your body.
The virus is not one we've experienced before... it's similar in effect, but slower in its methodology.
It will spread--*unabated*--until it consumes the host.
We've tried every blood replacement or purification method we could think of.

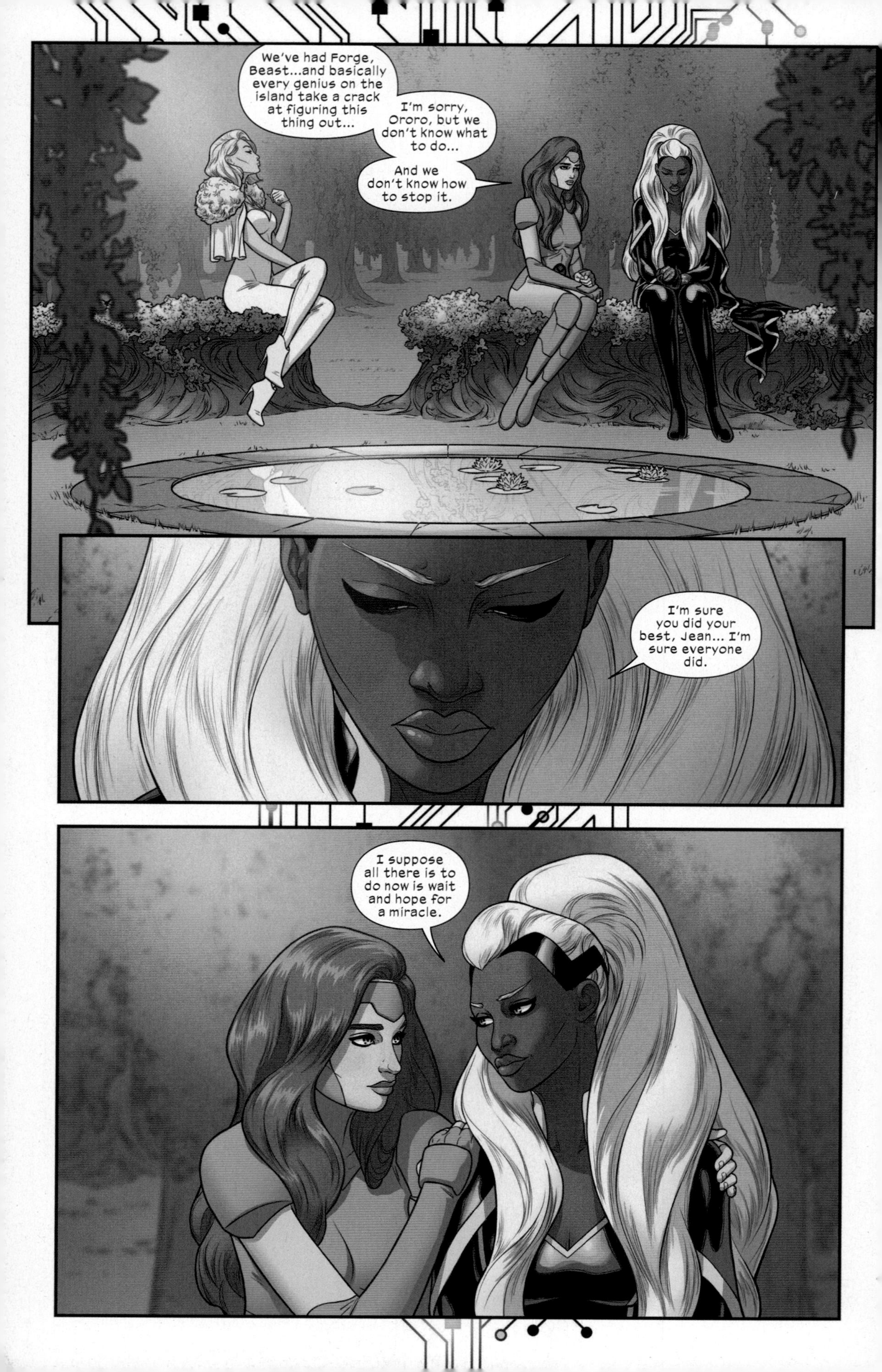
We've had Forge, Beast...and basically every genius on the island take a crack at figuring this thing out...
I'm sorry, Ororo, but we don't know what to do...
And we don't know how to stop it.
I'm sure you did your best, Jean... I'm sure everyone did.
I suppose all there is to do now is wait and hope for a miracle.

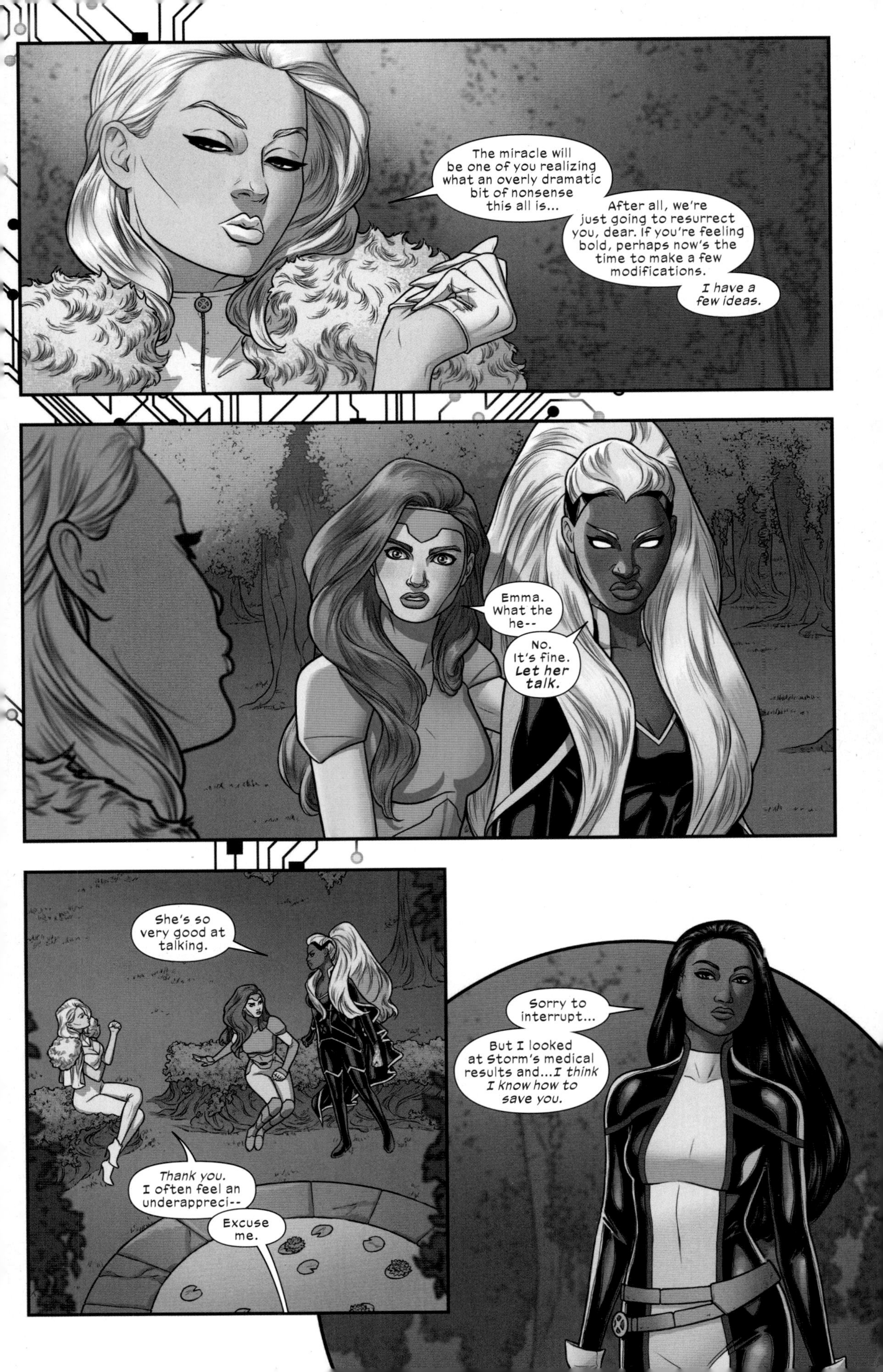

The miracle will be one of you realizing what an overly dramatic bit of nonsense this all is...
After all, we're just going to resurrect you, dear. If you're feeling bold, perhaps now's the time to make a few modifications.
I have a few ideas.
Emma. What the he--
No. It's fine. ***Let her talk.***
She's so very good at talking.
Thank you. I often feel an underappreci--
Excuse me.
Sorry to interrupt...
But I looked at Storm's medical results and...*I think I know how to save you.*

[00_mutants_of_X]
[00_the_world__X]

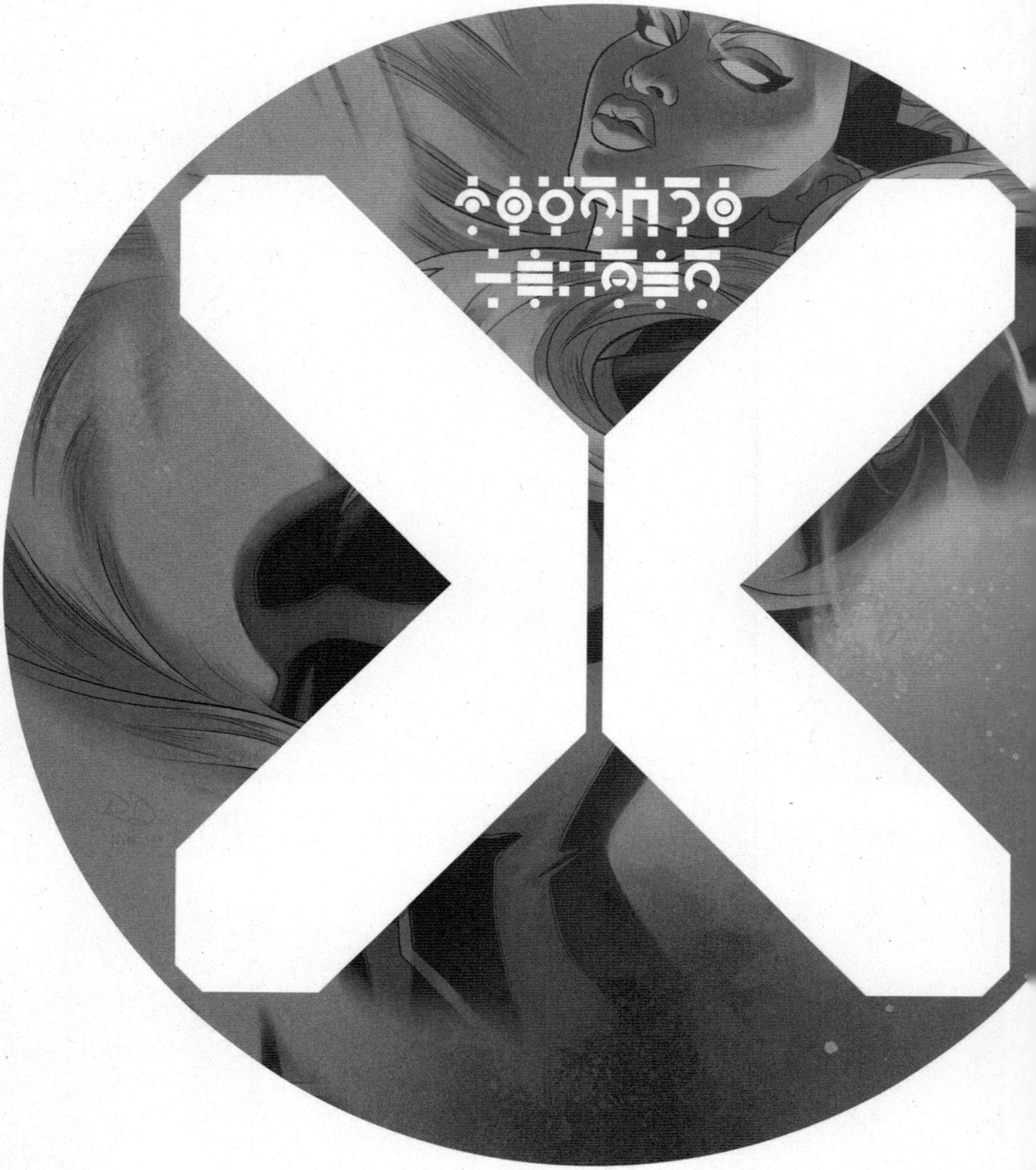

JONATHAN HICKMAN........................[STORY & WORDS]
RUSSELL DAUTERMAN.........................[STORY & ART]
MATTHEW WILSON............................[COLOR ARTIST]
VC's ARIANA MAHER.............................[LETTERER]
TOM MULLER......................................[DESIGN]

RUSSELL DAUTERMAN & MATTHEW WILSON......[COVER ARTISTS]
ALEX ROSS; JEN BARTEL...........[VARIANT COVER ARTISTS]

ANTHONY GAMBINO............................[PRODUCTION]

JONATHAN HICKMAN...........................[HEAD OF X]
ANNALISE BISSA......................[ASSISTANT EDITOR]
JORDAN D. WHITE...............................[EDITOR]
C.B. CEBULSKI........................[EDITOR IN CHIEF]

[01] GIANT SIZE X-MEN: STORM

[ISSUE ONE]................ DISINTEGRATION
X-MEN CREATED BY .... STAN LEE & JACK KIRBY

[00_mutants_of_X]
[00_the_world__X]

[00_CO...0]
[00_CO...1]

[00_⊾nite_]
[00_____]

[00_____]

[00_____X]

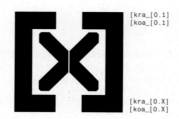

[kra_[0.1]
[koa_[0.1]

[kra_[0.X]
[koa_[0.X]

ANTIVIRAL

Following a fight against Orchis and the Children of the Vault, Jean Grey and Emma Frost discovered that Storm has been infected with a machine virus that will kill her in 30 days. Meanwhile, Fantomex has recruited a team to break into the high-tech laboratory known as the World...

Storm

Jean Grey

Emma Frost

Monet

Cypher

Fantomex

[kra_[0.1]...]
[koa_[0.1]...]

[A._New_World]

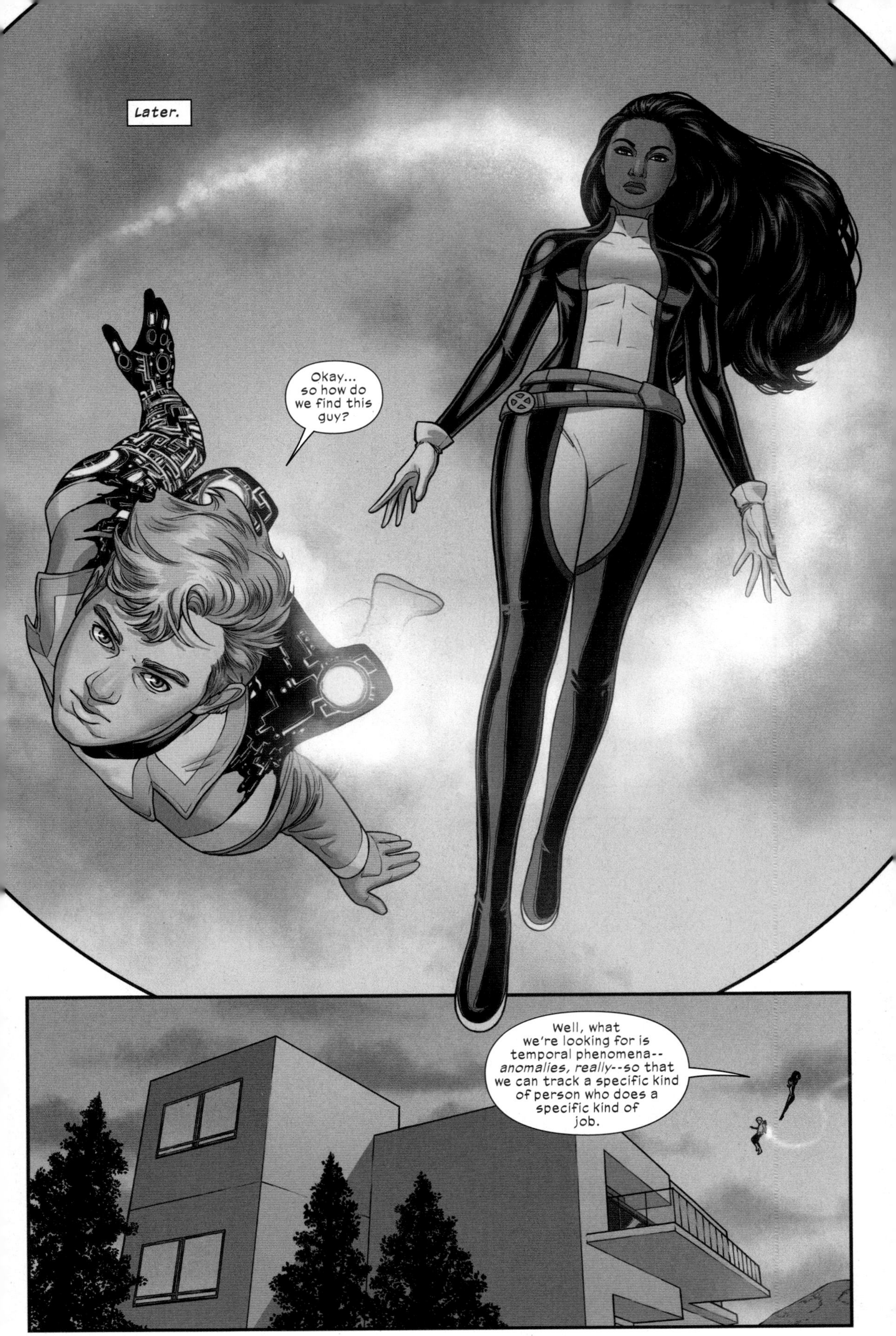
Later.
Okay... so how do we find this guy?
Well, what we're looking for is temporal phenomena-- *anomalies, really*--so that we can track a specific kind of person who does a specific kind of job.

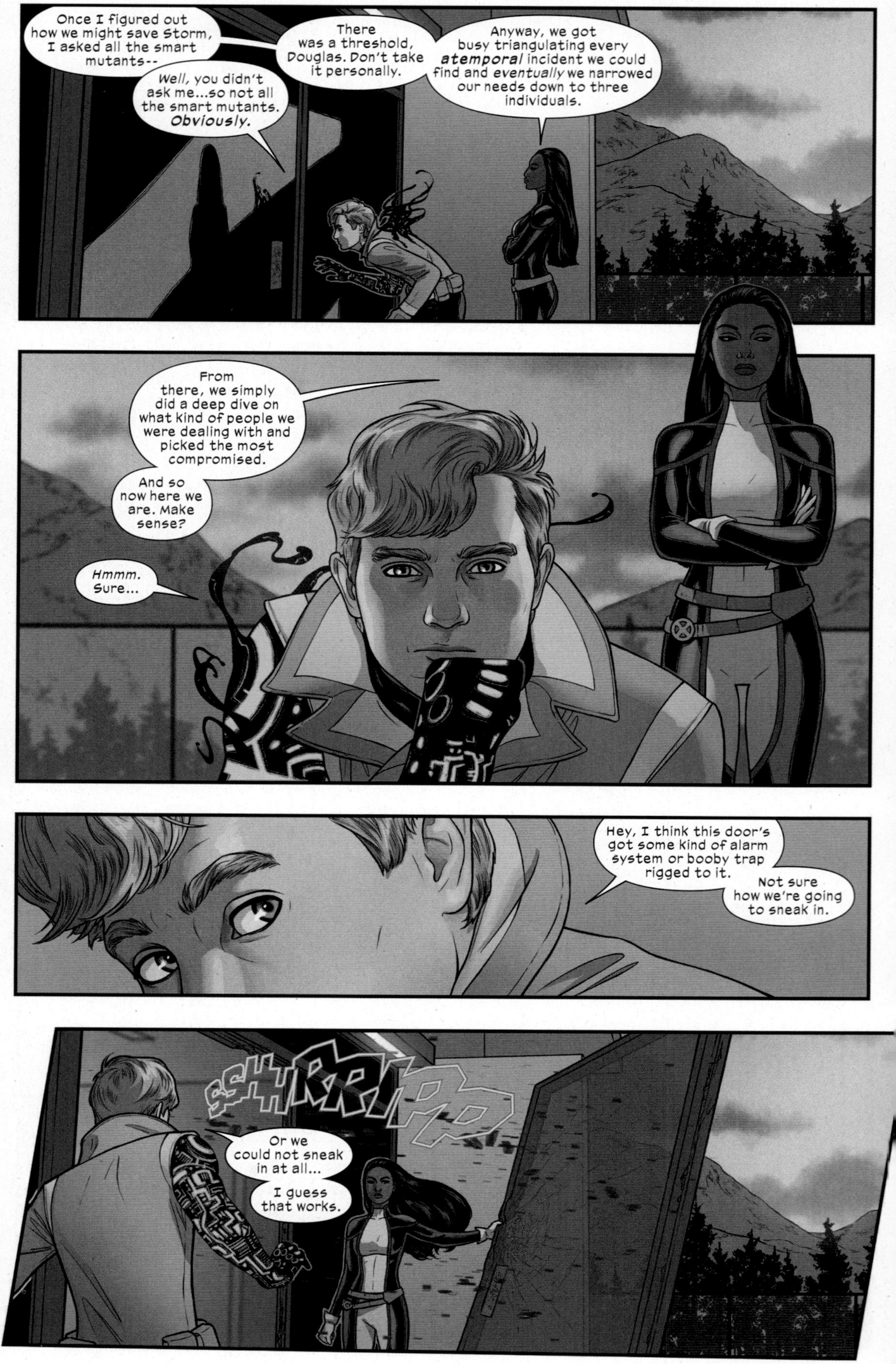
Once I figured out how we might save Storm, I asked all the smart mutants--
Well, you didn't ask me...so not all the smart mutants. Obviously.
There was a threshold, Douglas. Don't take it personally.
Anyway, we got busy triangulating every atemporal incident we could find and eventually we narrowed our needs down to three individuals.
From there, we simply did a deep dive on what kind of people we were dealing with and picked the most compromised.
And so now here we are. Make sense?
Hmmm. Sure...
Hey, I think this door's got some kind of alarm system or booby trap rigged to it.
Not sure how we're going to sneak in.
SSHRRRIPP
Or we could not sneak in at all...
I guess that works.

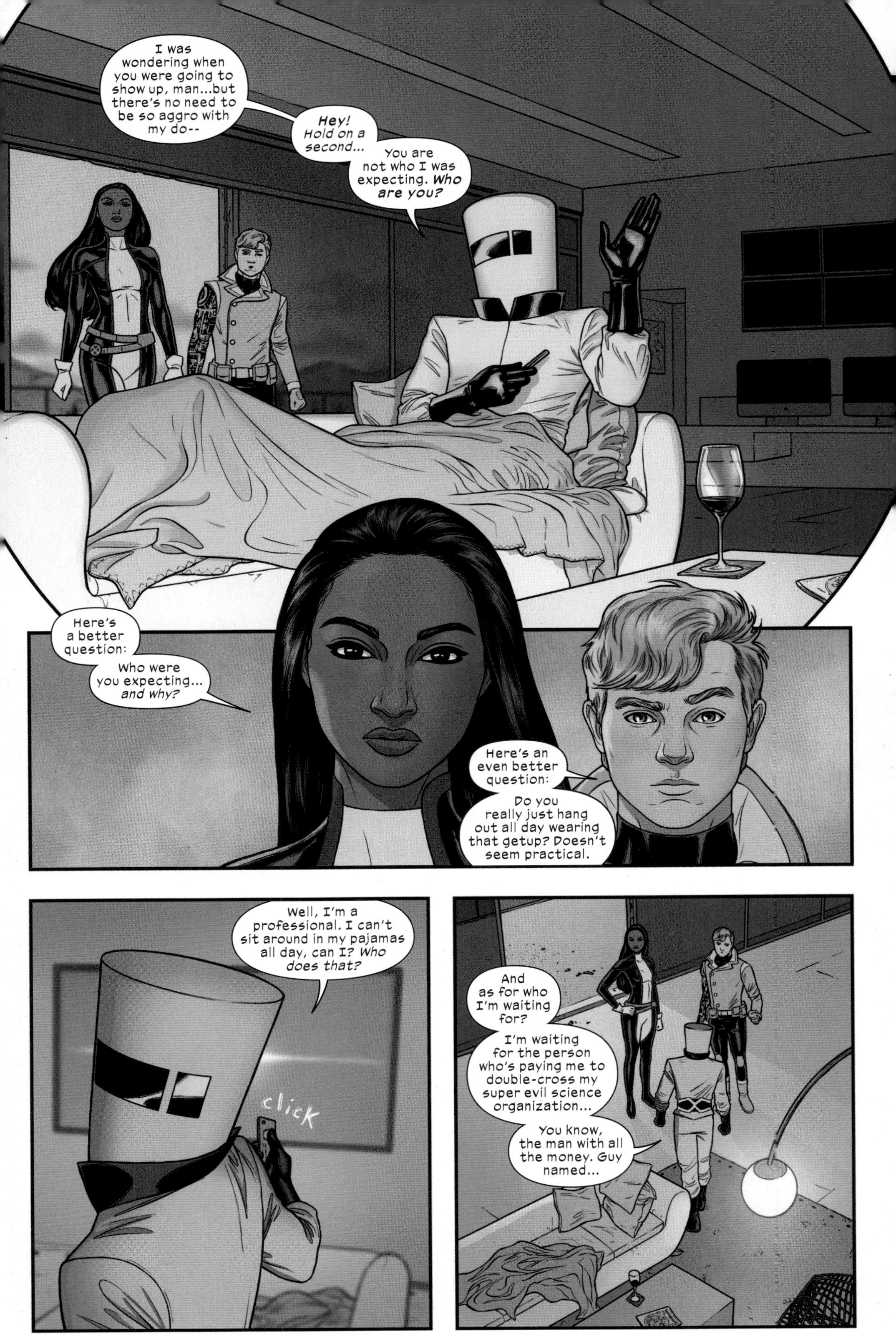

I was wondering when you were going to show up, man...but there's no need to be so aggro with my do--
Hey! Hold on a second...
You are not who I was expecting. Who are you?
Here's a better question:
Who were you expecting... and why?
Here's an even better question:
Do you really just hang out all day wearing that getup? Doesn't seem practical.
Well, I'm a professional. I can't sit around in my pajamas all day, can I? Who does that?
click
And as for who I'm waiting for?
I'm waiting for the person who's paying me to double-cross my super evil science organization...
You know, the man with all the money. Guy named...

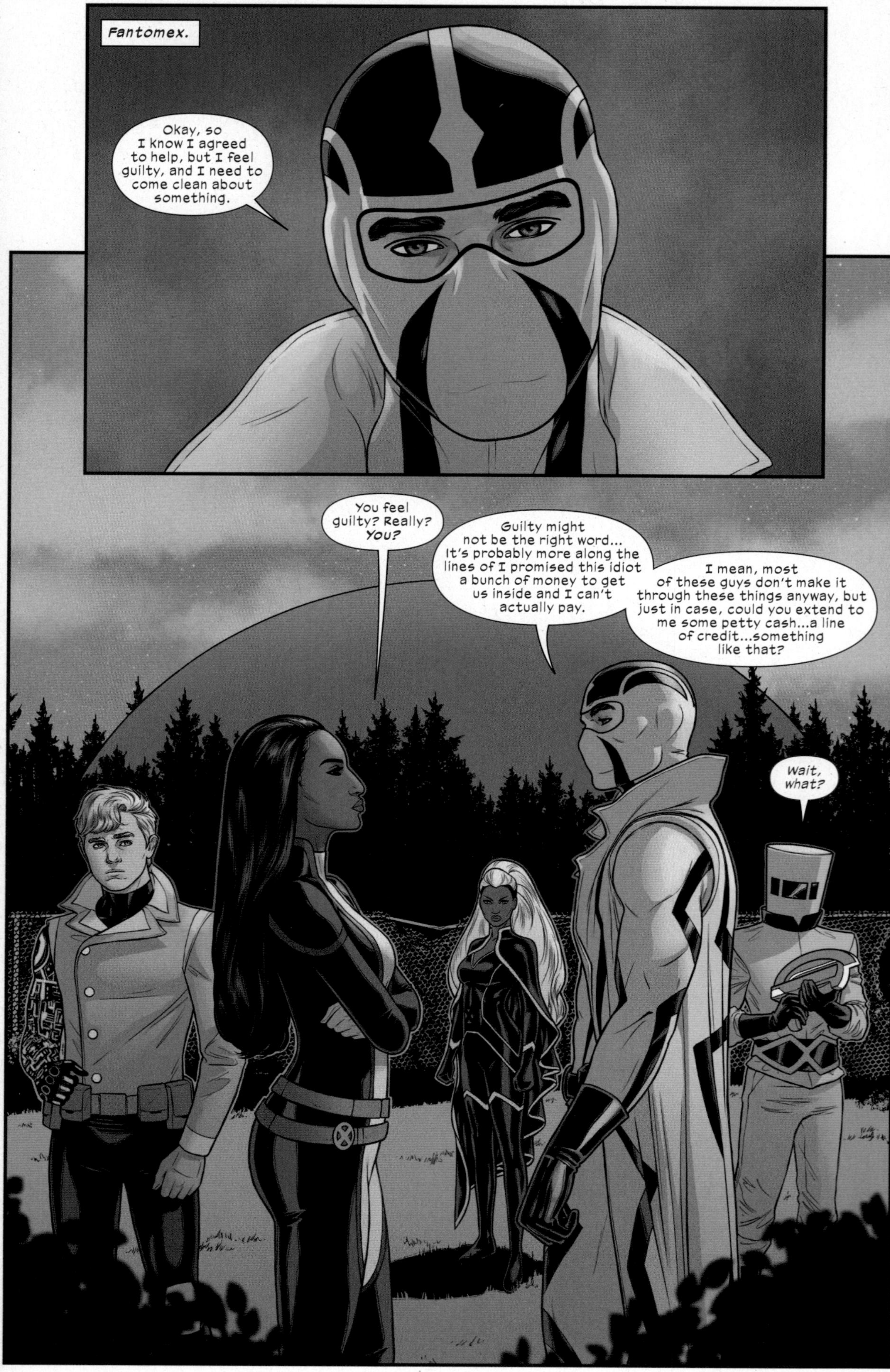
Fantomex.
Okay, so I know I agreed to help, but I feel guilty, and I need to come clean about something.
You feel guilty? Really? YOU?
Guilty might not be the right word... It's probably more along the lines of I promised this idiot a bunch of money to get us inside and I can't actually pay.
I mean, most of these guys don't make it through these things anyway, but just in case, could you extend to me some petty cash...a line of credit...something like that?
Wait, what?

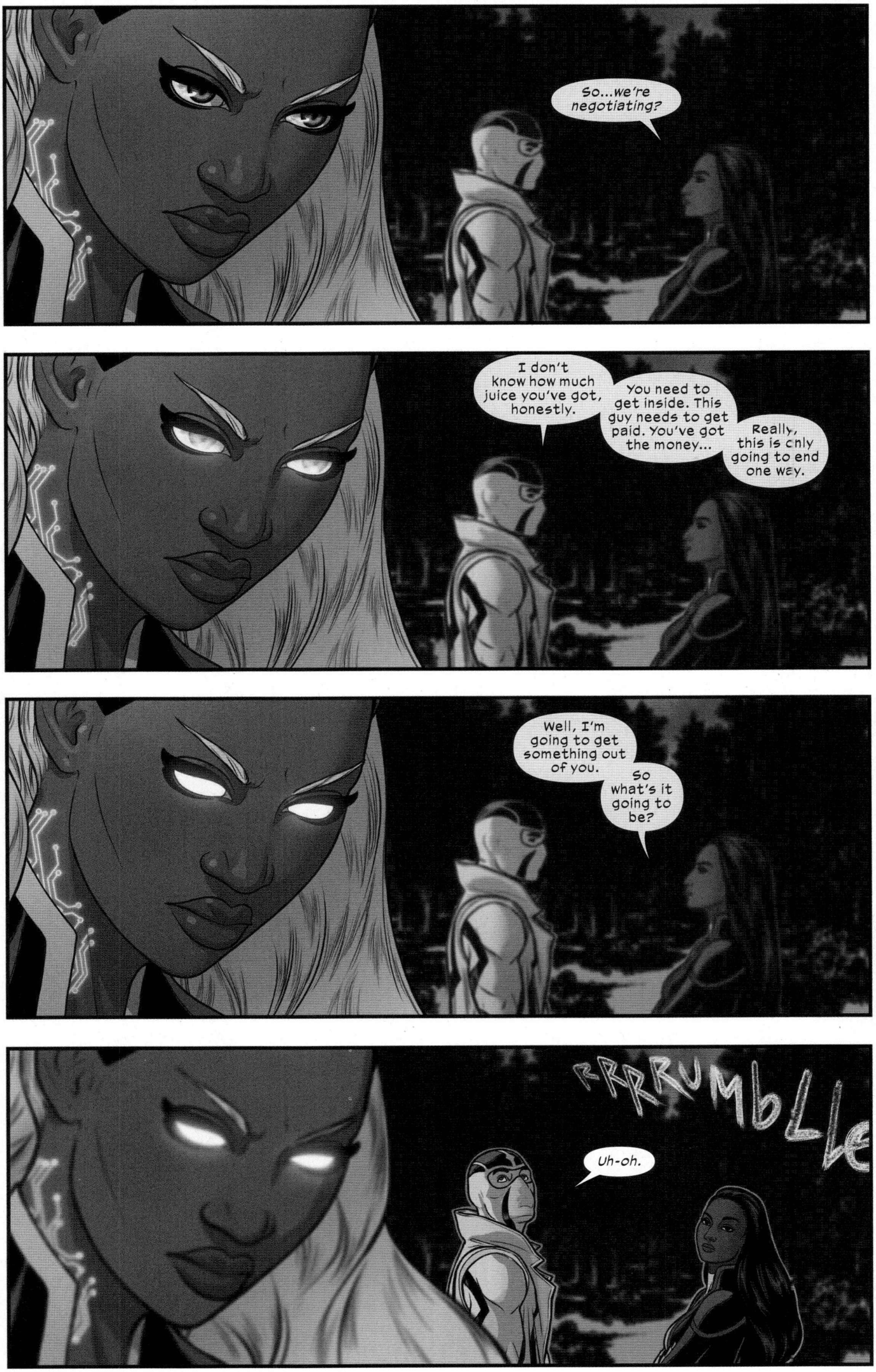
So...we're negotiating?
I don't know how much juice you've got, honestly.
You need to get inside. This guy needs to get paid. You've got the money...
Really, this is cnly going to end one way.
Well, I'm going to get something out of you.
So what's it going to be?
RRRRUMBLLE
Uh-oh.

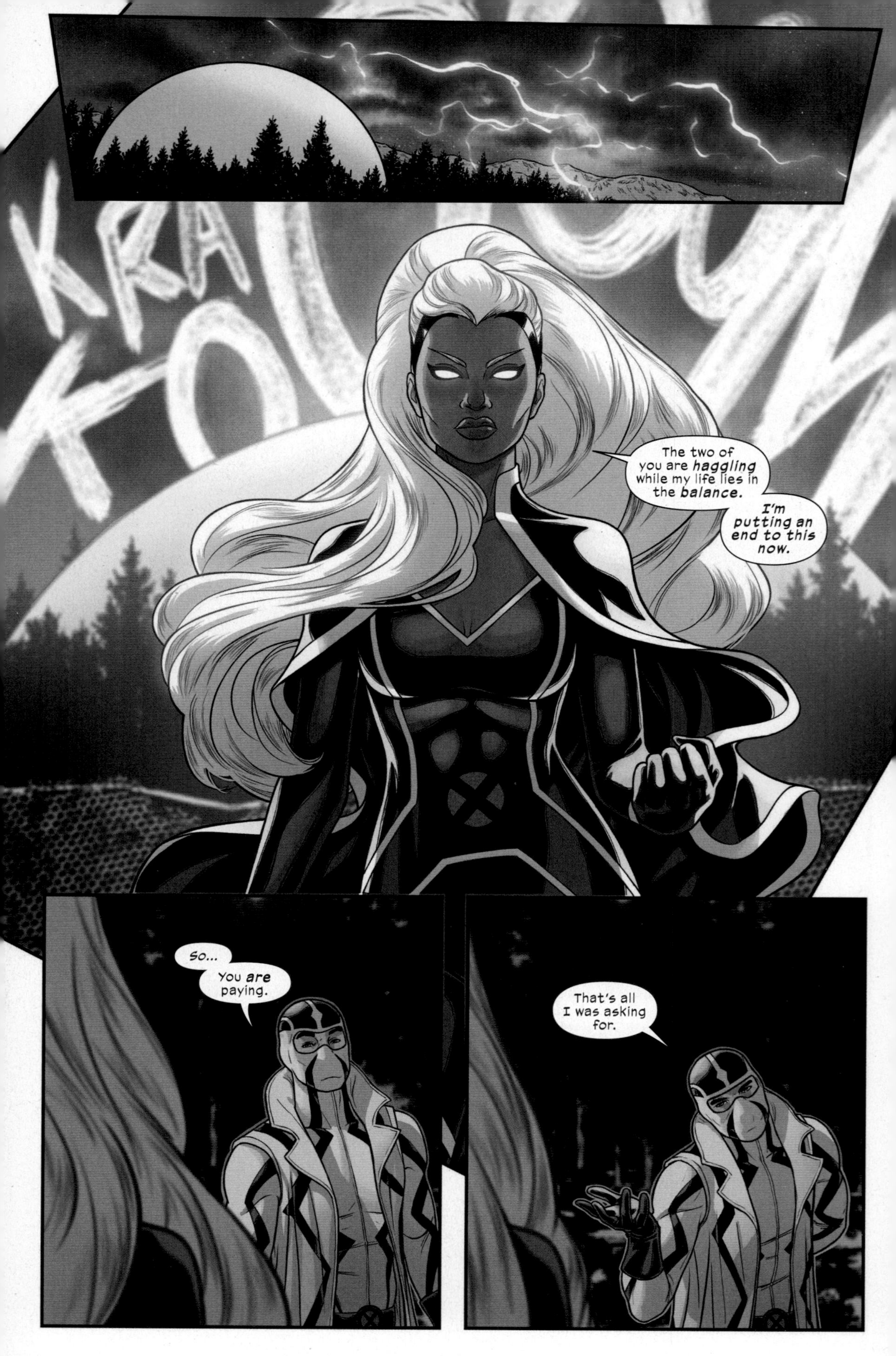
KRA KOOM
The two of you are haggling while my life lies in the balance.
I'm putting an end to this now.
So...
You are paying.
That's all I was asking for.

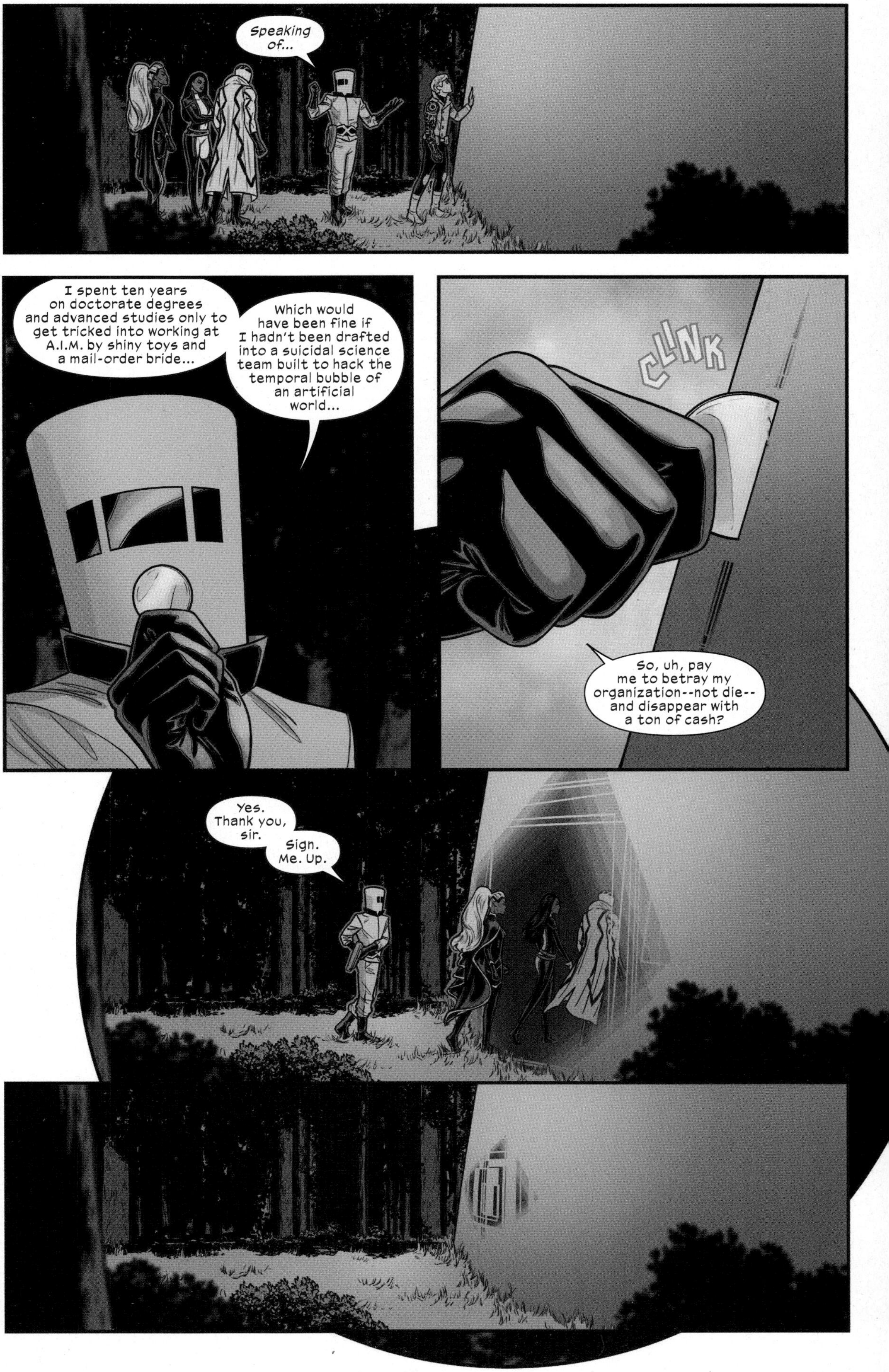
Speaking of...
I spent ten years on doctorate degrees and advanced studies only to get tricked into working at A.I.M. by shiny toys and a mail-order bride...
Which would have been fine if I hadn't been drafted into a suicidal science team built to hack the temporal bubble of an artificial world...
CLINK
So, uh, pay me to betray my organization--not die--and disappear with a ton of cash?
Yes. Thank you, sir.
Sign. Me. Up.

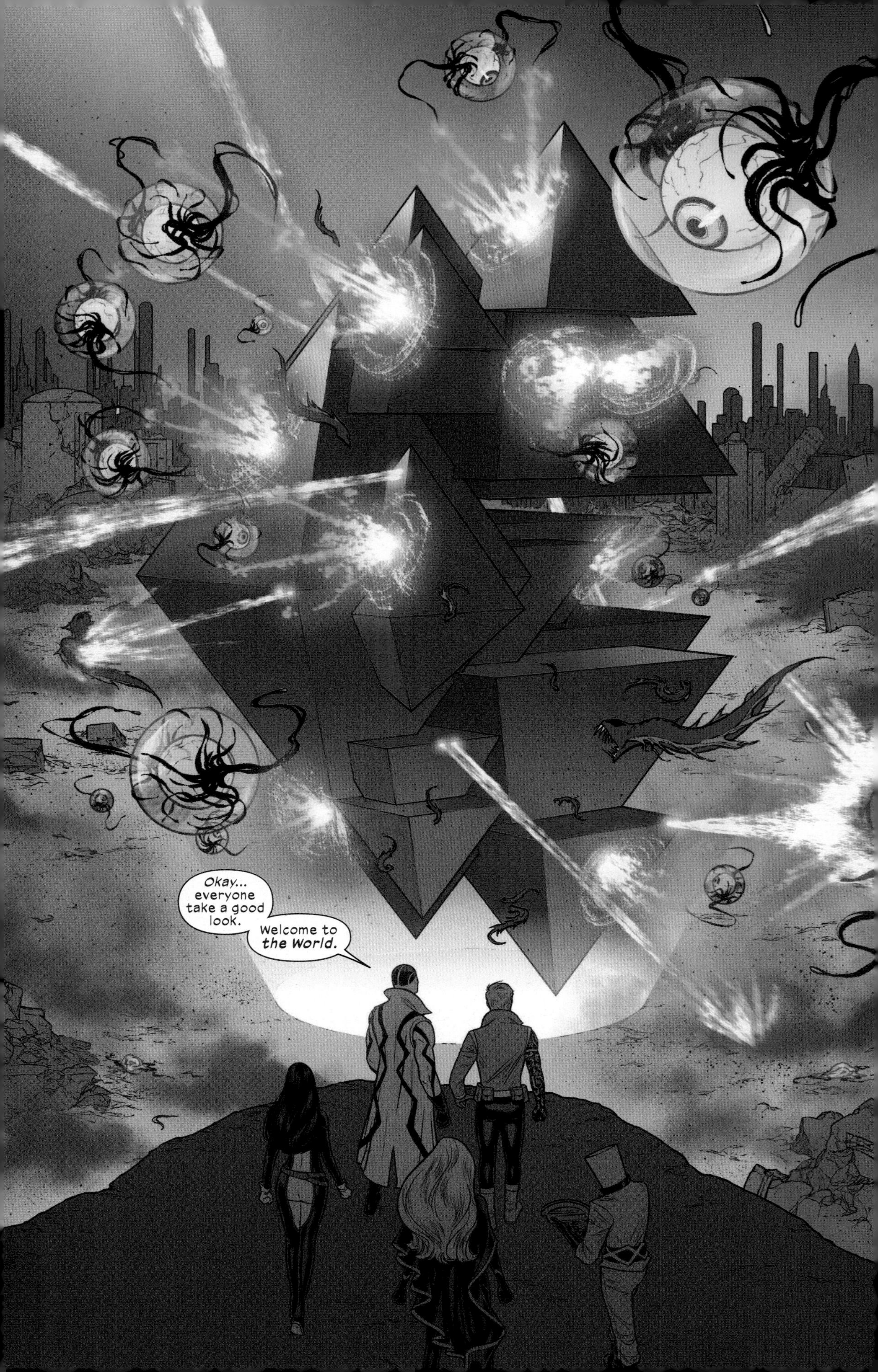
Okay... everyone take a good look.
Welcome to the World.

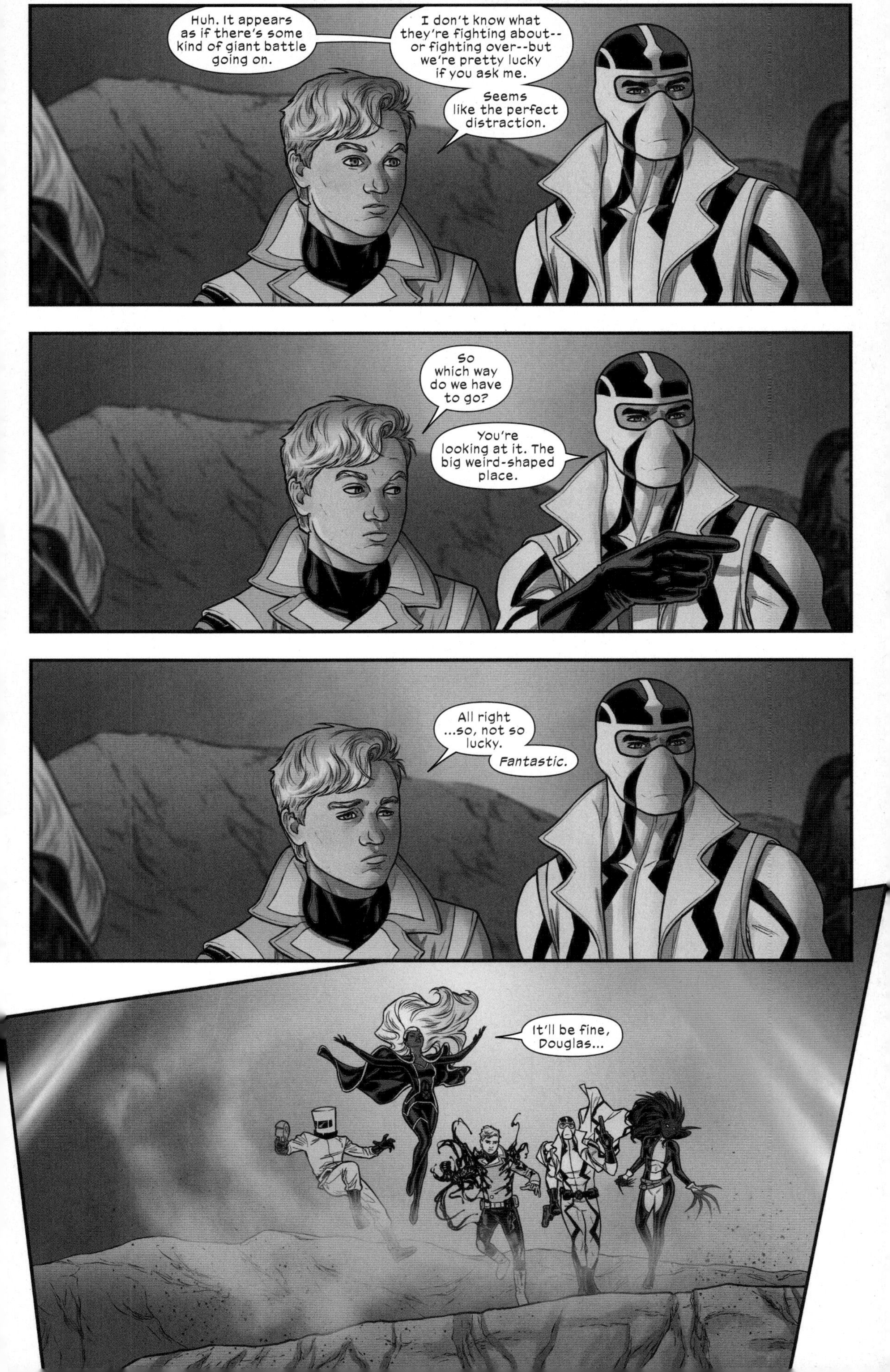
Huh. It appears as if there's some kind of giant battle going on.
I don't know what they're fighting about--or fighting over--but we're pretty lucky if you ask me.
Seems like the perfect distraction.
So which way do we have to go?
You're looking at it. The big weird-shaped place.
All right ...so, not so lucky.
Fantastic.
It'll be fine, Douglas...

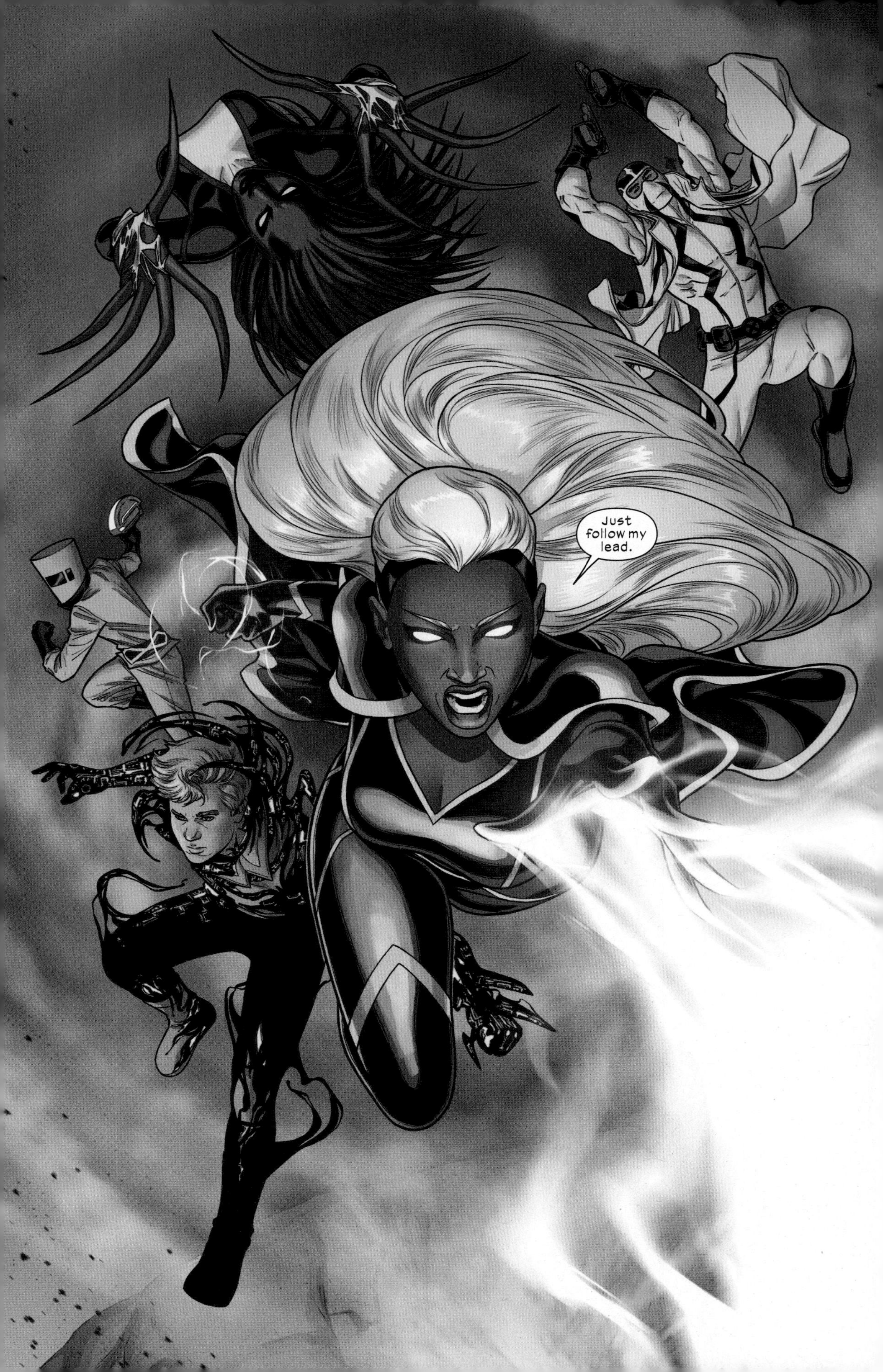
Just follow my lead.

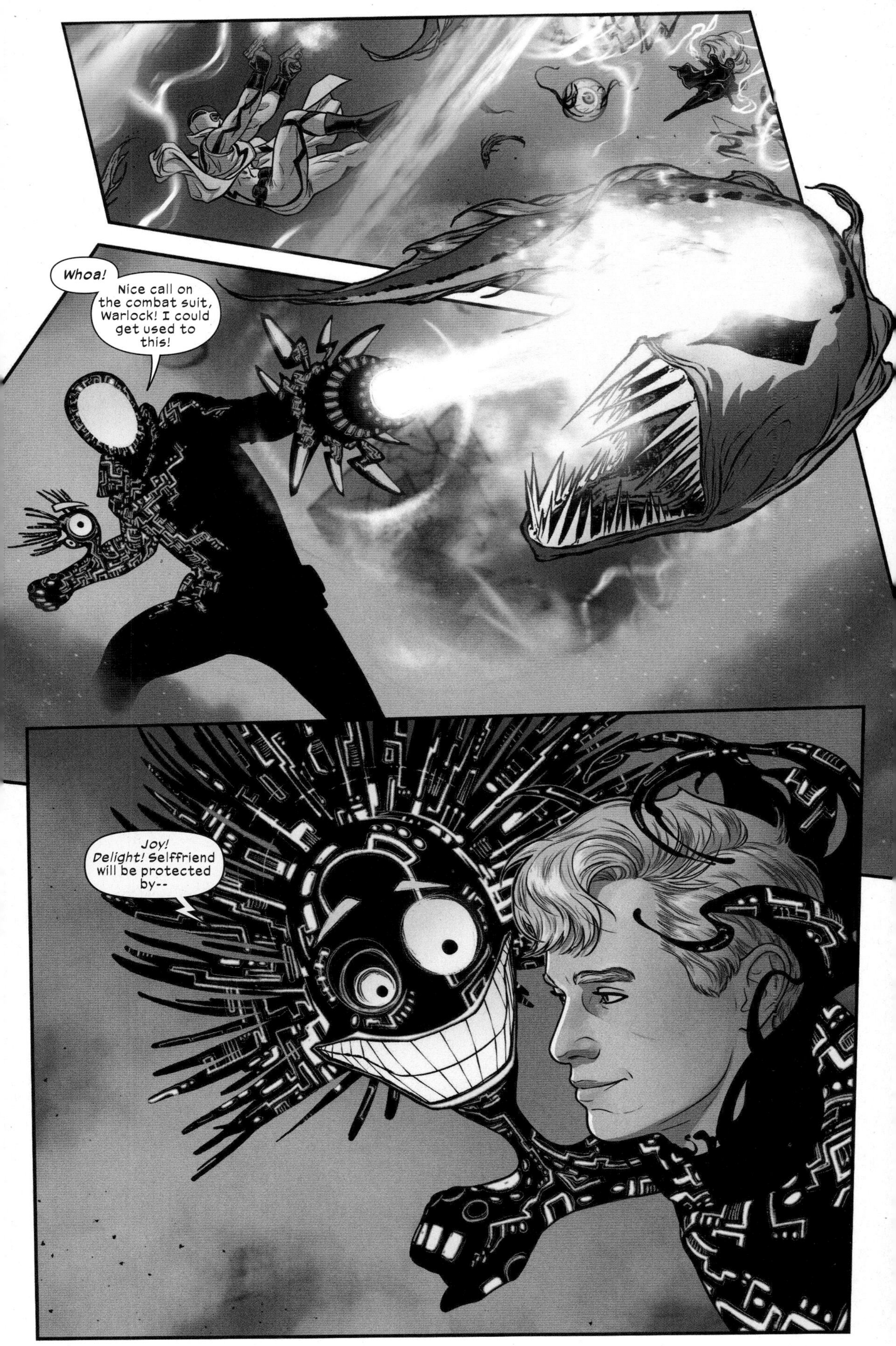
Whoa!
Nice call on the combat suit, Warlock! I could get used to this!
Joy! Delight! Selffriend will be protected by--

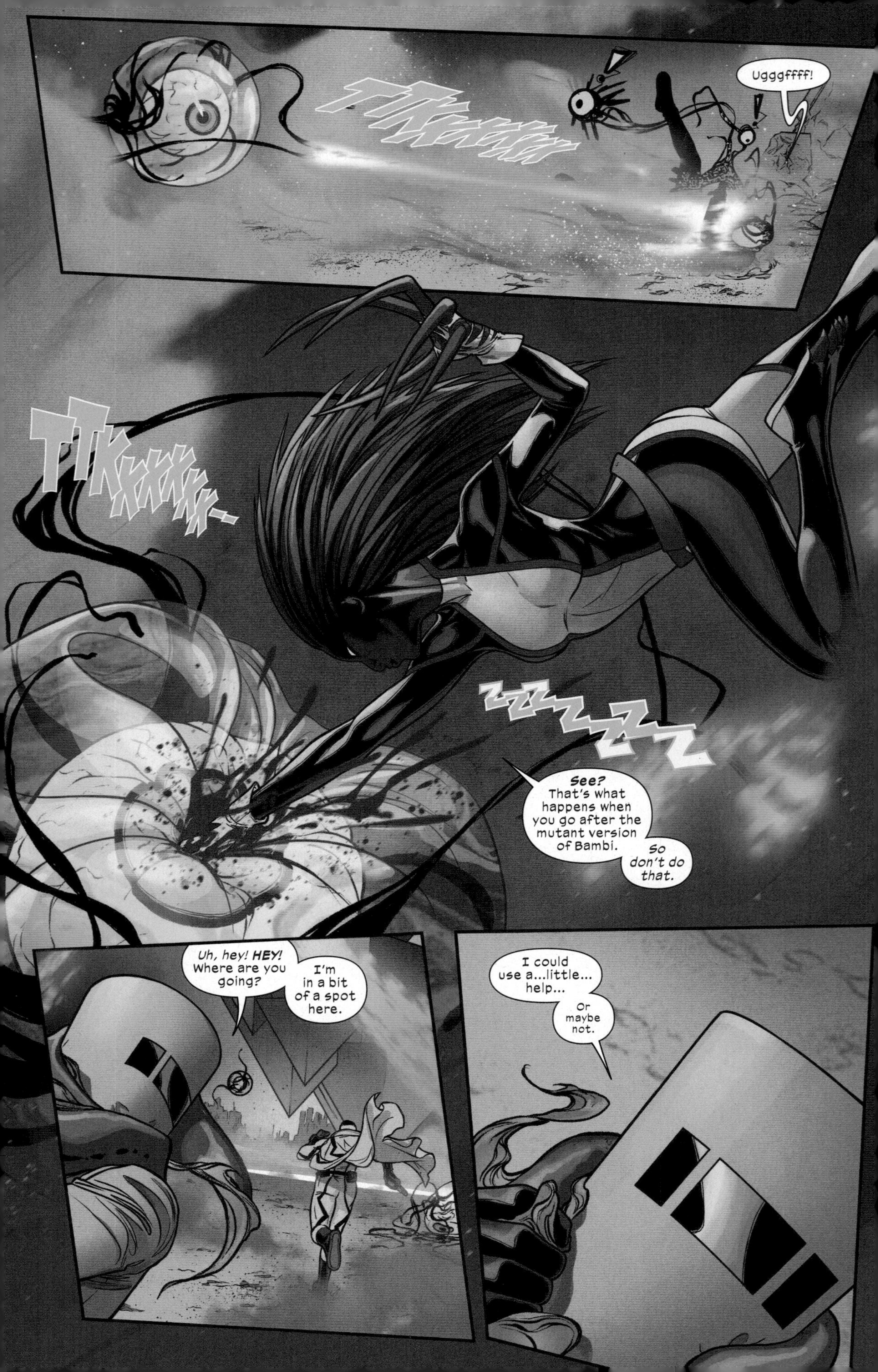
TTKKKKKKKKK
Ugggffff!
!
!
TTKKKKKKK--
ZZZZZZZ
See? That's what happens when you go after the mutant version of Bambi.
So don't do that.
Uh, hey! HEY! Where are you going?
I'm in a bit of a spot here.
I could use a...little... help...
Or maybe not.

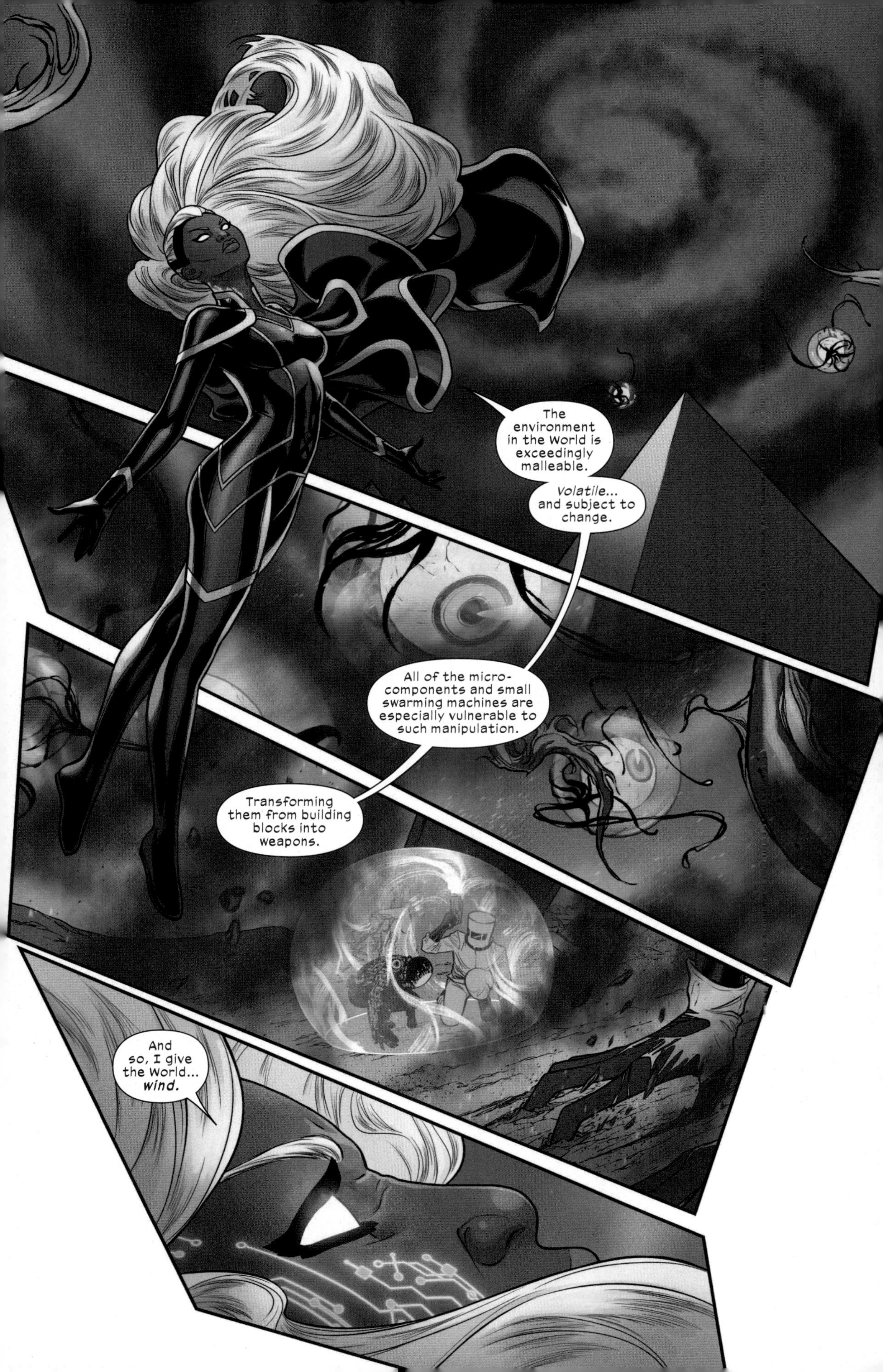

The environment in the World is exceedingly malleable.
Volatile... and subject to change.
All of the micro-components and small swarming machines are especially vulnerable to such manipulation.
Transforming them from building blocks into weapons.
And so, I give the World... ***wind.***

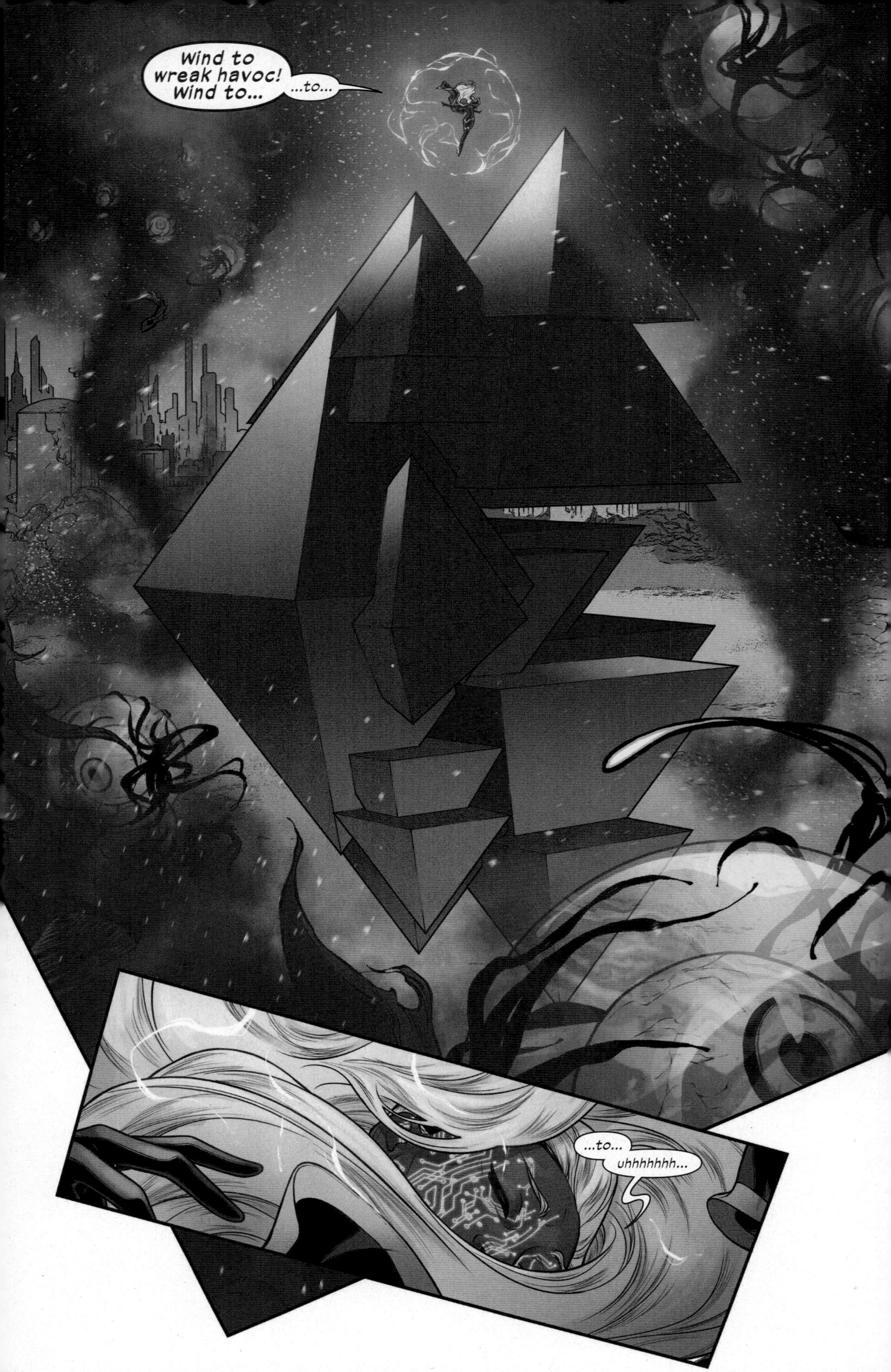
Wind to wreak havoc! Wind to...
...to...
...to...
uhhhhhhh...

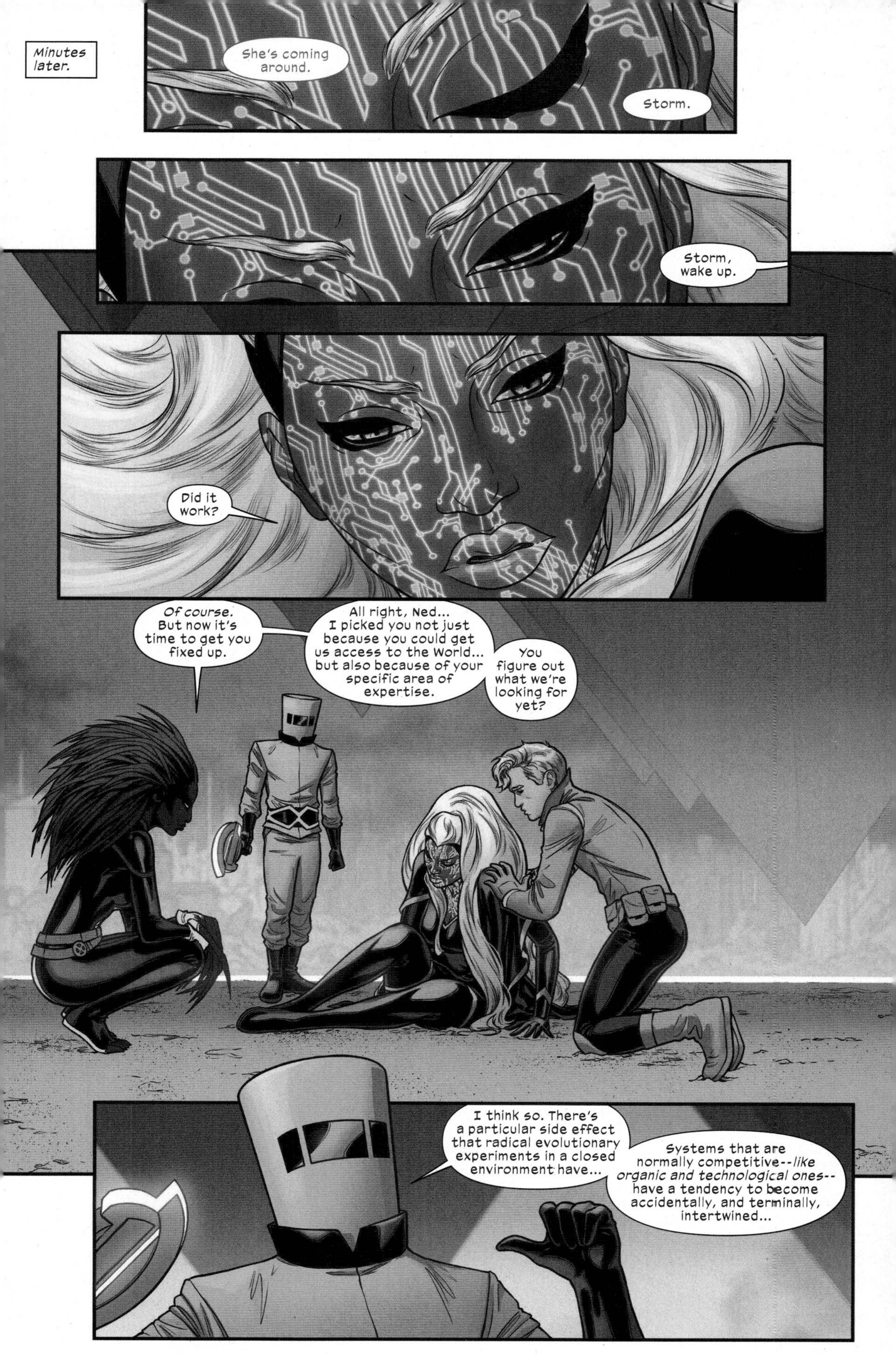
Minutes later.
She's coming around.
Storm.
Storm, wake up.
Did it work?
Of course. But now it's time to get you fixed up.
All right, Ned... I picked you not just because you could get us access to the World... but also because of your specific area of expertise.
You figure out what we're looking for yet?
I think so. There's a particular side effect that radical evolutionary experiments in a closed environment have...
Systems that are normally competitive--like organic and technological ones--have a tendency to become accidentally, and terminally, intertwined...

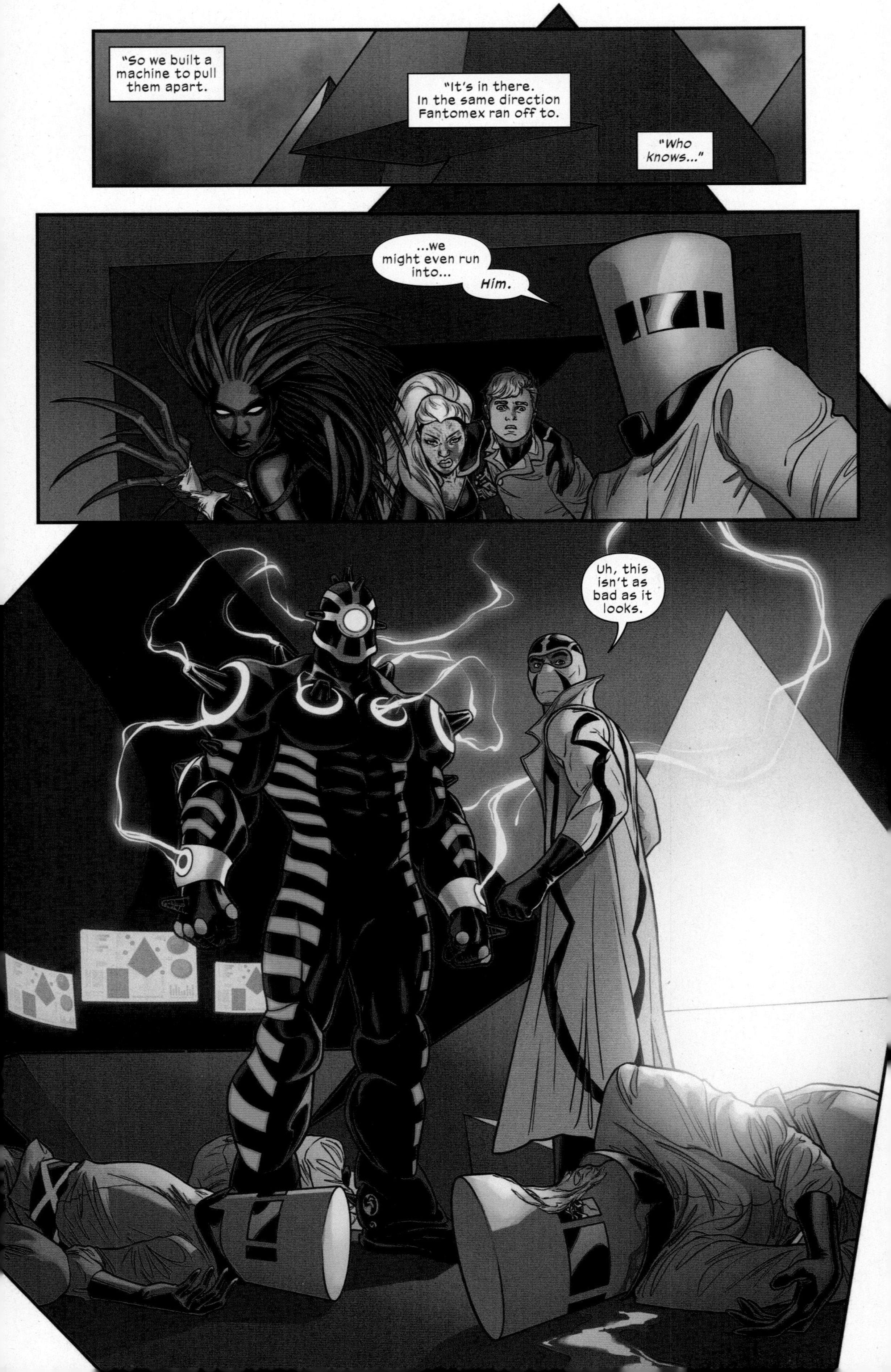
"So we built a machine to pull them apart.
"It's in there. In the same direction Fantomex ran off to.
"Who knows..."
...we might even run into...
Him.
Uh, this isn't as bad as it looks.

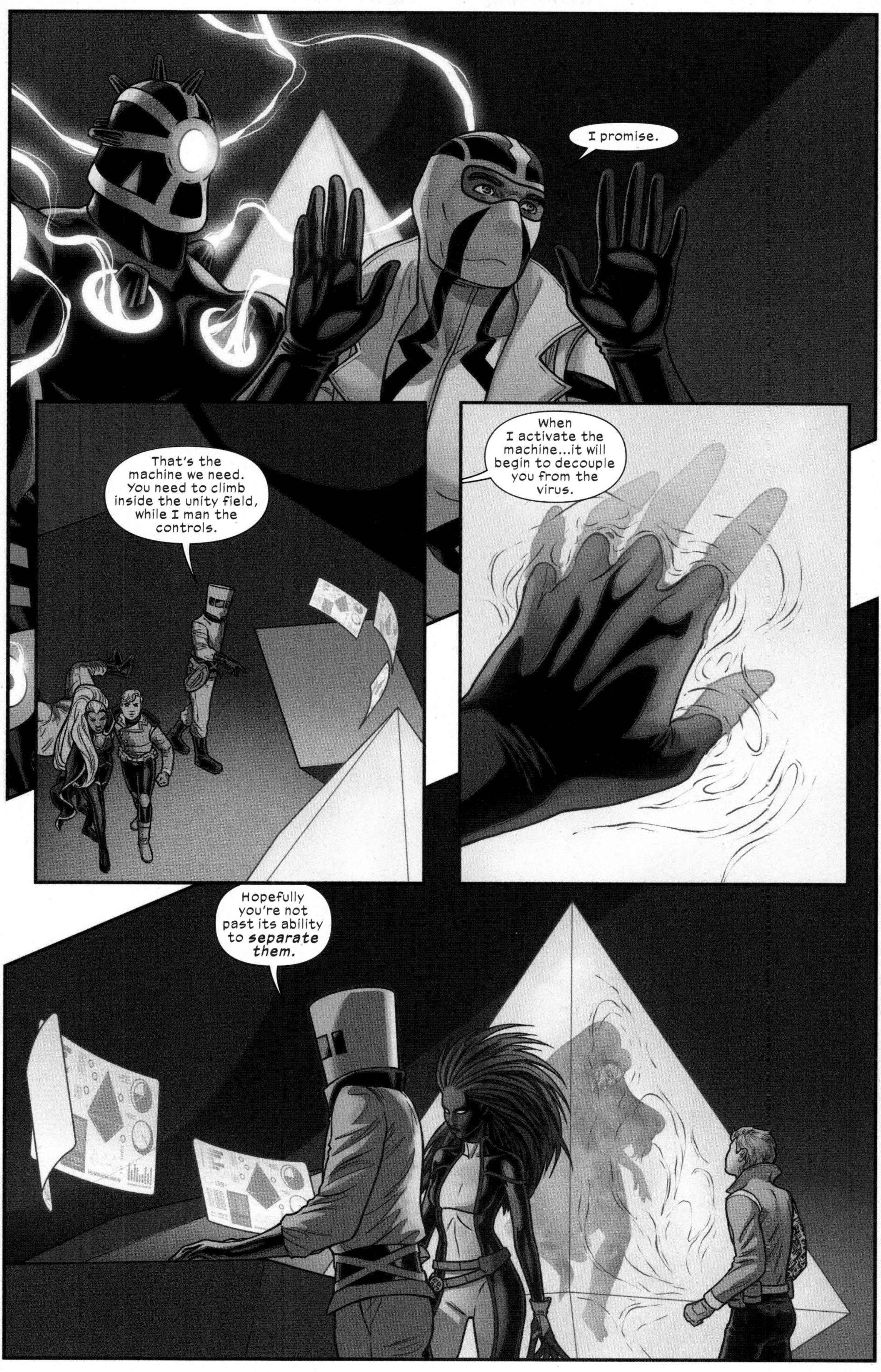
I promise.
That's the machine we need. You need to climb inside the unity field, while I man the controls.
When I activate the machine...it will begin to decouple you from the virus.
Hopefully you're not past its ability to *separate them.*

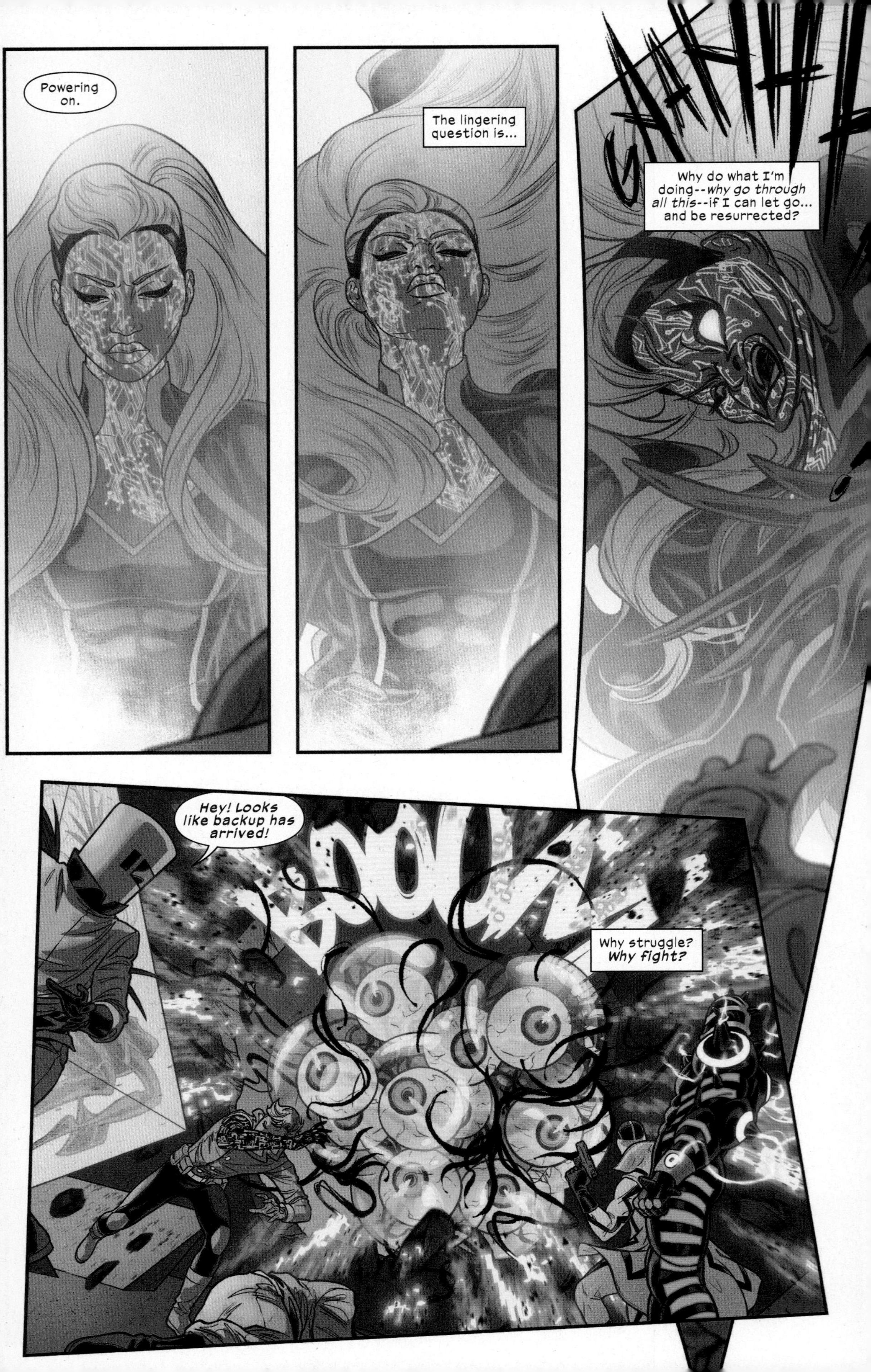
Powering on.
The lingering question is...
Why do what I'm doing--*why go through all this*--if I can let go... and be resurrected?
Hey! Looks like backup has arrived!
BOOM
Why struggle? *Why fight?*

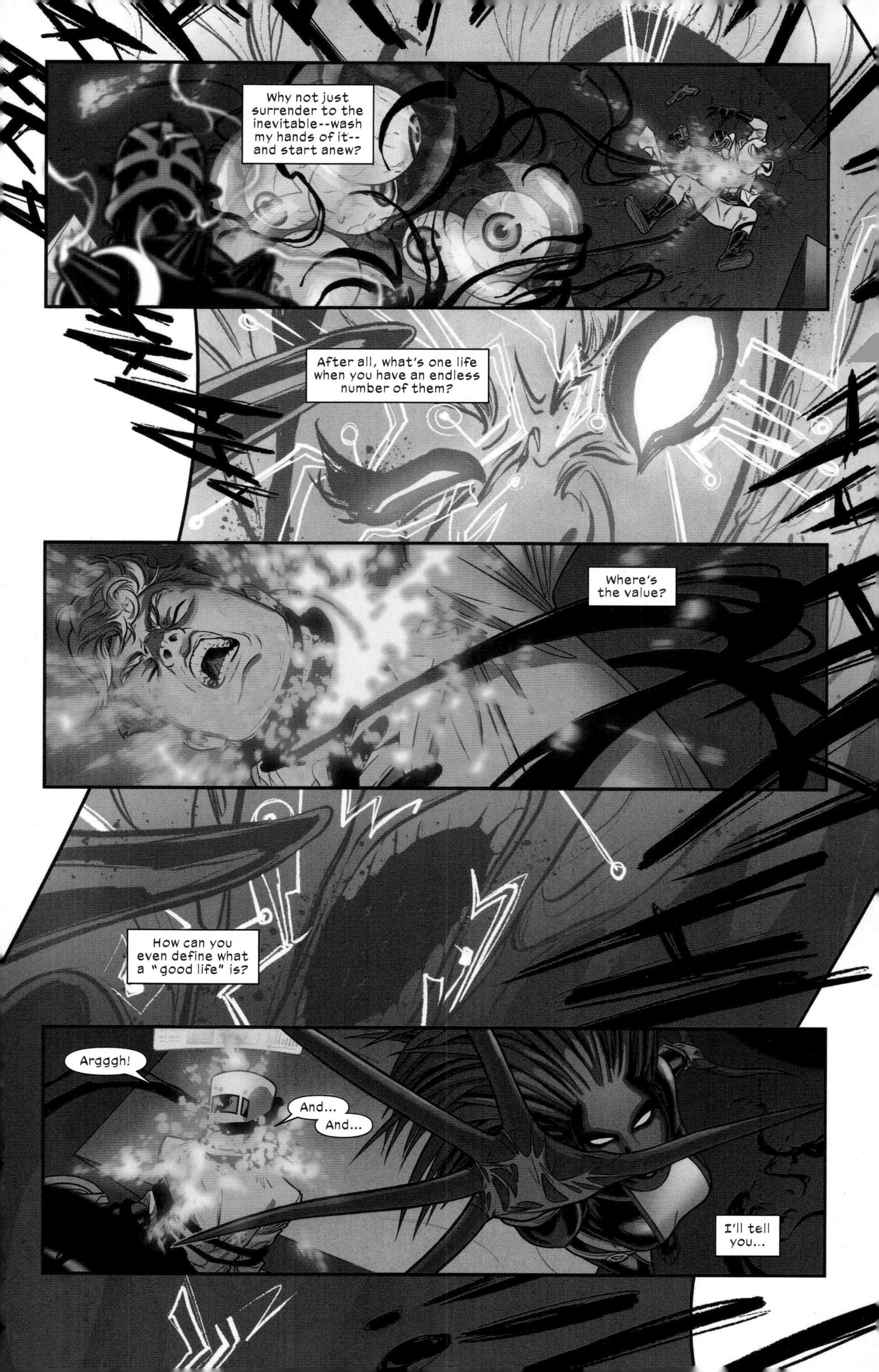
Why not just surrender to the inevitable--wash my hands of it--and start anew?
After all, what's one life when you have an endless number of them?
Where's the value?
How can you even define what a "good life" is?
Arggh!
And...
And...
I'll tell you...

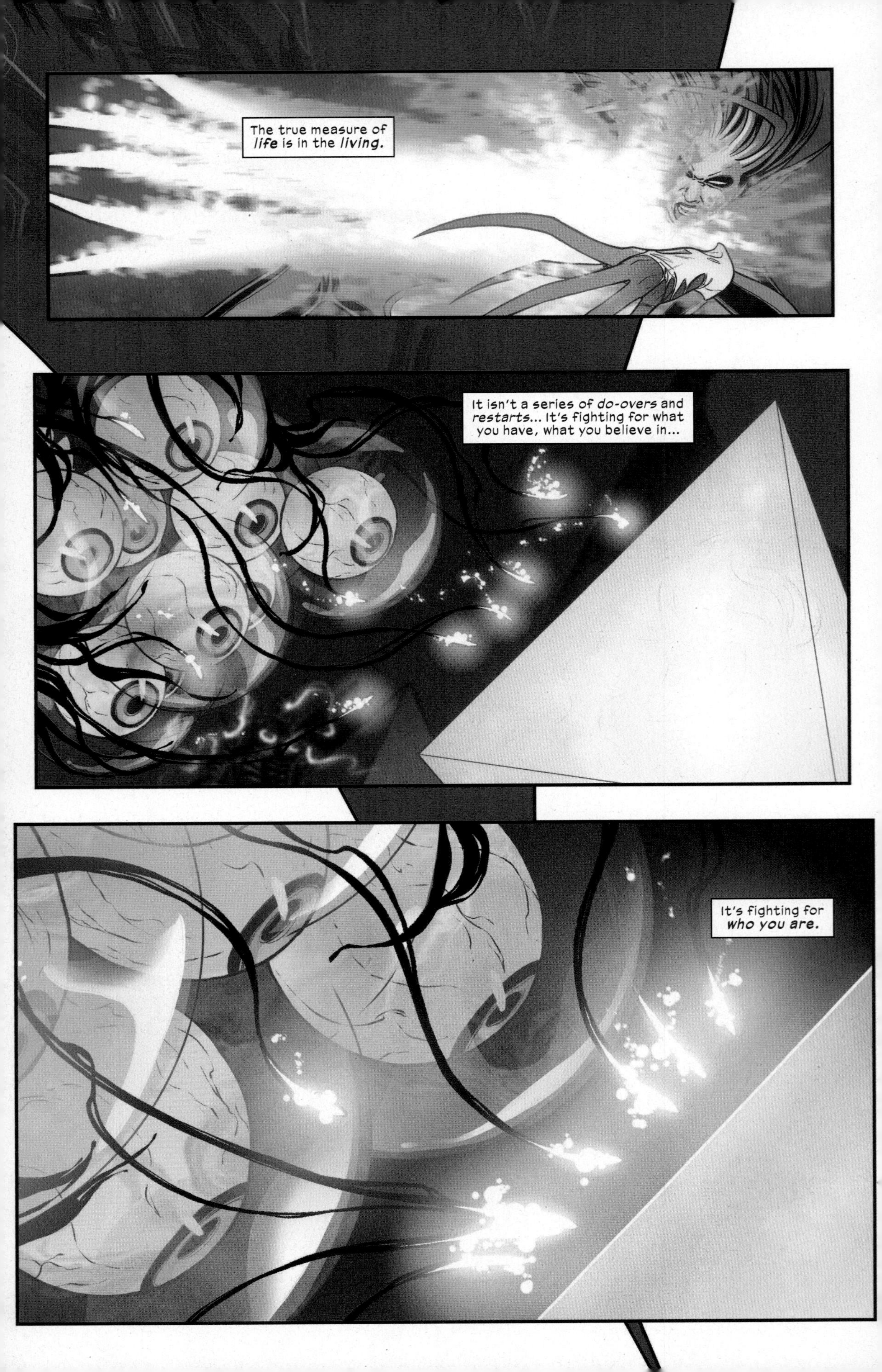
The true measure of *life* is in the *living.*
It isn't a series of *do-overs* and *restarts*... It's fighting for what you have, what you believe in...
It's fighting for *who you are.*

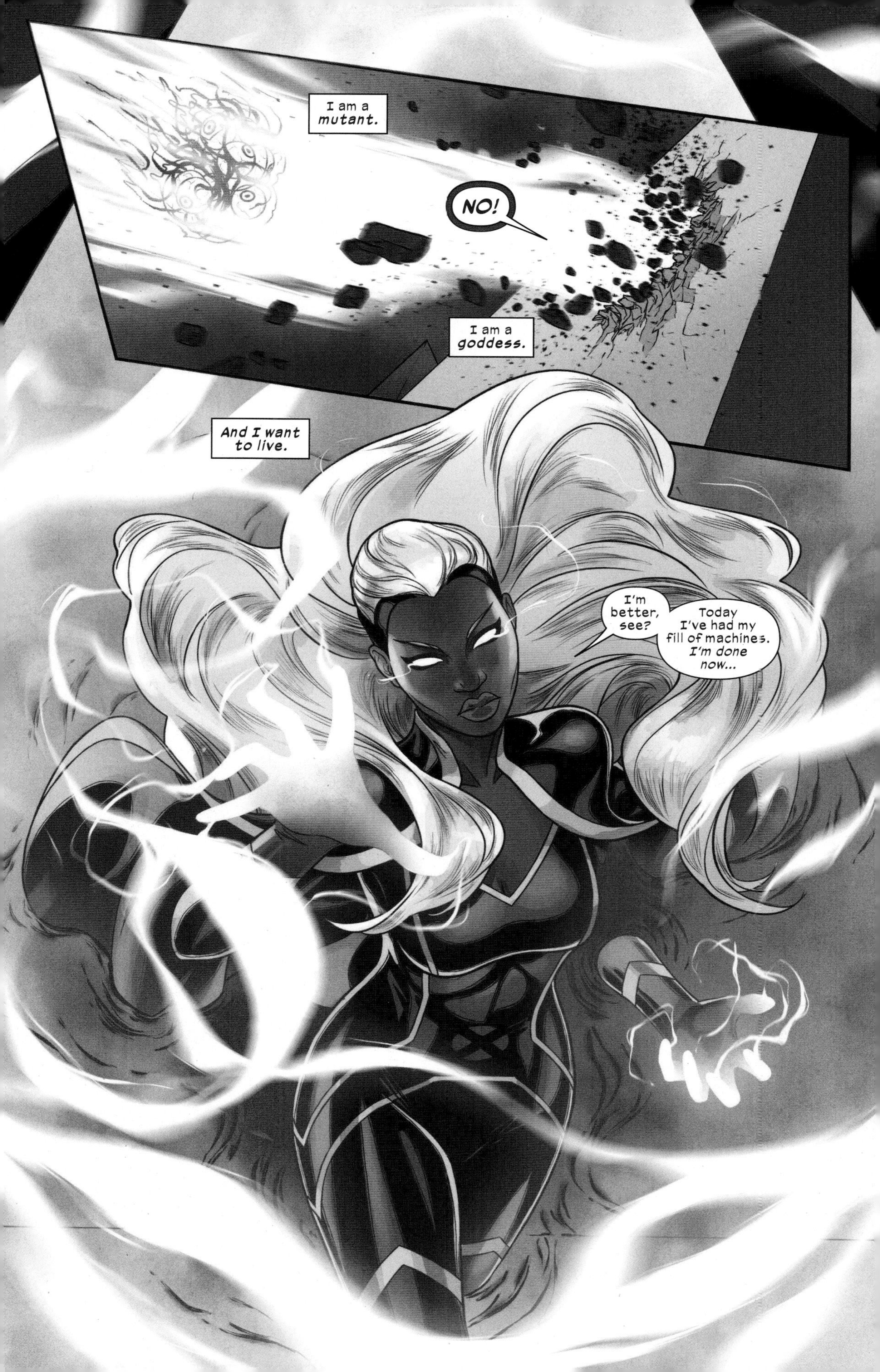
I am a mutant.
NO!
I am a goddess.
And I want to live.
I'm better, see?
Today I've had my fill of machines. I'm done now...

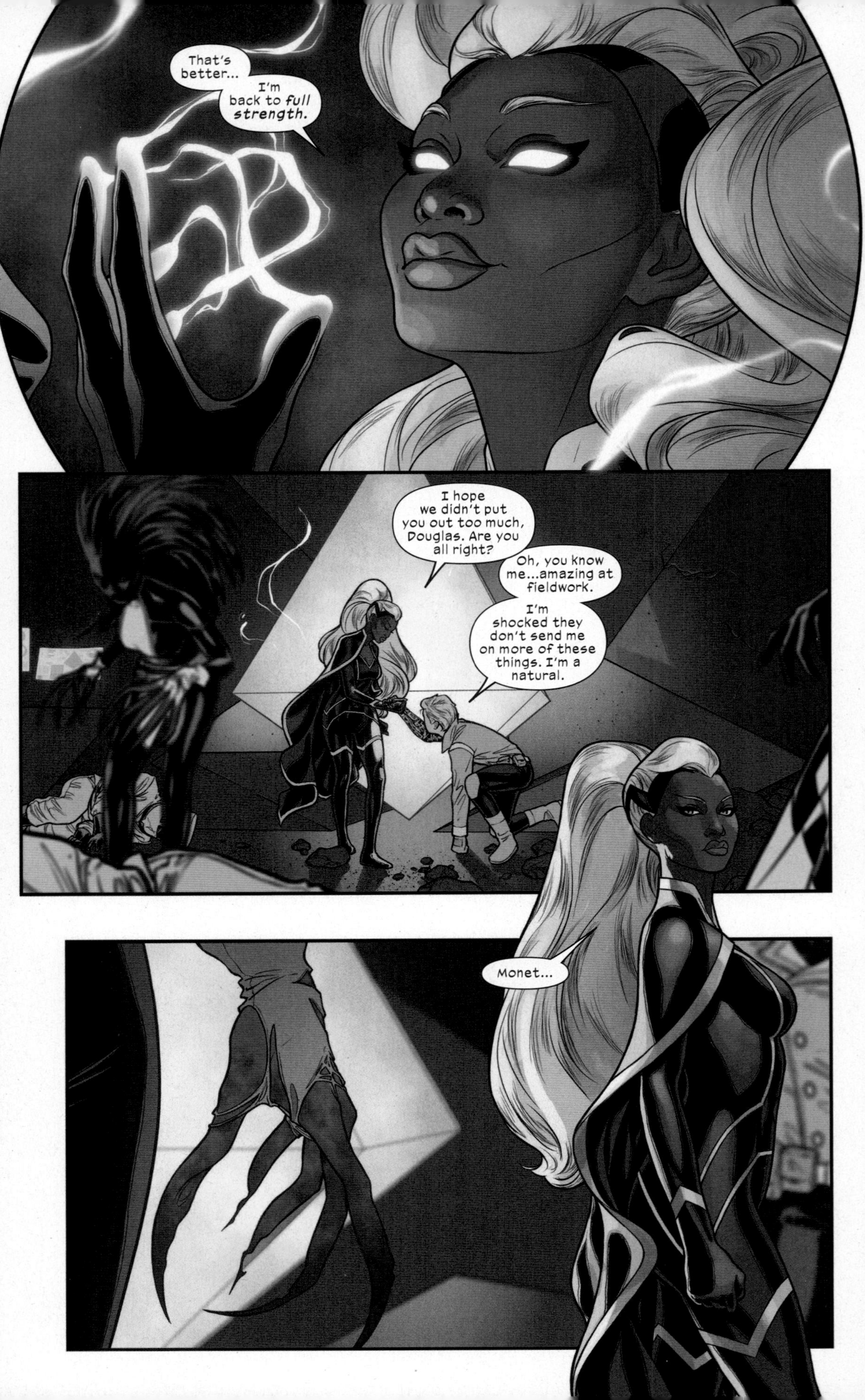
That's better... I'm back to *full strength.*
I hope we didn't put you out too much, Douglas. Are you all right?
Oh, you know me...amazing at fieldwork.
I'm shocked they don't send me on more of these things. I'm a natural.
Monet...

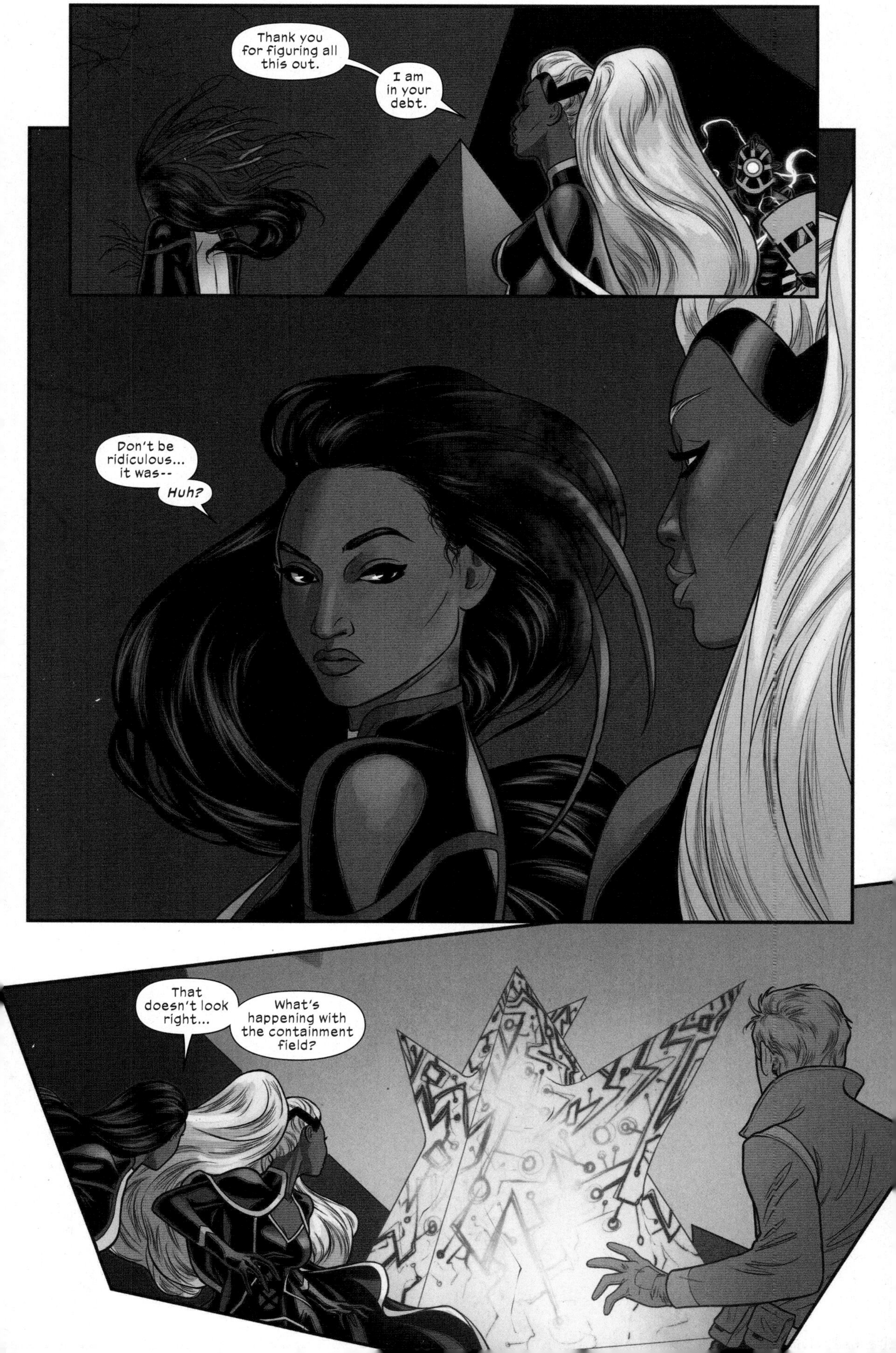
Thank you for figuring all this out.
I am in your debt.
Don't be ridiculous... it was--
Huh?
That doesn't look right...
What's happening with the containment field?

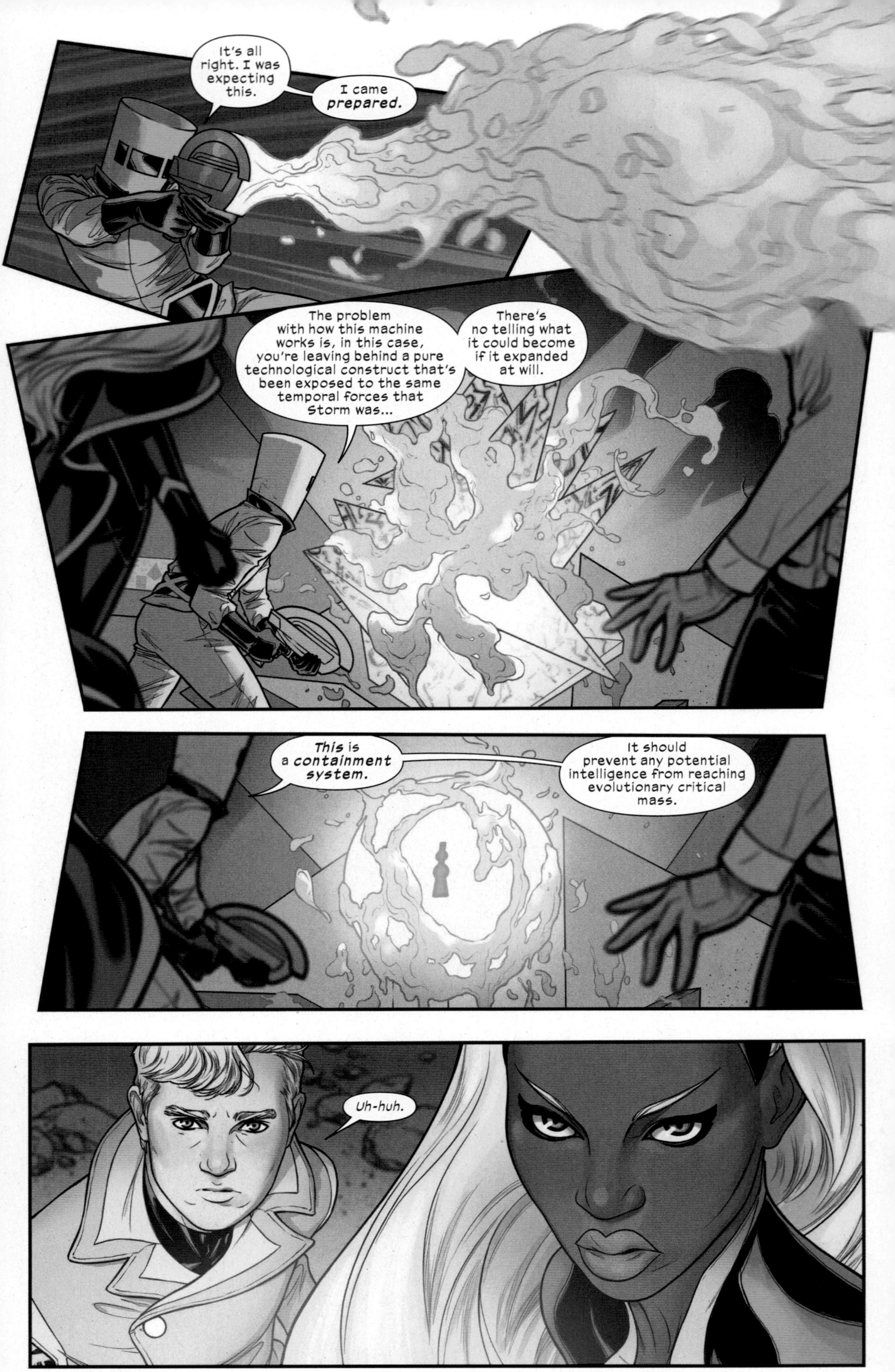

It's all right. I was expecting this.
I came *prepared.*
The problem with how this machine works is, in this case, you're leaving behind a pure technological construct that's been exposed to the same temporal forces that Storm was...
There's no telling what it could become if it expanded at will.
This is a *containment system.*
It should prevent any potential intelligence from reaching evolutionary critical mass.
Uh-huh.

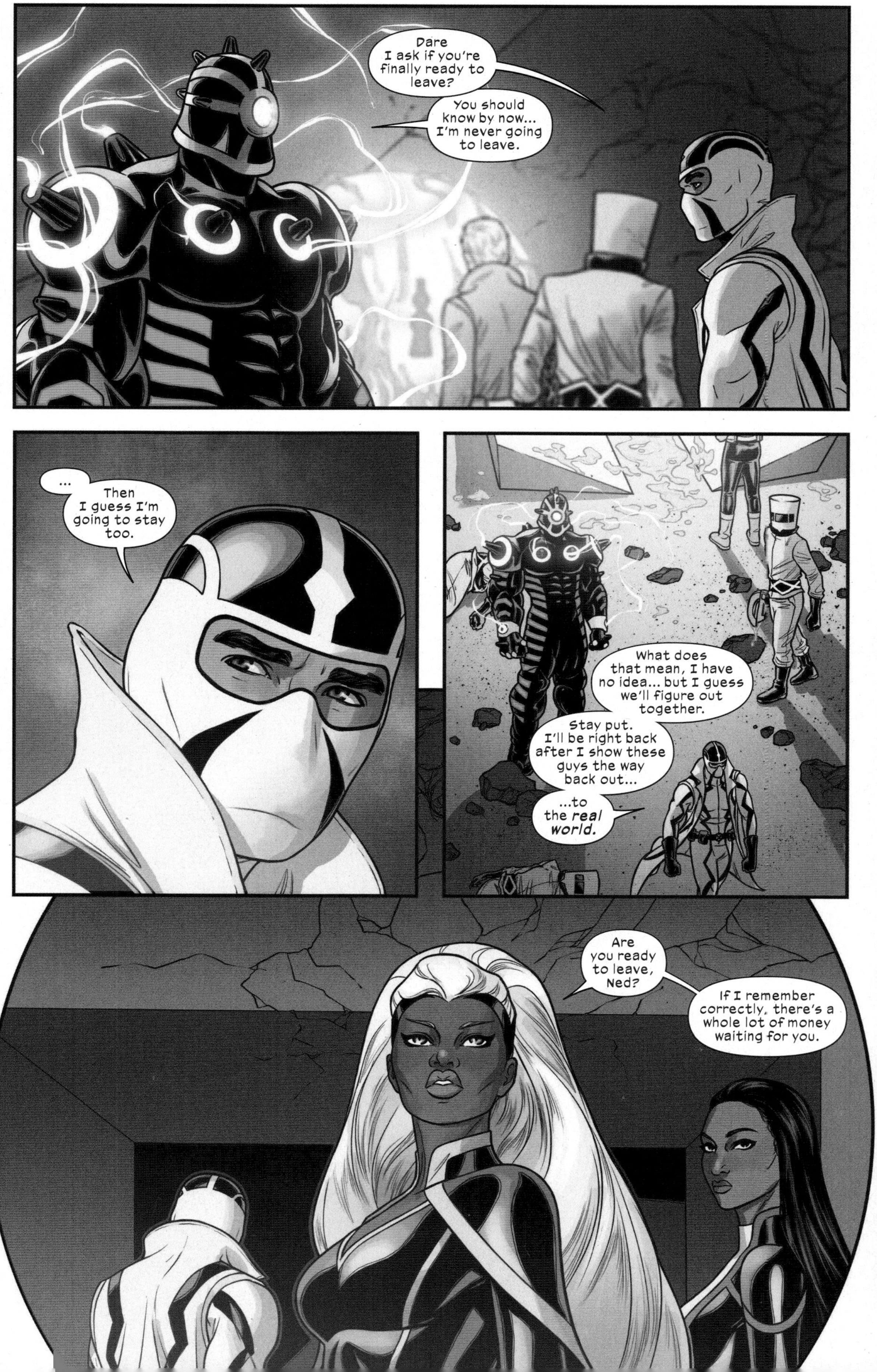
Dare I ask if you're finally ready to leave?
You should know by now... I'm never going to leave.
... Then I guess I'm going to stay too.
What does that mean, I have no idea... but I guess we'll figure out together.
Stay put. I'll be right back after I show these guys the way back out...
...to the *real world.*
Are you ready to leave, Ned?
If I remember correctly, there's a whole lot of money waiting for you.

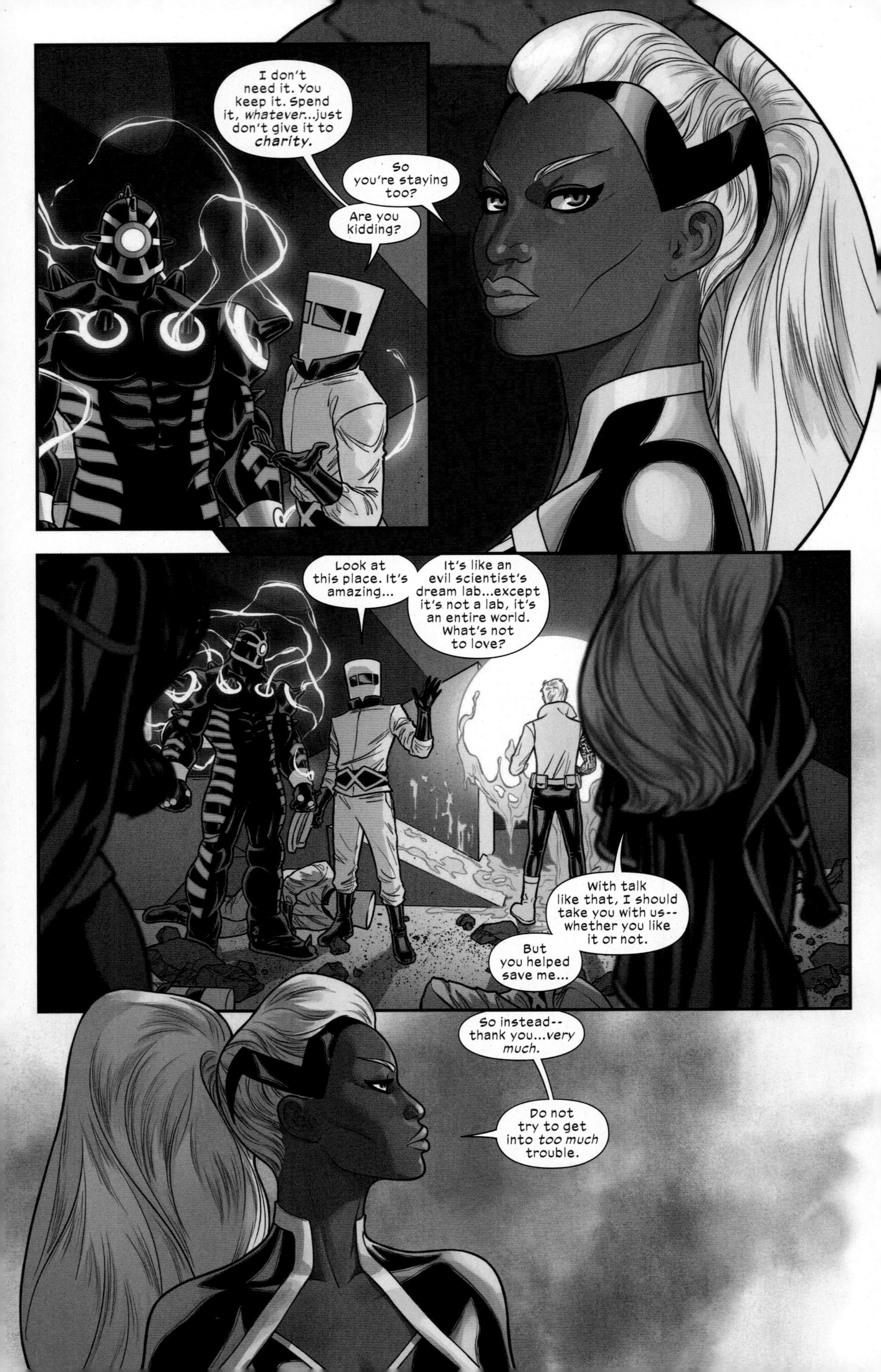

I don't need it. You keep it. Spend it, *whatever*...just don't give it to ***charity.***
So you're staying too?
Are you kidding?
Look at this place. It's amazing...
It's like an evil scientist's dream lab...except it's not a lab, it's an entire world. What's not to love?
With talk like that, I should take you with us--whether you like it or not.
But you helped save me...
So instead--thank you...*very much.*
Do not try to get into *too much* trouble.

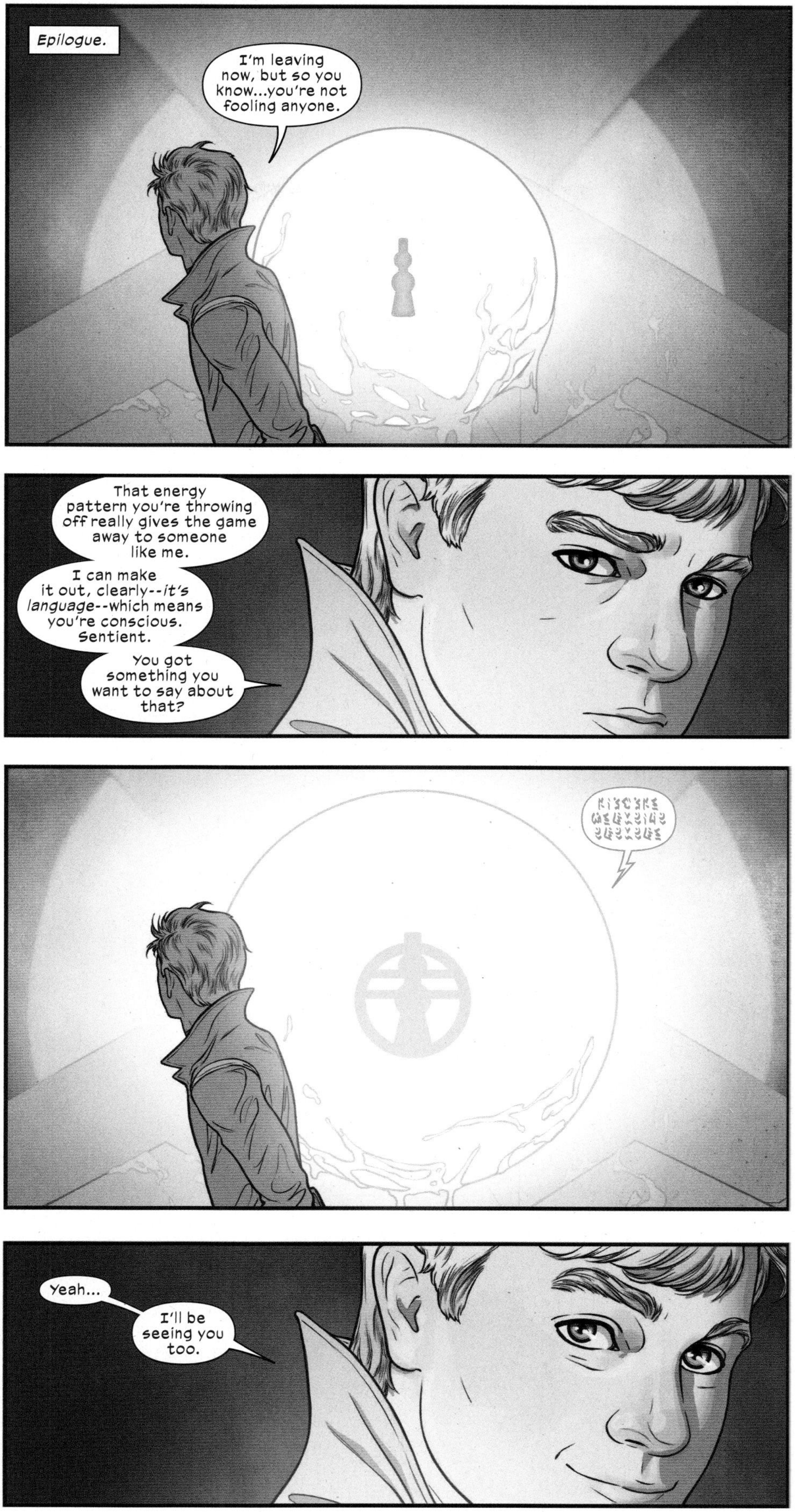
Epilogue.
I'm leaving now, but so you know...you're not fooling anyone.
That energy pattern you're throwing off really gives the game away to someone like me.
I can make it out, clearly--*it's language*--which means you're conscious. Sentient.
You got something you want to say about that?
Yeah...
I'll be seeing you too.

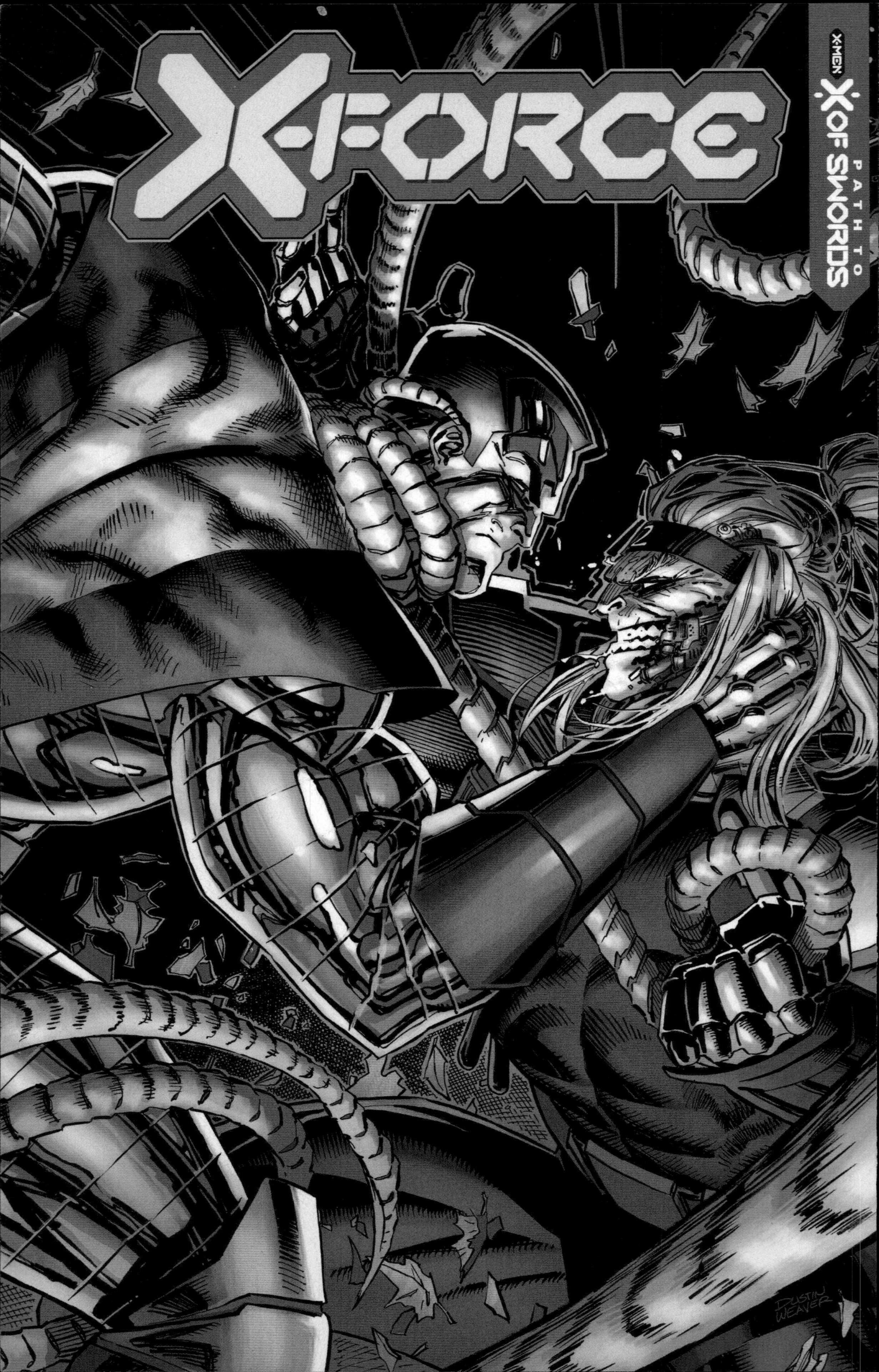

X-FORCE
X-MEN
PATH TO
X OF SWORDS
DUSTIN WEAVER

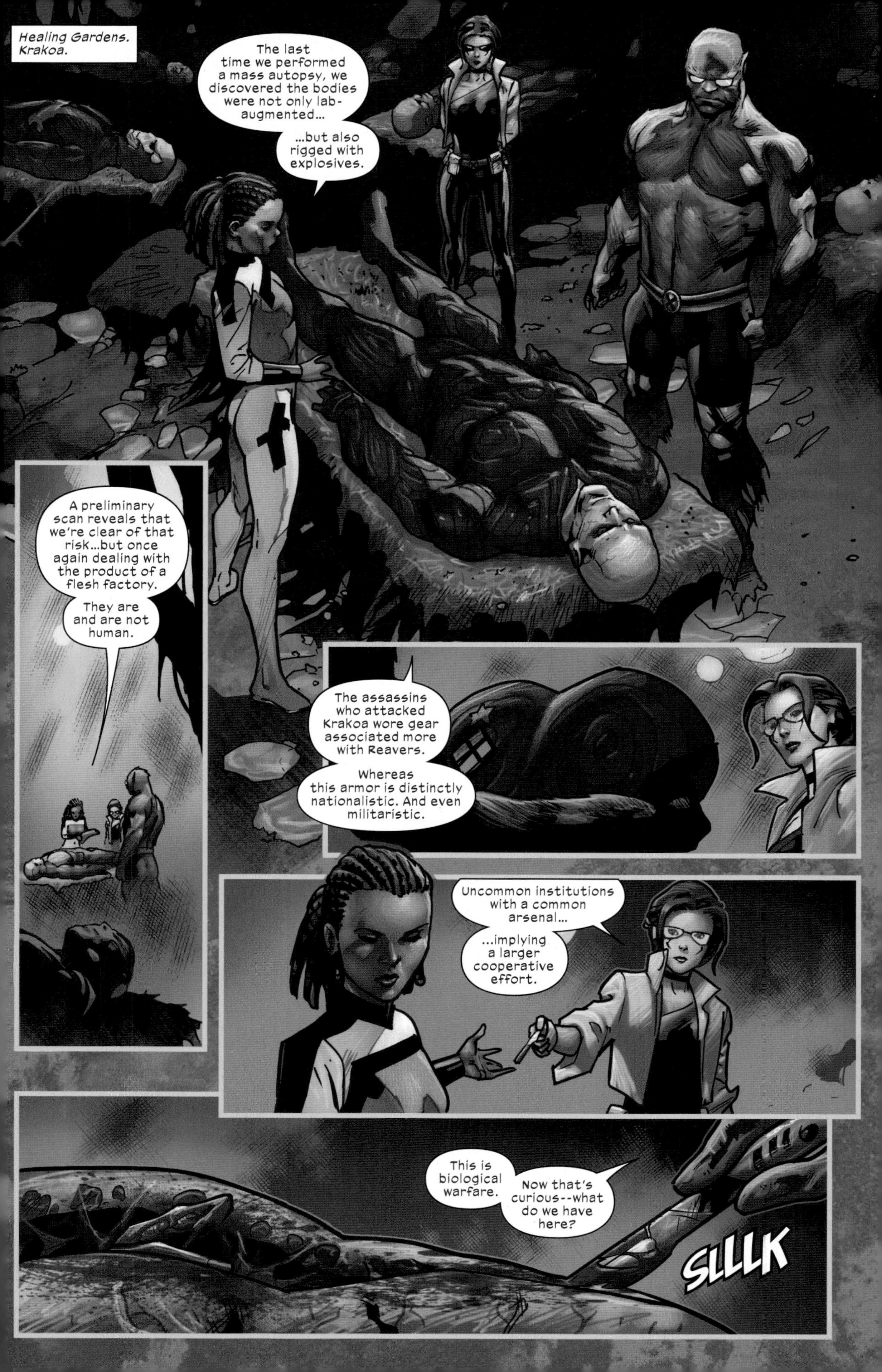
Healing Gardens. Krakoa.
The last time we performed a mass autopsy, we discovered the bodies were not only lab-augmented...
...but also rigged with explosives.
A preliminary scan reveals that we're clear of that risk...but once again dealing with the product of a flesh factory.
They are and are not human.
The assassins who attacked Krakoa wore gear associated more with Reavers.
Whereas this armor is distinctly nationalistic. And even militaristic.
Uncommon institutions with a common arsenal...
...implying a larger cooperative effort.
This is biological warfare.
Now that's curious--what do we have here?
SLLLK

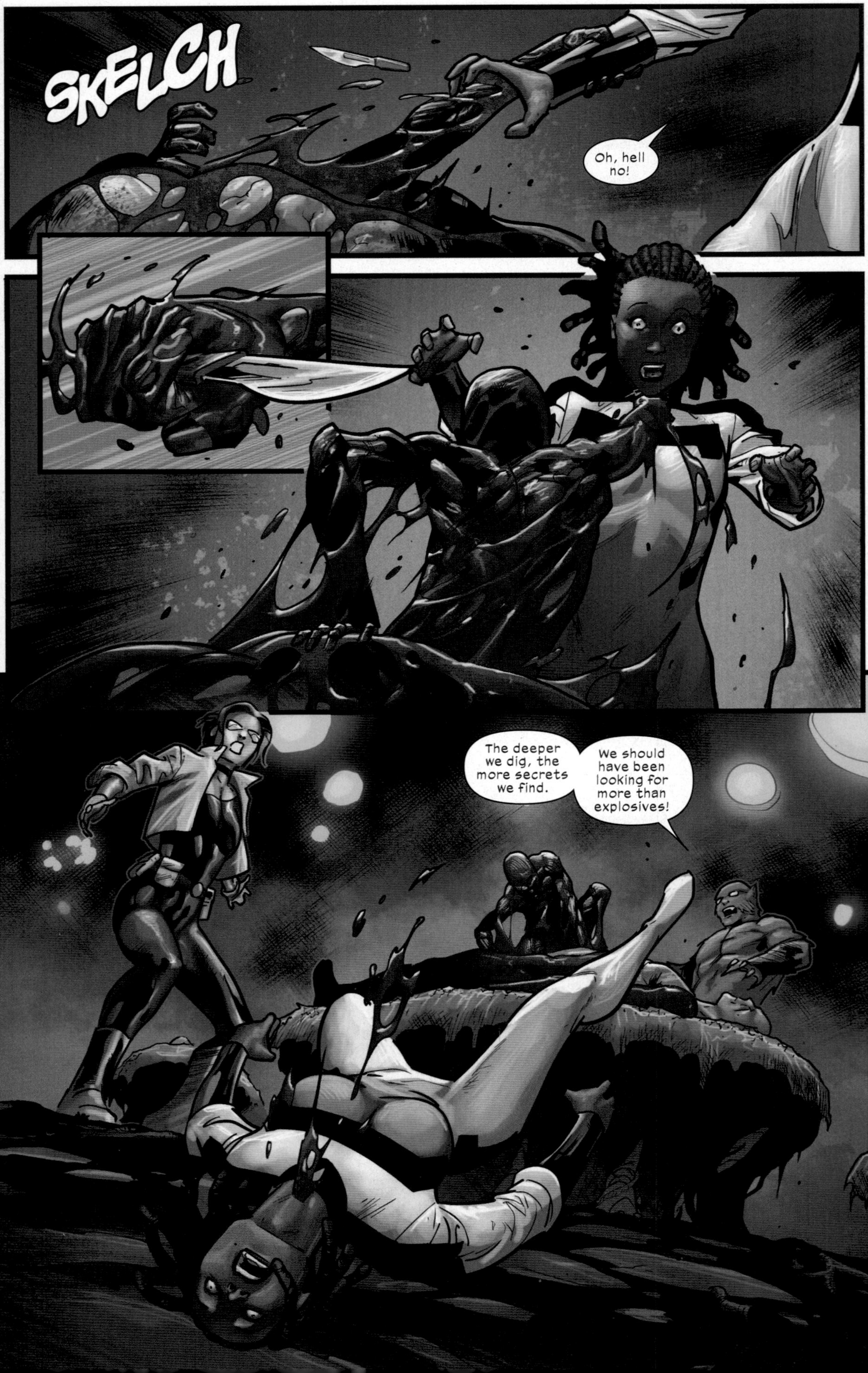
SKELCH
Oh, hell no!
The deeper we dig, the more secrets we find.
We should have been looking for more than explosives!

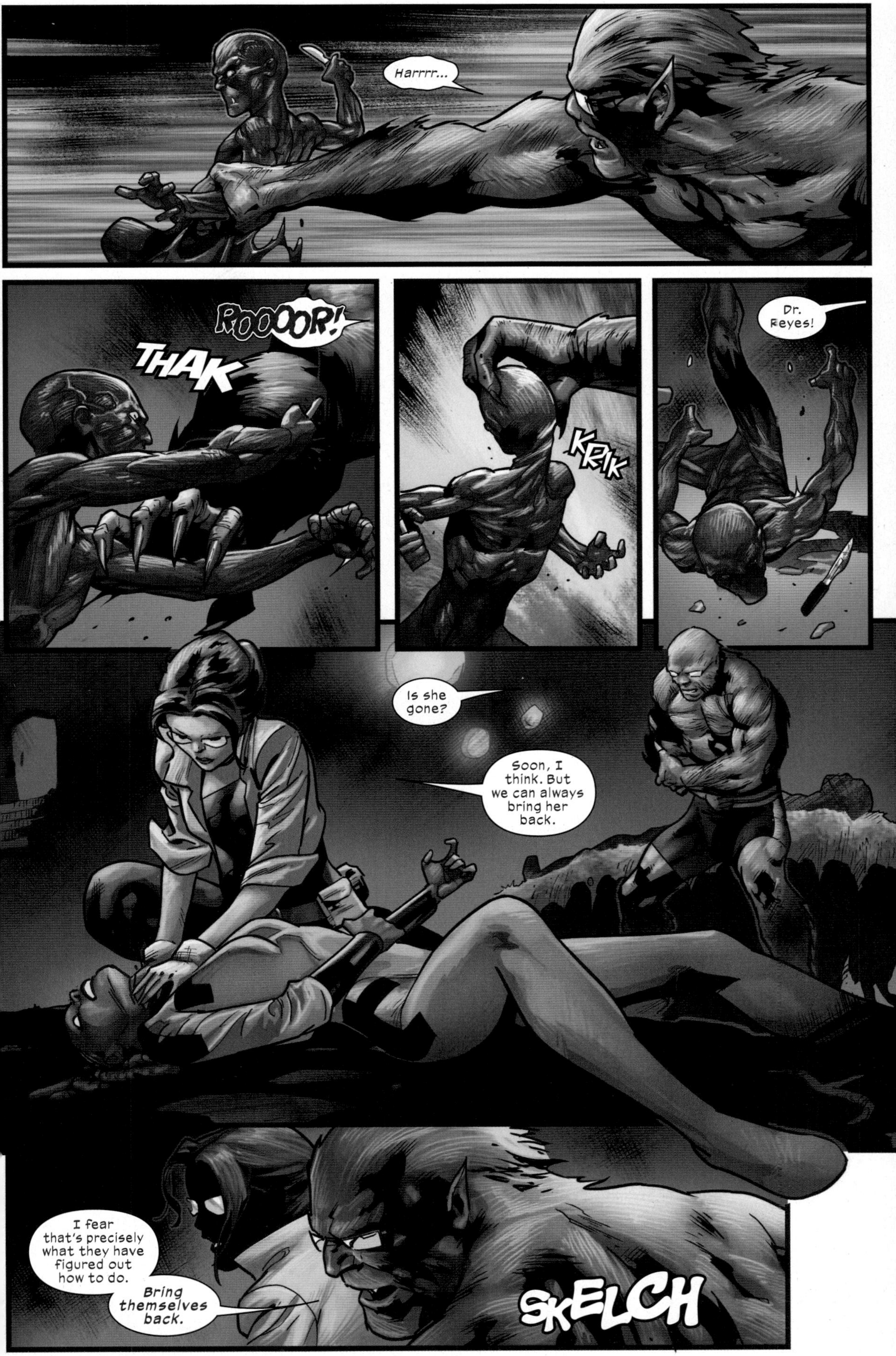
Harrrr...
ROOOOR!
THAK
KRIK
Dr. Reyes!
Is she gone?
Soon, I think. But we can always bring her back.
I fear that's precisely what they have figured out how to do.
Bring themselves back.
SKELCH

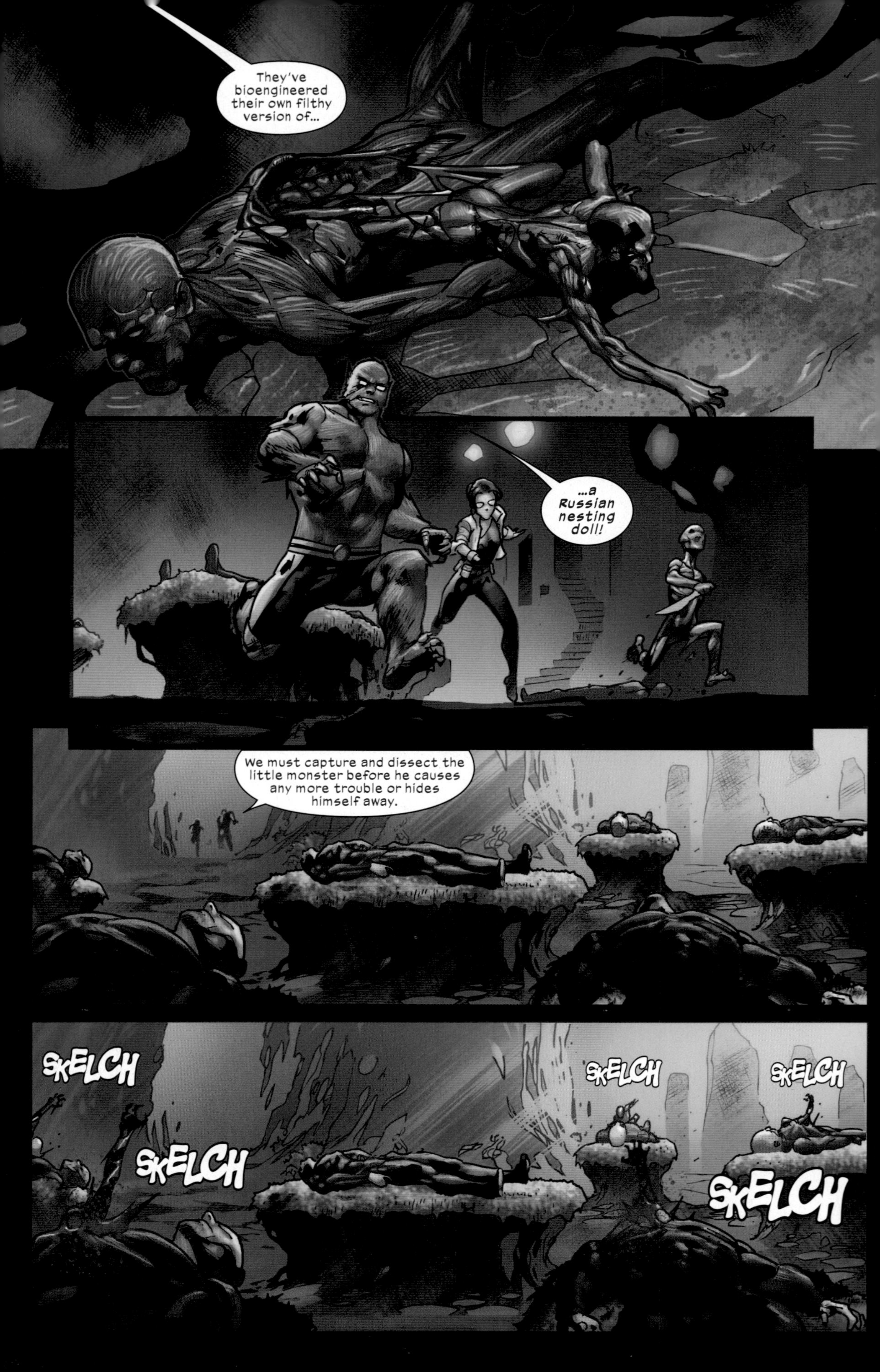
They've bioengineered their own filthy version of...
...a Russian nesting doll!
We must capture and dissect the little monster before he causes any more trouble or hides himself away.
SKELCH
SKELCH
SKELCH
SKELCH
SKELCH

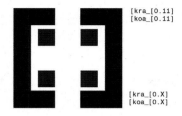

[kra_[0.11]
[koa_[0.11]

[kra_[0.X]
[koa_[0.X]

THE ENEMY WITHIN

After Wolverine and the Marauders took down a criminal organization that was stealing Krakoan medicine, a group of mysterious Russian super-soldiers was discovered and captured...

Beast

Sage

Cecilia Reyes

Colossus

Domino

[kra_[0.11]...]
[koa_[0.11]...]

[A._Spy_Agency]

[00_mutant_espionage]
[00_law_order___X___]

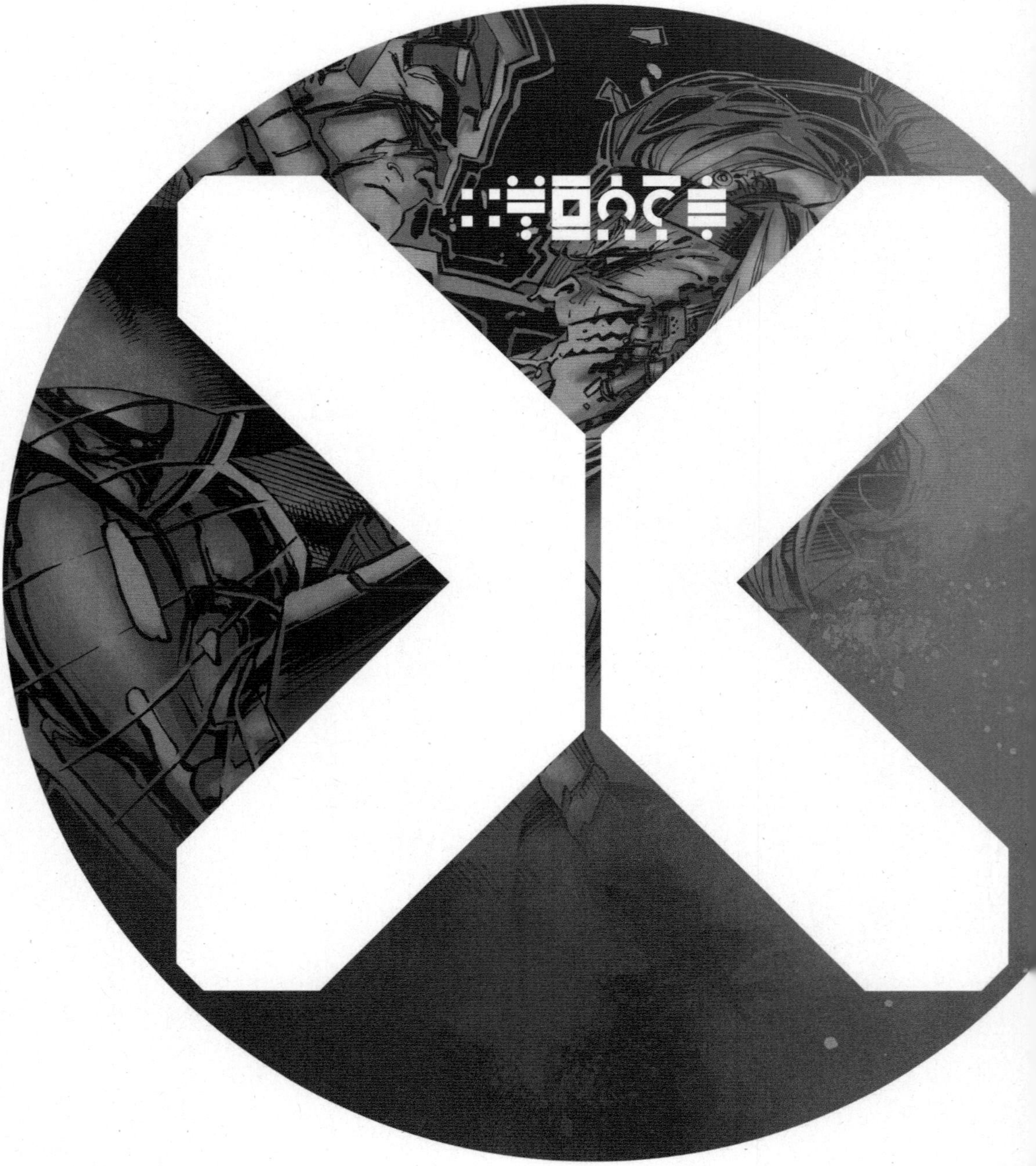

[00_mutant_espionage]
[00_law_order___X___]

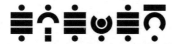

BENJAMIN PERCY................................[WRITER]
JAN BAZALDUA..................................[ARTIST]
GURU-eFX..............................[COLOR ARTIST]
VC's JOE CARAMAGNA.........................[LETTERER]
TOM MULLER....................................[DESIGN]

DUSTIN WEAVER & EDGAR DELGADO...........[COVER ARTISTS]

NICK RUSSELL..............................[PRODUCTION]

JONATHAN HICKMAN............................[HEAD OF X]
CHRIS ROBINSON......................[ASSISTANT EDITOR]
JORDAN D. WHITE...............................[EDITOR]
C.B. CEBULSKI.........................[EDITOR IN CHIEF]

[11] X-FORCE

[ISSUE ELEVEN].....................RED DAWN

[00_mutant_espionage]
[00_law_order___X___]

[00_00...0]
[00_00..11]

[00_probe_]
[00_______]

[00_______]

[00______X]

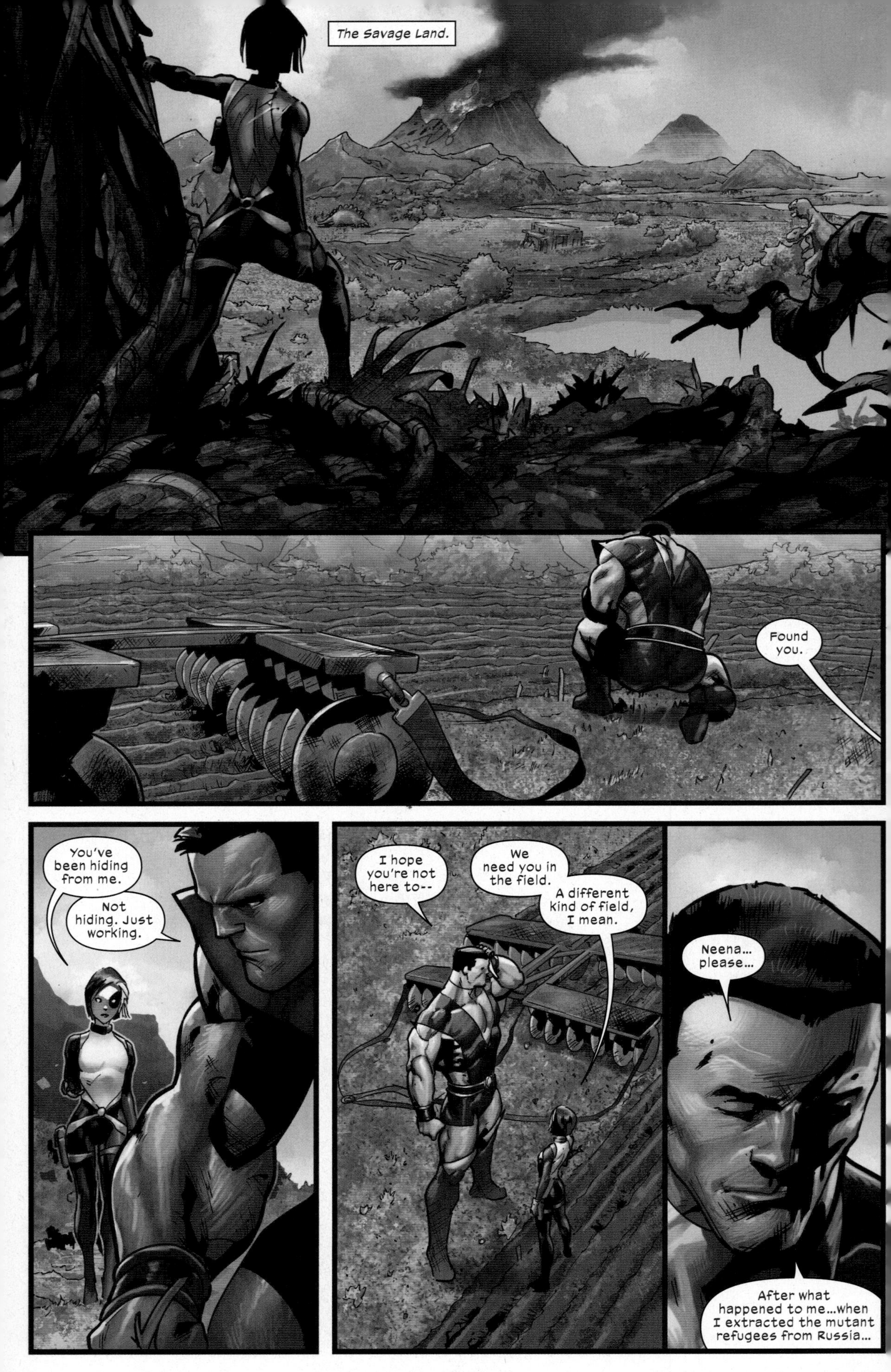
The Savage Land.
Found you.
You've been hiding from me.
Not hiding. Just working.
I hope you're not here to--
We need you in the field.
A different kind of field, I mean.
Neena... please...
After what happened to me...when I extracted the mutant refugees from Russia...

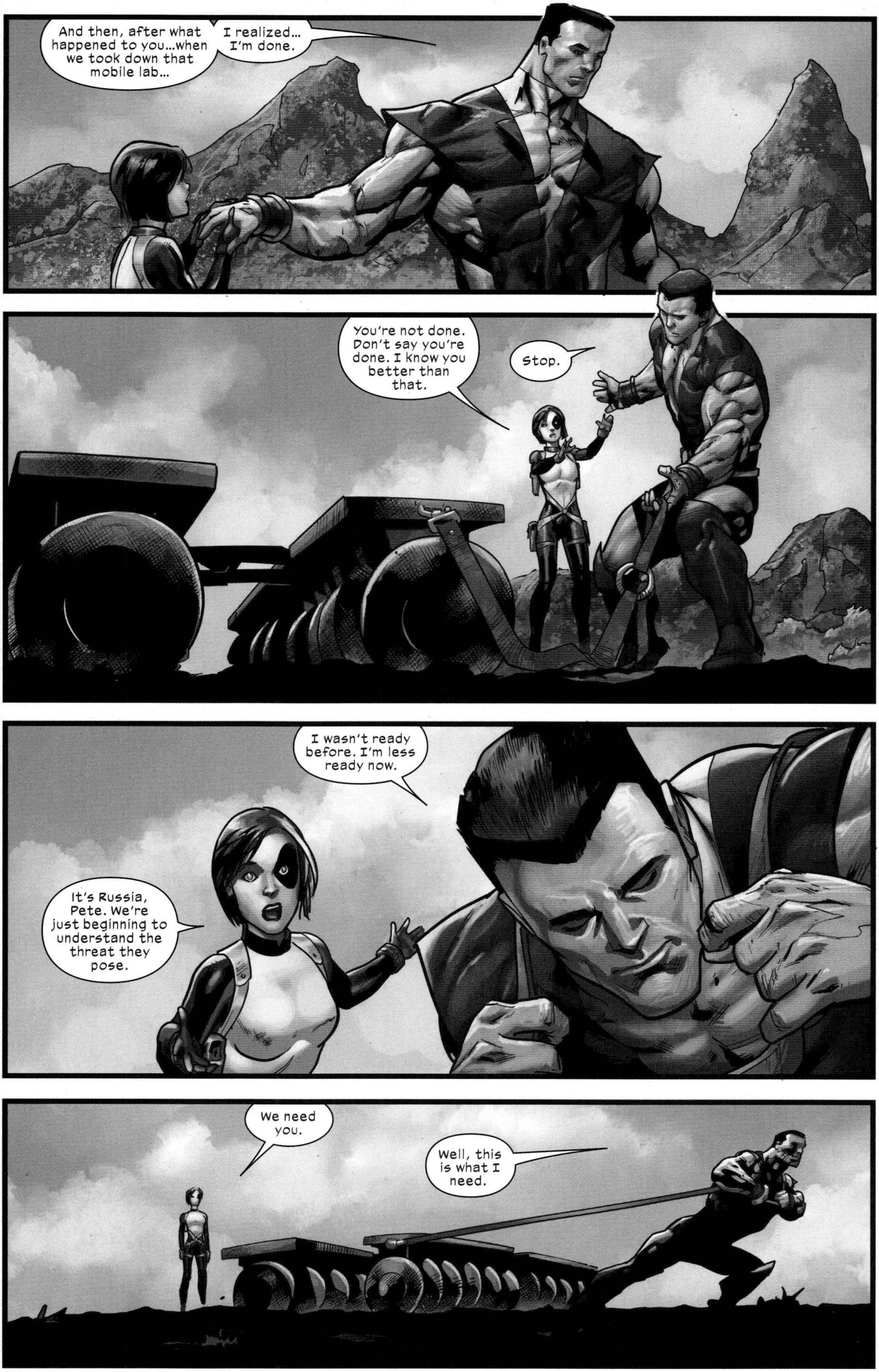
And then, after what happened to you...when we took down that mobile lab...
I realized... I'm done.
You're not done. Don't say you're done. I know you better than that.
Stop.
I wasn't ready before. I'm less ready now.
It's Russia, Pete. We're just beginning to understand the threat they pose.
We need you.
Well, this is what I need.

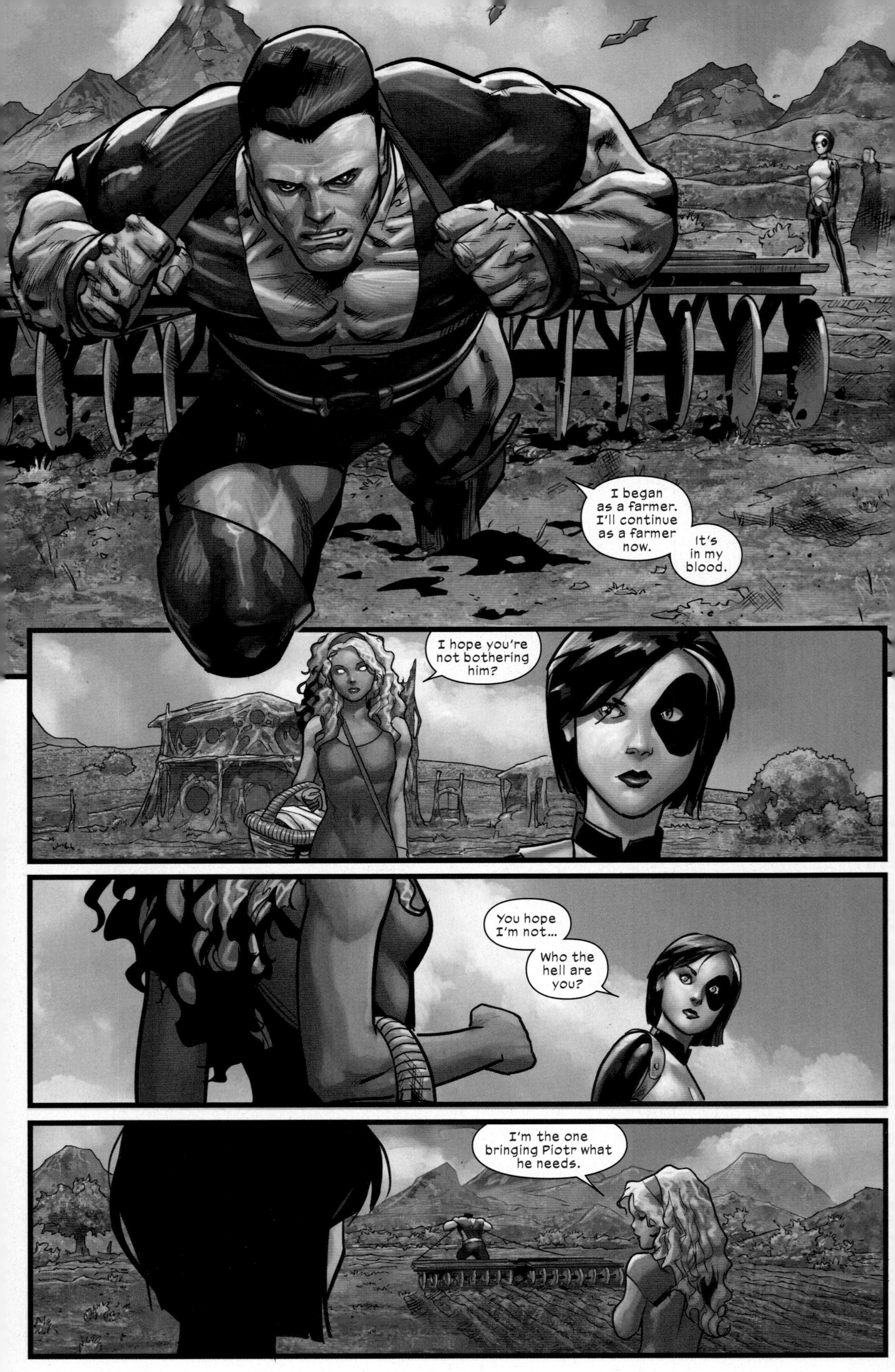
I began as a farmer. I'll continue as a farmer now.
It's in my blood.
I hope you're not bothering him?
You hope I'm not...
Who the hell are you?
I'm the one bringing Piotr what he needs.

CHAPTER 1

Drink is a writer's affliction. The need for it. The belief that it can lubricate the imagination or help an overactive mind finally find sleep. I suppose alcoholism is the only occupational hazard of my trade besides bleary eyes, a bad back, the occasional paper cut. Madness does tend to find us.

When I started making money off my writing, I didn't really know what to do with it. I don't care for luxurious clothes or expensive cars or international travel. I only wish to be home with my work. I've bought a few paintings, some first-edition novels, but wine is my investment of choice.

My cellar is rather elaborate and a point of guilty pride. Among its many treasures are: a 1945 Château Mouton Rothschild, with its hints of coffee and chocolate and black currants. The powerfully complex and nuanced 1921 Château d'Yquem. And a 1982 Pichon Longueville Comtesse de Lalande, a Bourdeaux that offers an unmatched velvety sweetness.

And it was here, in the cellar, that he found me.

Mutton was on the menu for dinner, and I went hunting for a leathery pinot noir to pair with it. The scrape of his boot startled me. He filled the doorway so that only a little light filtered through. His hair was more like the coarse, dark fur of the bear that he resembled. He wore a costume of armor. When he spoke, his voice was subterranean in its bass.

To be continued...

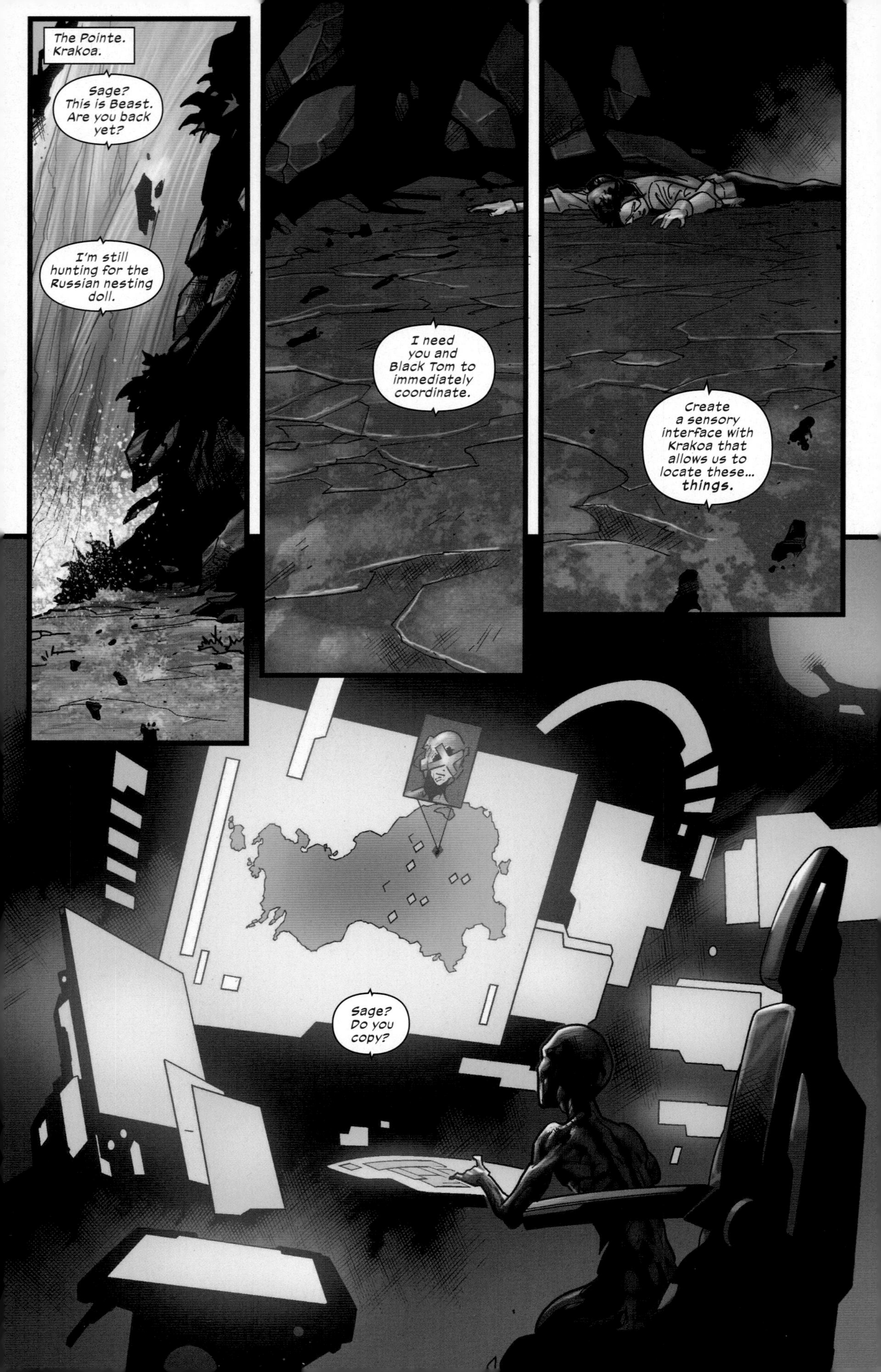
The Pointe.
Krakoa.
Sage? This is Beast. Are you back yet?
I'm still hunting for the Russian nesting doll.
I need you and Black Tom to immediately coordinate.
Create a sensory interface with Krakoa that allows us to locate these... things.
Sage? Do you copy?

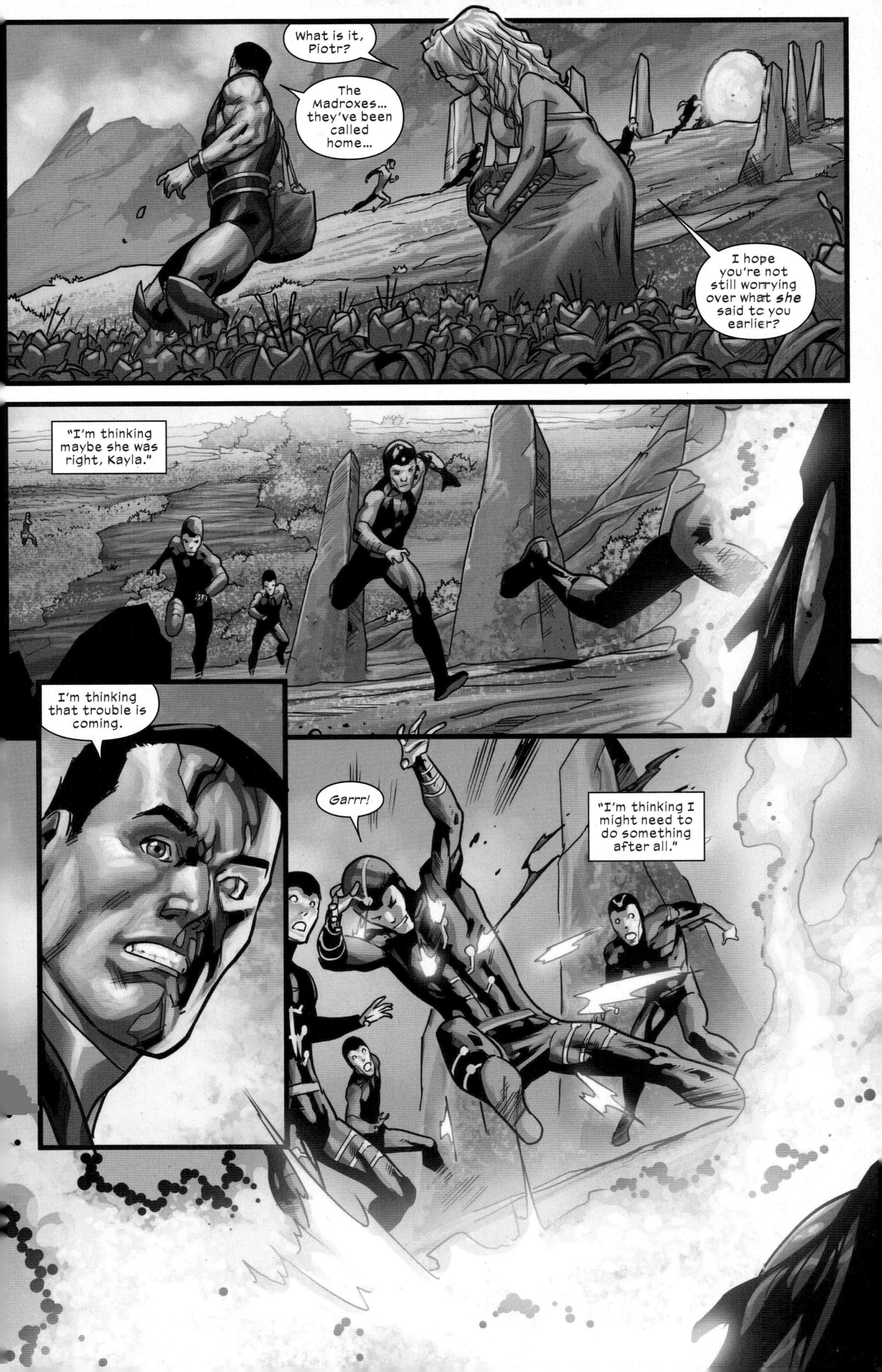
What is it, Piotr?
The Madroxes... they've been called home...
I hope you're not still worrying over what *she* said to you earlier?
"I'm thinking maybe she was right, Kayla."
I'm thinking that trouble is coming.
Garrr!
"I'm thinking I might need to do something after all."

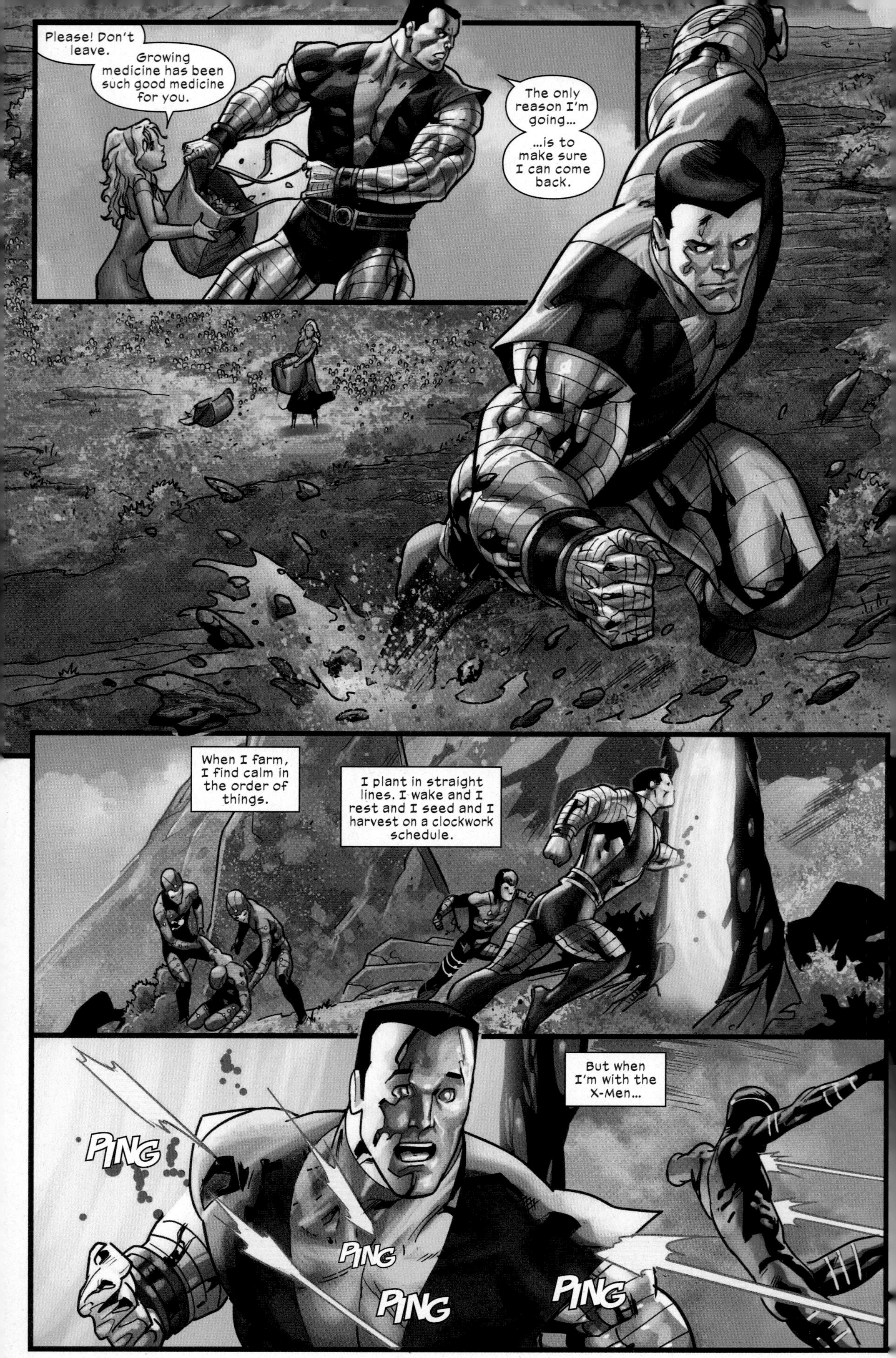

Please! Don't leave.
Growing medicine has been such good medicine for you.
The only reason I'm going...
...is to make sure I can come back.
When I farm, I find calm in the order of things.
I plant in straight lines. I wake and I rest and I seed and I harvest on a clockwork schedule.
But when I'm with the X-Men...
PING
PING
PING
PING

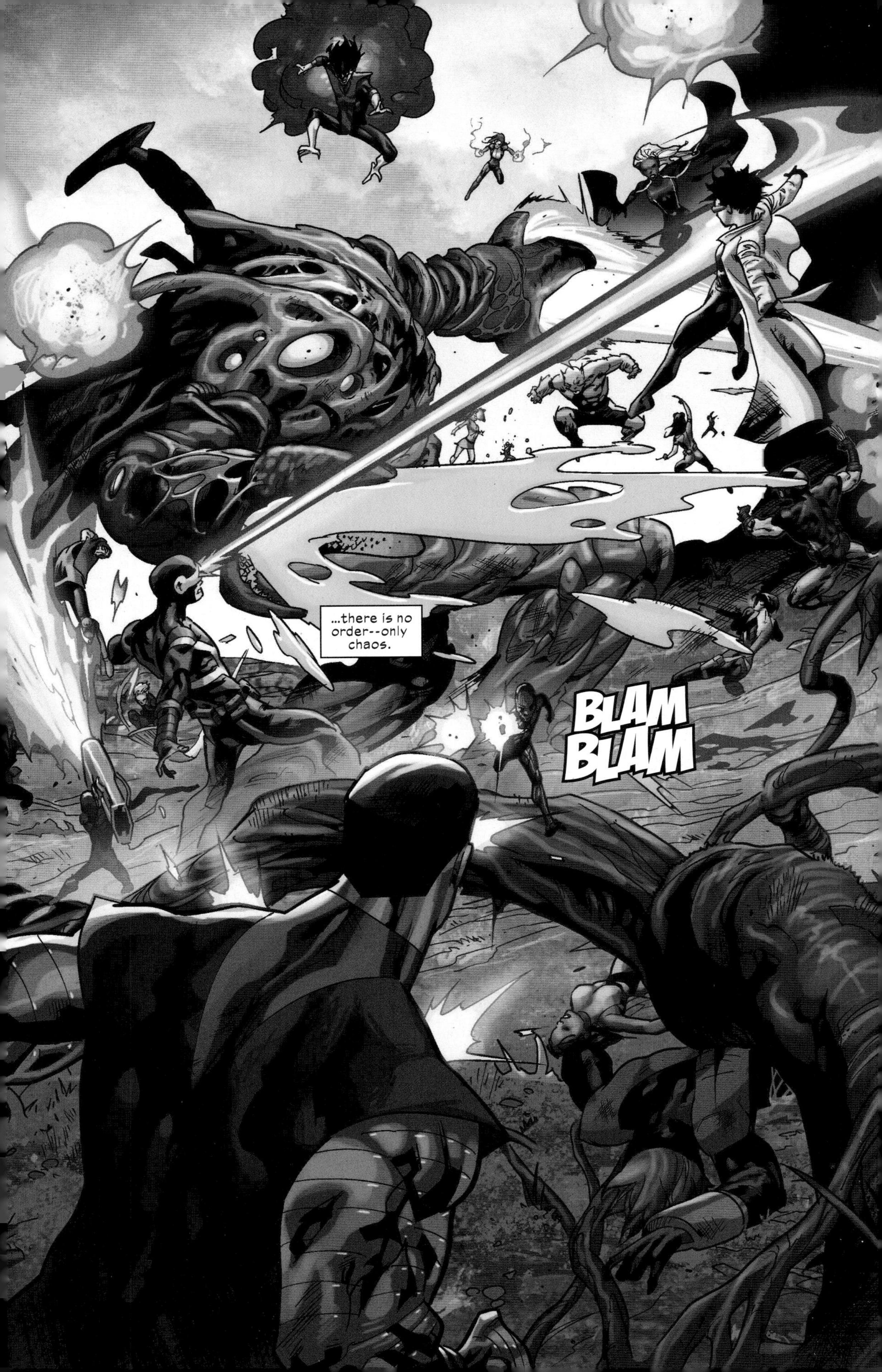
...there is no order--only chaos.
BLAM BLAM

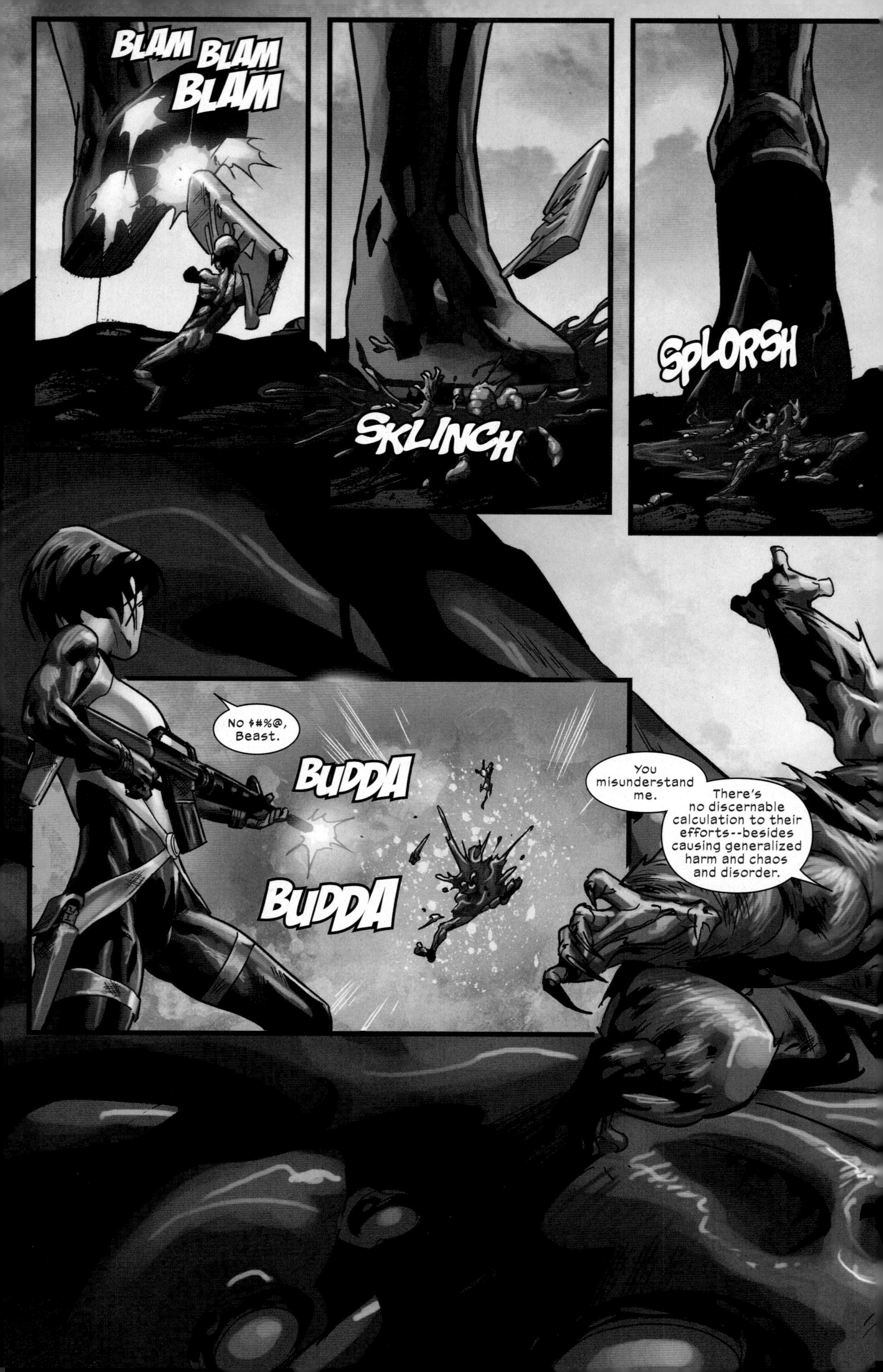
BLAM BLAM BLAM
SKLINCH
SPLORSH
No $#%@, Beast.
BUDDA
BUDDA
You misunderstand me.
There's no discernable calculation to their efforts--besides causing generalized harm and chaos and disorder.

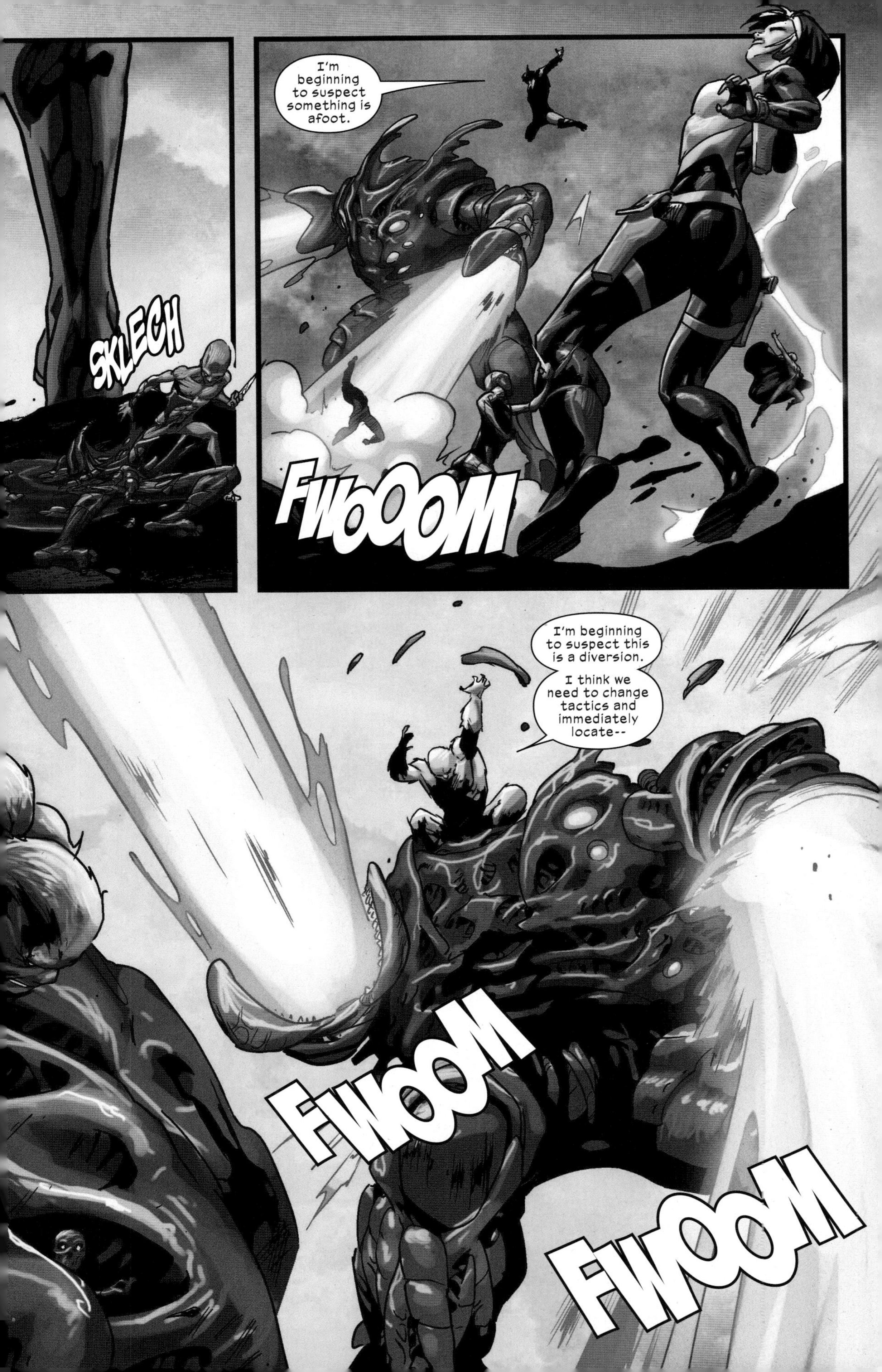

SKLECH
I'm beginning to suspect something is afoot.
FWOOOM
I'm beginning to suspect this is a diversion.
I think we need to change tactics and immediately locate--
FWOOM
FWOOM

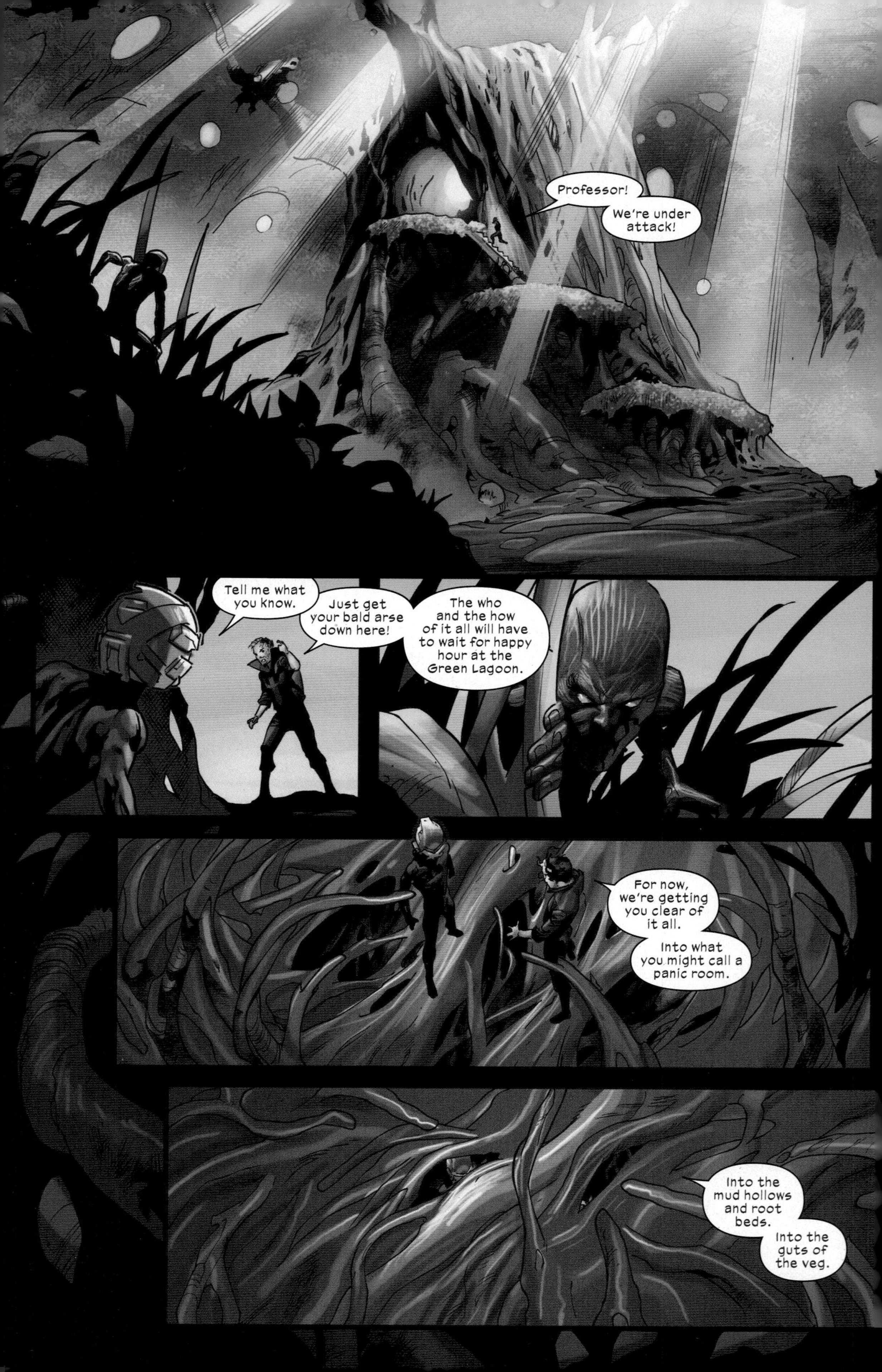
Professor!
We're under attack!
Tell me what you know.
Just get your bald arse down here!
The who and the how of it all will have to wait for happy hour at the Green Lagoon.
For now, we're getting you clear of it all.
Into what you might call a panic room.
Into the mud hollows and root beds.
Into the guts of the veg.

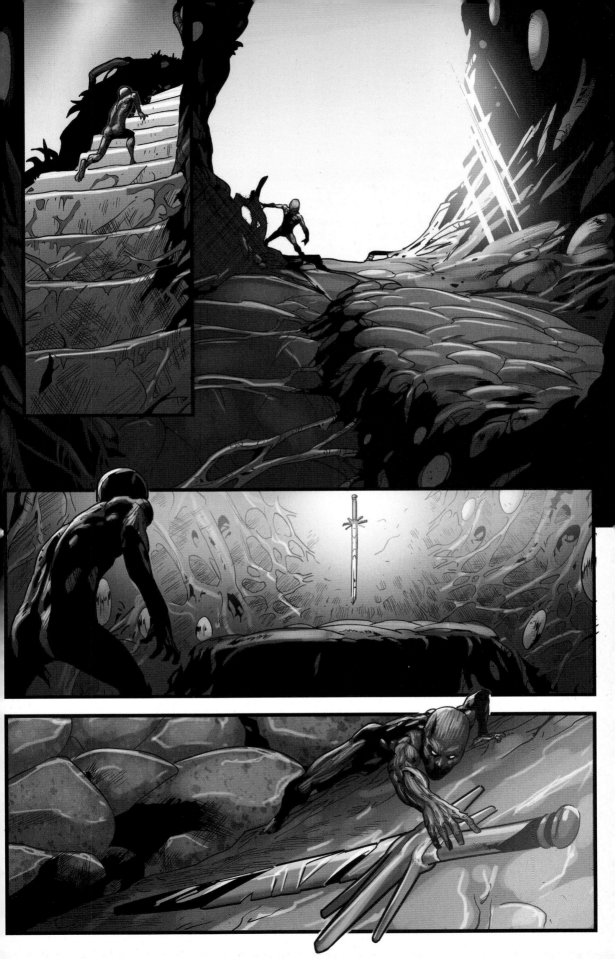

CHAPTER 2

He said that he admired my writing very much. Russia has had many greats, he said. Dostoevsky. Tolstoy. Turgenev. Chekov. "But you," he said. "You are the most *powerful*."

But what had I done with that power? Won some prizes? Made a few people weep in their armchairs? Animate some dinnertime conversations? "You are capable of so much more."

But I don't want for much, I told him. I only want a quiet life. I only want to do my best to illuminate the human condition.

"You must recognize your superiority and use it to celebrate the superiority of your country."

"I am not," I said, stammering some, as he approached. "We are *not* superior."

He swung out an arm then, and I flinched. Though it was clear he did not mean to strike me, something came rolling off him, like a big block of energy. The air thrummed. And I heard a great rustling tear. By the time I had recovered my senses, I saw that every wine bottle was suddenly bare.

"No," I said. "No!" And I fell to my knees, hurrying through the shed labels, trying desperately to match them with their bottles.

"You see," he said. "You do believe in superiority after all." He held out his giant hand to me. "Now come."

летописец

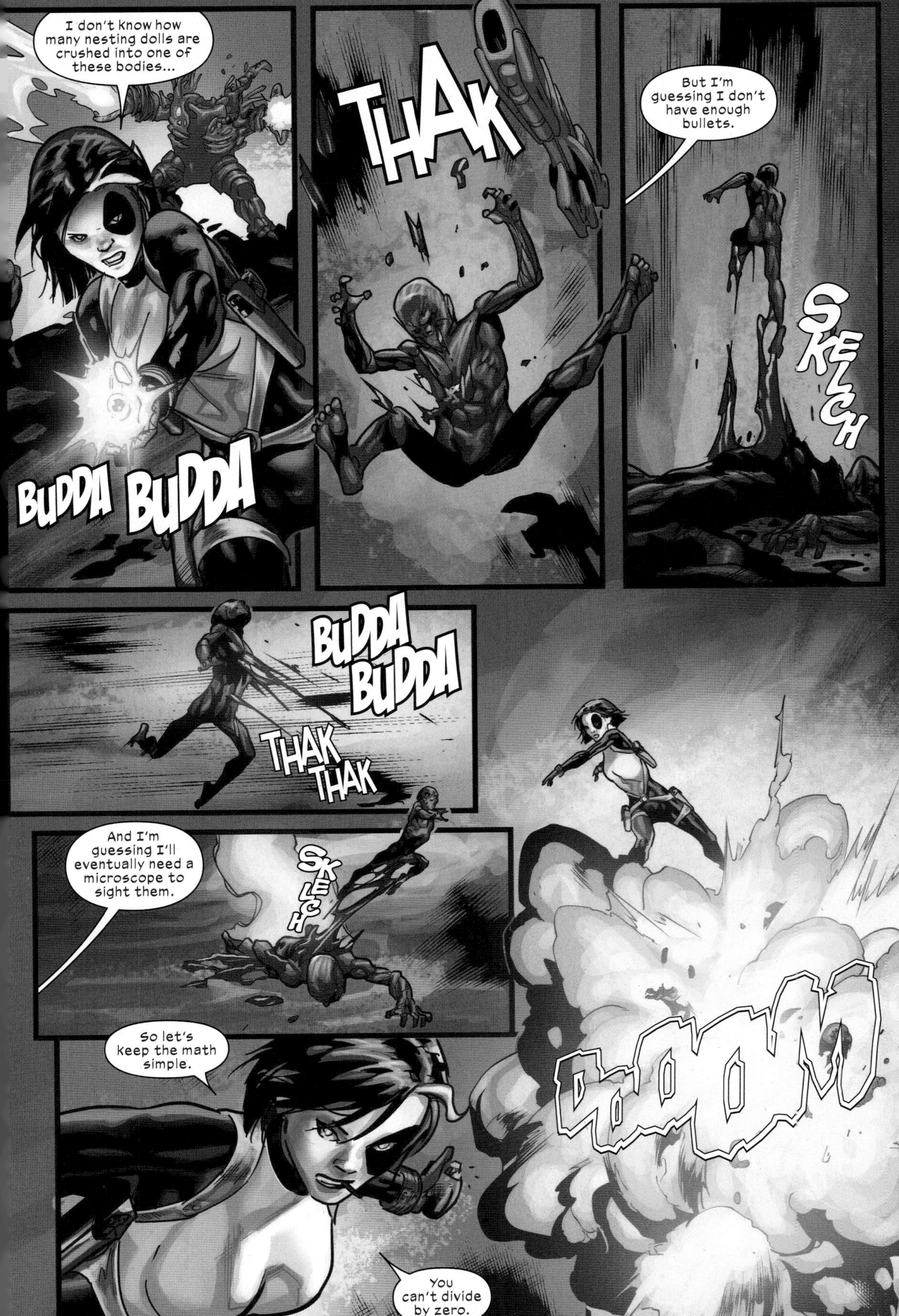

I don't know how many nesting dolls are crushed into one of these bodies...
BUDDA BUDDA
THAK
But I'm guessing I don't have enough bullets.
SKELCH
BUDDA BUDDA
THAK THAK
And I'm guessing I'll eventually need a microscope to sight them.
SKELCH
So let's keep the math simple.
You can't divide by zero.
DOOOM

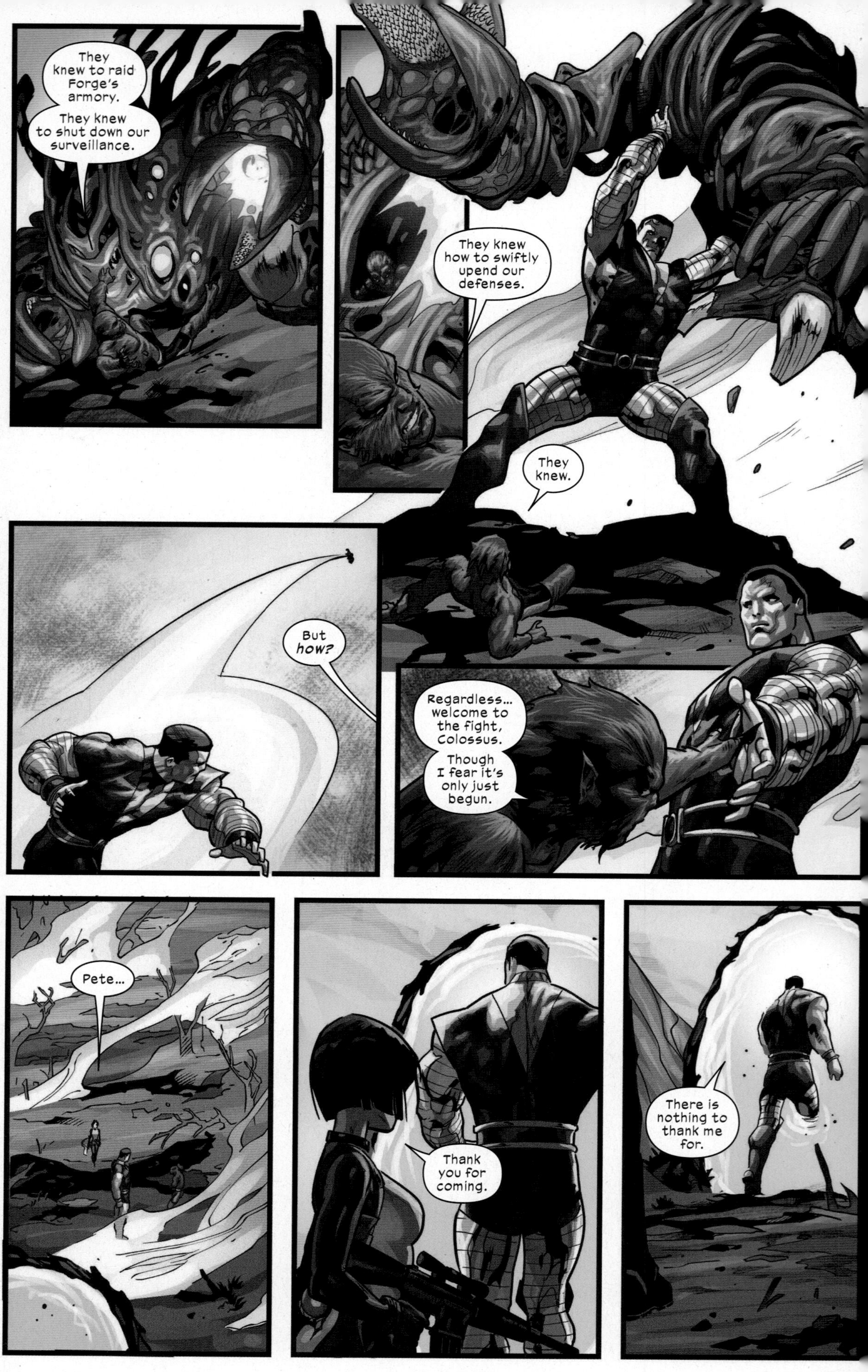
They knew to raid Forge's armory.
They knew to shut down our surveillance.
They knew how to swiftly upend our defenses.
They knew.
But *how?*
Regardless... welcome to the fight, Colossus.
Though I fear it's only just begun.
Pete...
Thank you for coming.
There is nothing to thank me for.

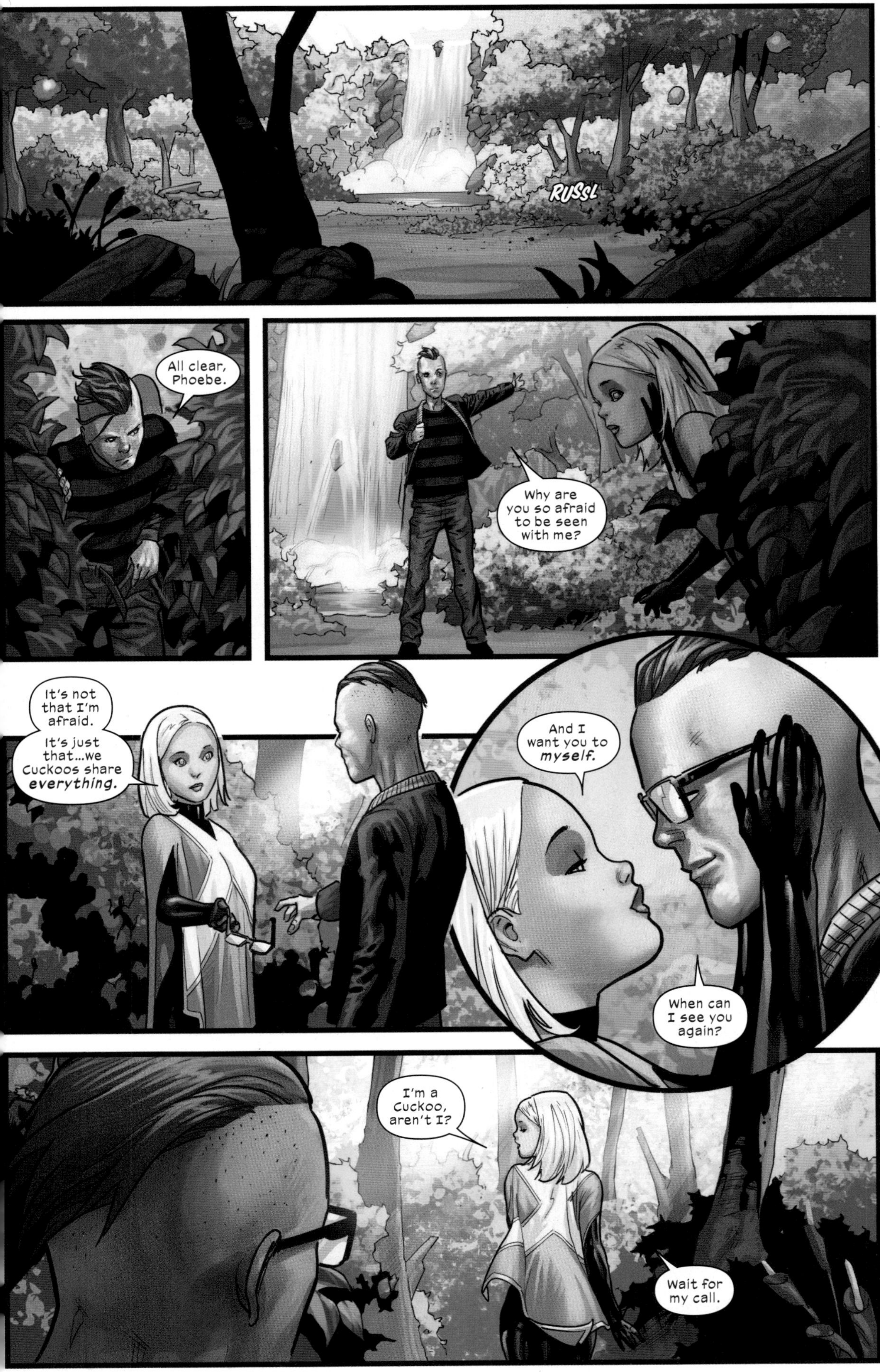
RUSSL
All clear, Phoebe.
Why are you so afraid to be seen with me?
It's not that I'm afraid.
It's just that...we Cuckoos share *everything.*
And I want you to *myself.*
When can I see you again?
I'm a Cuckoo, aren't I?
Wait for my call.

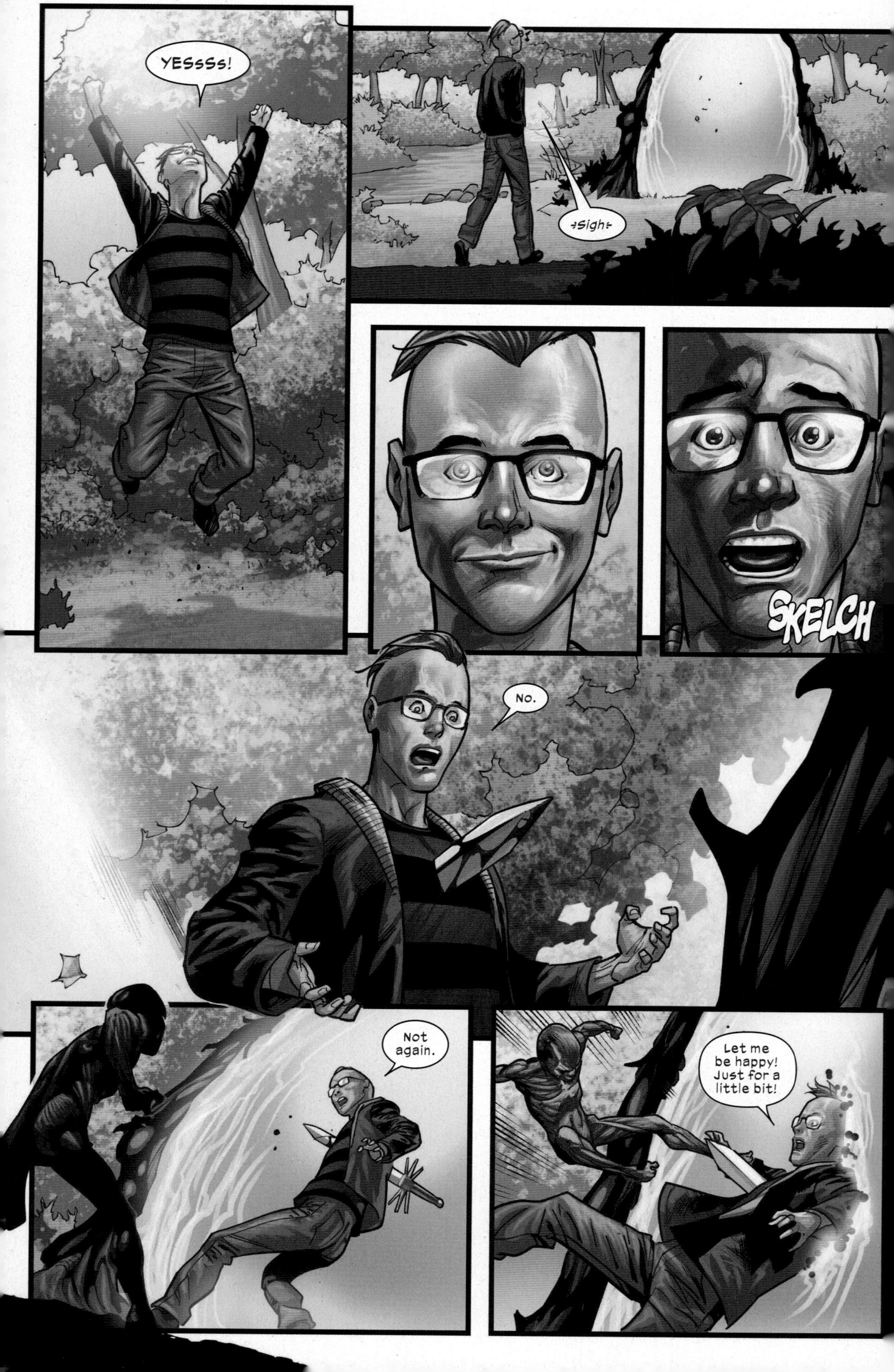
YESSSS!
⇾Sigh⇽
SKELCH
No.
Not again.
Let me be happy! Just for a little bit!

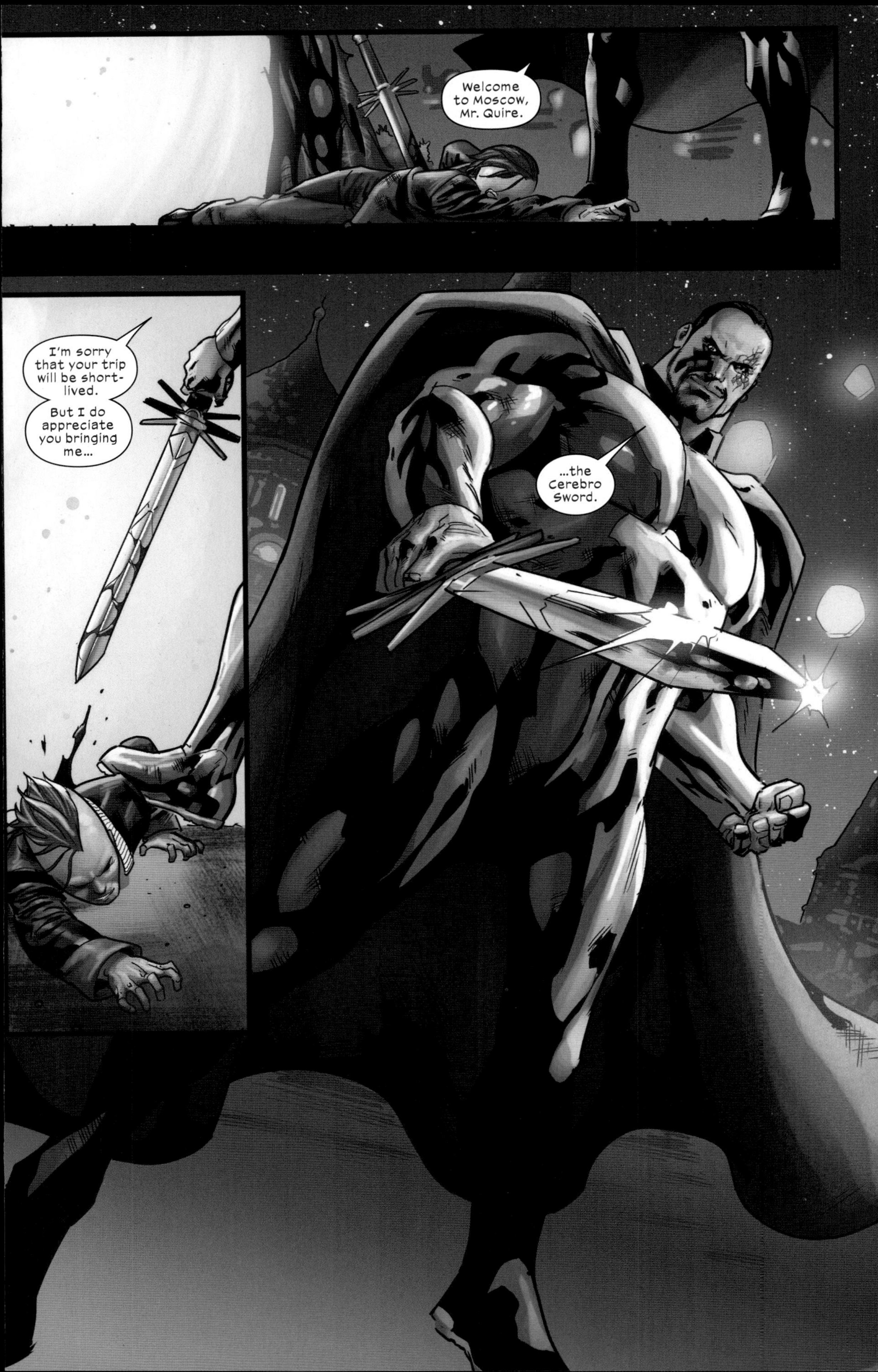
Welcome to Moscow, Mr. Quire.
I'm sorry that your trip will be short-lived.
But I do appreciate you bringing me...
...the Cerebro Sword.

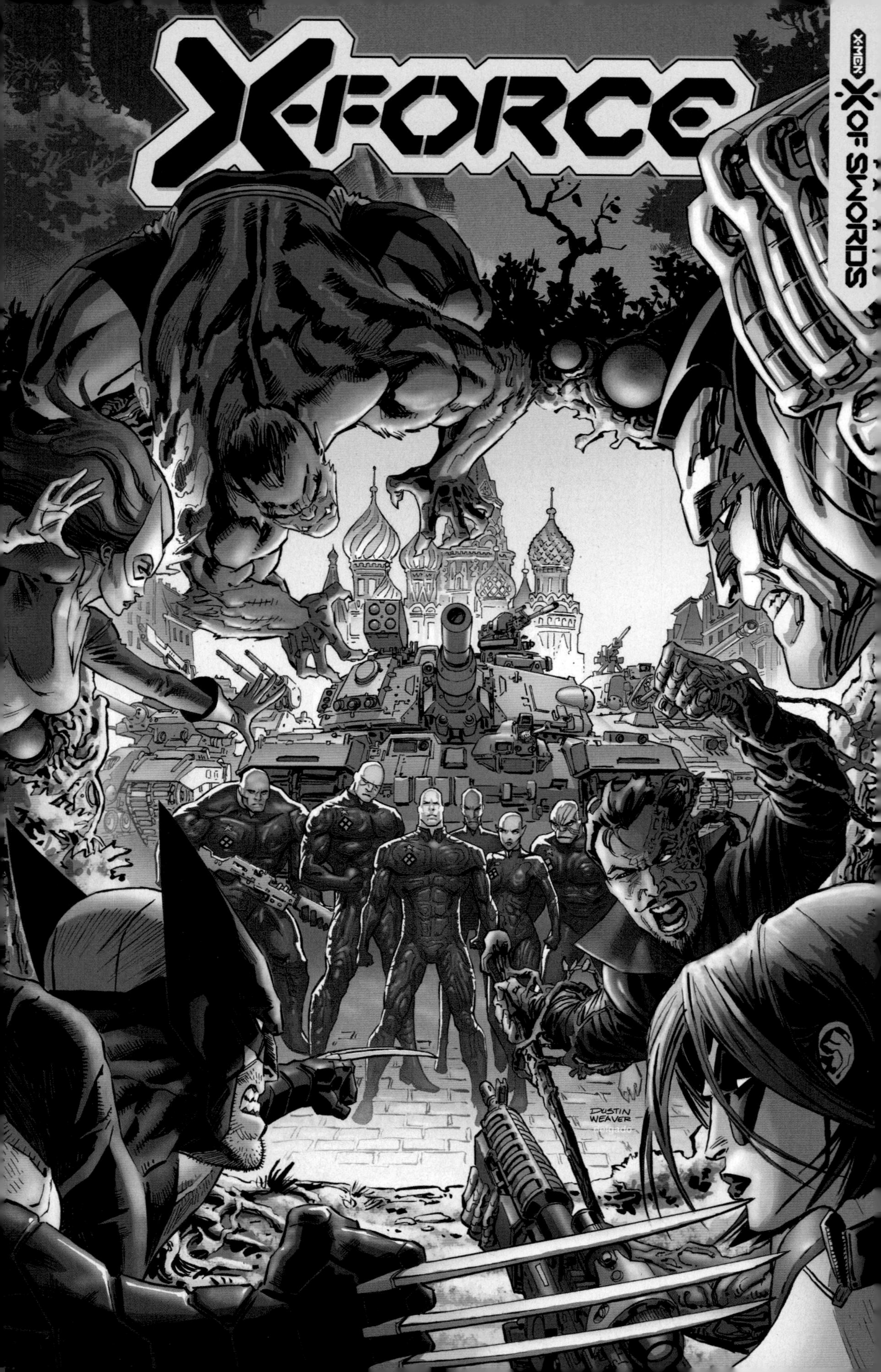
X-FORCE
X-MEN
X OF SWORDS
DUSTIN WEAVER

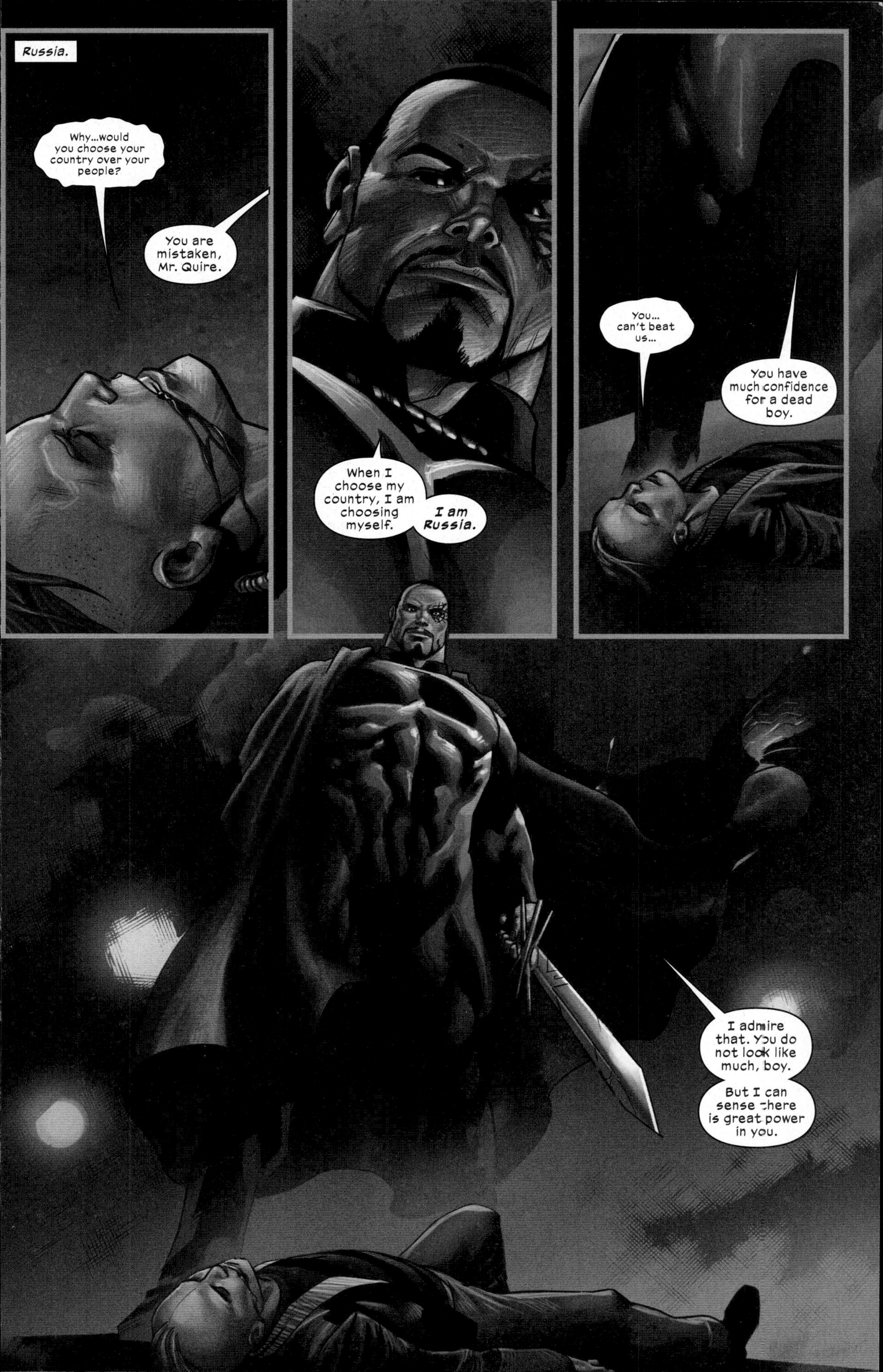

Russia.
Why...would you choose your country over your people?
You are mistaken, Mr. Quire.
When I choose my country, I am choosing myself.
I am Russia.
You... can't beat us...
You have much confidence for a dead boy.
I admire that. You do not look like much, boy.
But I can sense there is great power in you.

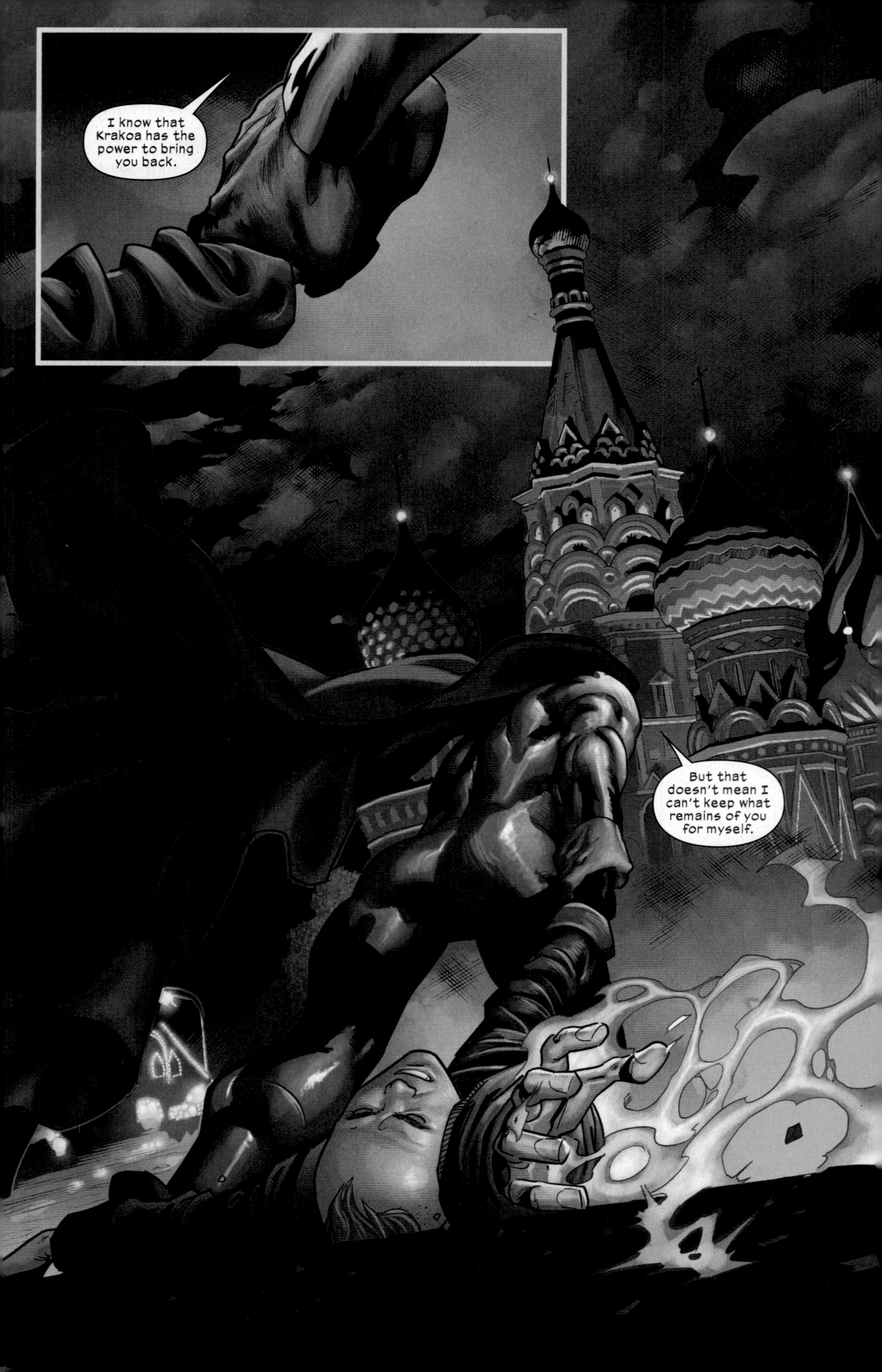
I know that Krakoa has the power to bring you back.
But that doesn't mean I can't keep what remains of you for myself.

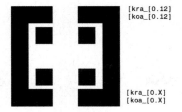

[kra_[0.12]
[koa_[0.12]

[kra_[0.X]
[koa_[0.X]

DEADLY ALLIANCE

Beast, Sage and Cecilia Reyes discovered the armored Russian super-soldiers that attacked Krakoa are bioengineered to have a smaller agent nested inside.

Kid Omega was ambushed by one of these escaped agents, who stabbed him with the stolen Cerebro Sword and kicked him through a portal to Moscow, into the clutches of the mysterious Mikhail.

Beast

Sage

Cecilia Reyes

Colossus

Domino

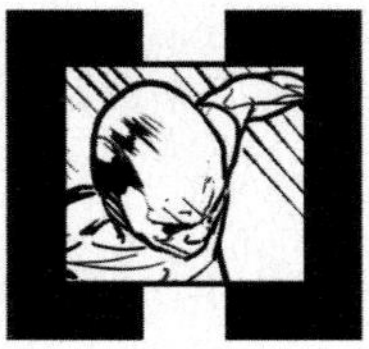

Kid Omega

Mikhail

[kra_[0.12]...]
[koa_[0.12]...]

[A._Spy_Agency]

[00_mutant_espionage]
[00_law_order___X___]

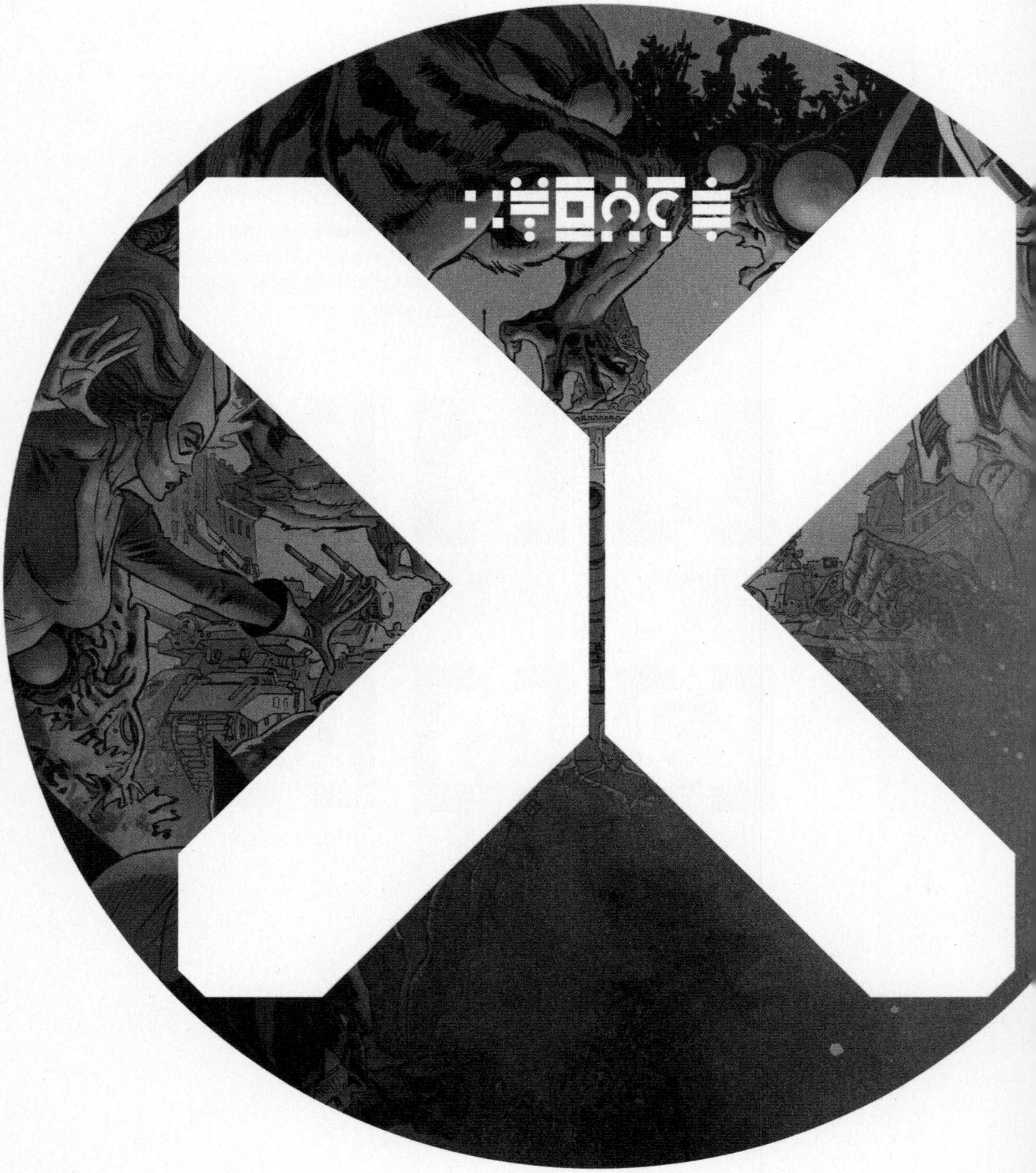

BENJAMIN PERCY...................................[WRITER]
JAN BAZALDUA....................................[ARTIST]
GURU-eFX...................................[COLOR ARTIST]
VC's JOE CARAMAGNA...........................[LETTERER]
TOM MULLER......................................[DESIGN]

DUSTIN WEAVER & EDGAR DELGADO...........[COVER ARTISTS]

NICK RUSSELL.............................[PRODUCTION]

JONATHAN HICKMAN...........................[HEAD OF X]
CHRIS ROBINSON & LAUREN AMARO ......[ASSISTANT EDITORS]
JORDAN D. WHITE & MARK BASSO.................[EDITORS]
C.B. CEBULSKI........................[EDITOR IN CHIEF]

[12] X-FORCE

[ISSUE TWELVE]..........THE CEREBRO SWORD

[00_mutant_espionage]
[00_law_order___X___]

[00_O■...O]
[00_O■..12]

[00_probe_]
[00_____]

[00_____]

[00_____X]

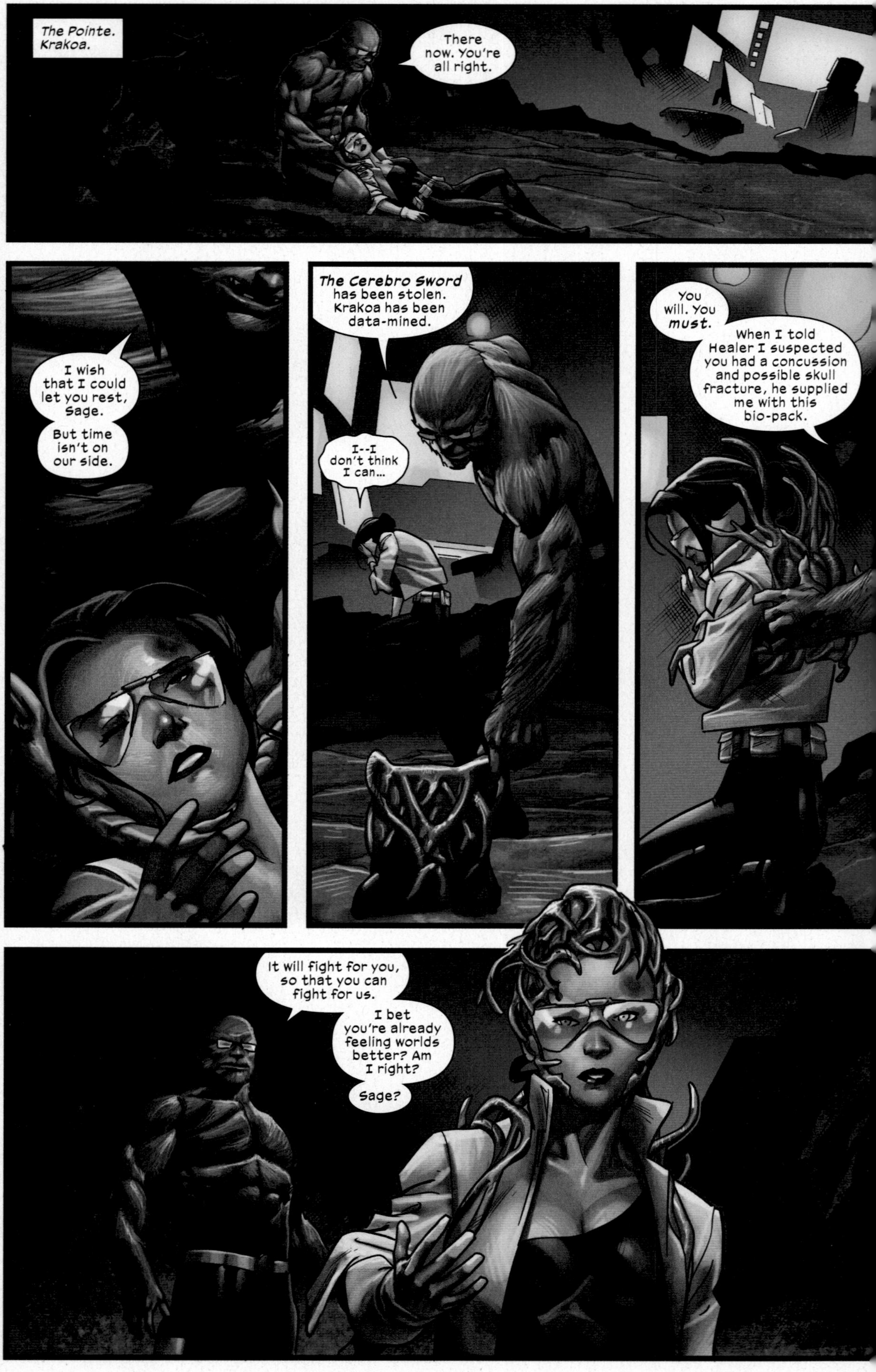

The Pointe. Krakoa.
There now. You're all right.
I wish that I could let you rest, Sage.
But time isn't on our side.
The Cerebro Sword has been stolen. Krakoa has been data-mined.
I--I don't think I can...
You will. You must.
When I told Healer I suspected you had a concussion and possible skull fracture, he supplied me with this bio-pack.
It will fight for you, so that you can fight for us.
I bet you're already feeling worlds better? Am I right?
Sage?

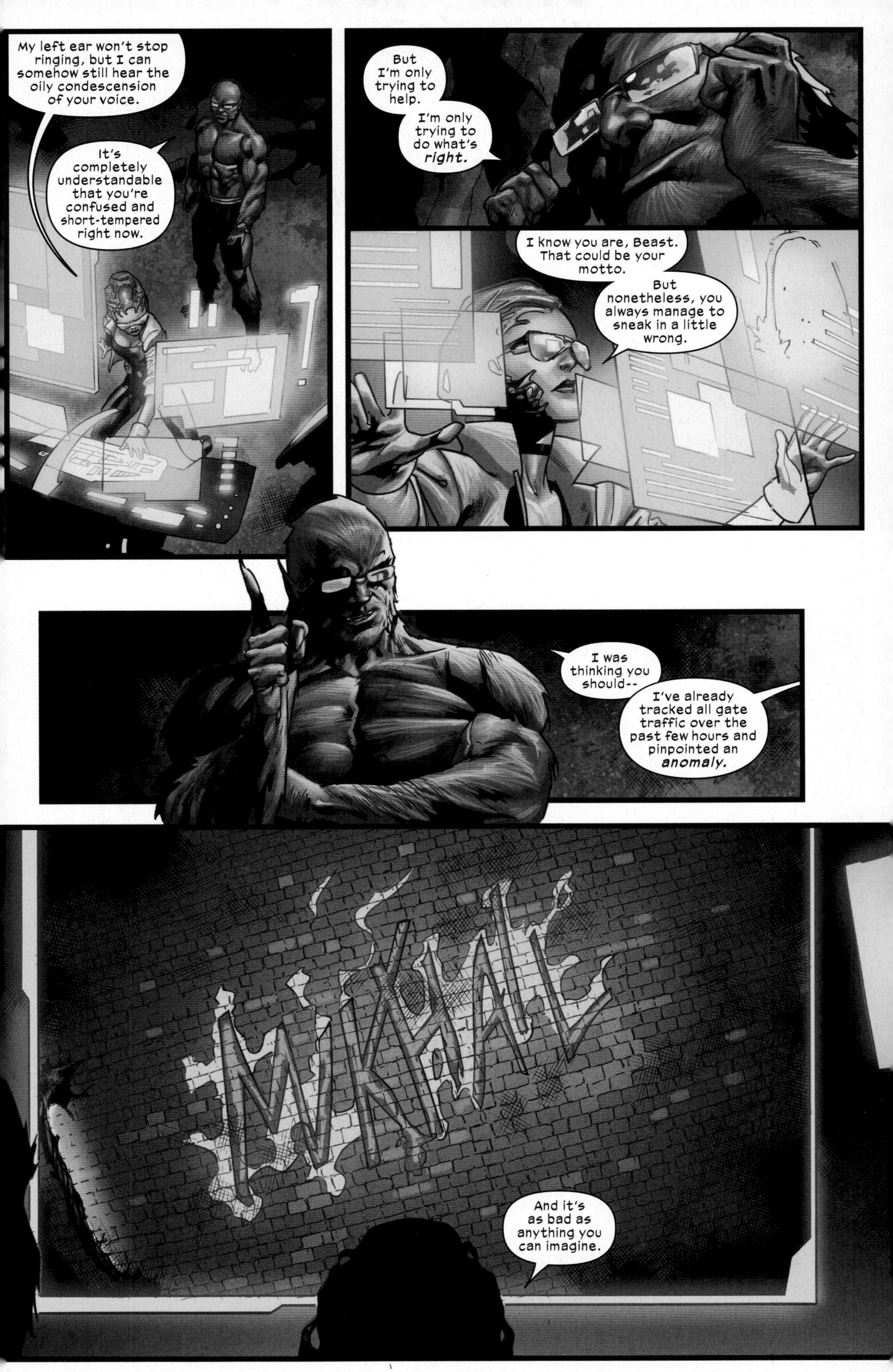
My left ear won't stop ringing, but I can somehow still hear the oily condescension of your voice.
It's completely understandable that you're confused and short-tempered right now.
But I'm only trying to help.
I'm only trying to do what's *right.*
I know you are, Beast. That could be your motto.
But nonetheless, you always manage to sneak in a little wrong.
I was thinking you should--
I've already tracked all gate traffic over the past few hours and pinpointed an *anomaly.*
And it's as bad as anything you can imagine.

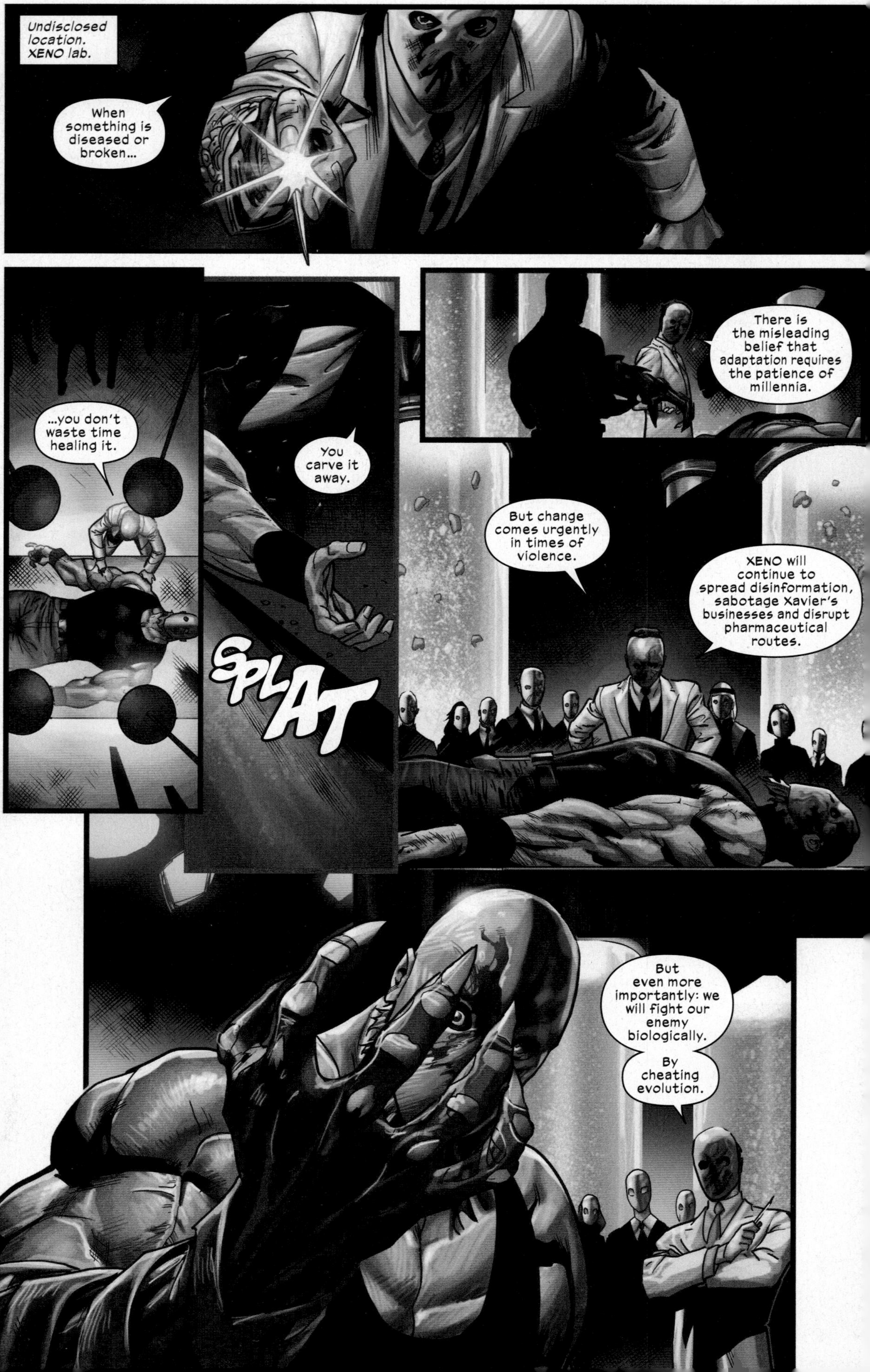
Undisclosed location. XENO lab.
When something is diseased or broken...
...you don't waste time healing it.
You carve it away.
SPLAT
There is the misleading belief that adaptation requires the patience of millennia.
But change comes urgently in times of violence.
XENO will continue to spread disinformation, sabotage Xavier's businesses and disrupt pharmaceutical routes.
But even more importantly: we will fight our enemy biologically.
By cheating evolution.

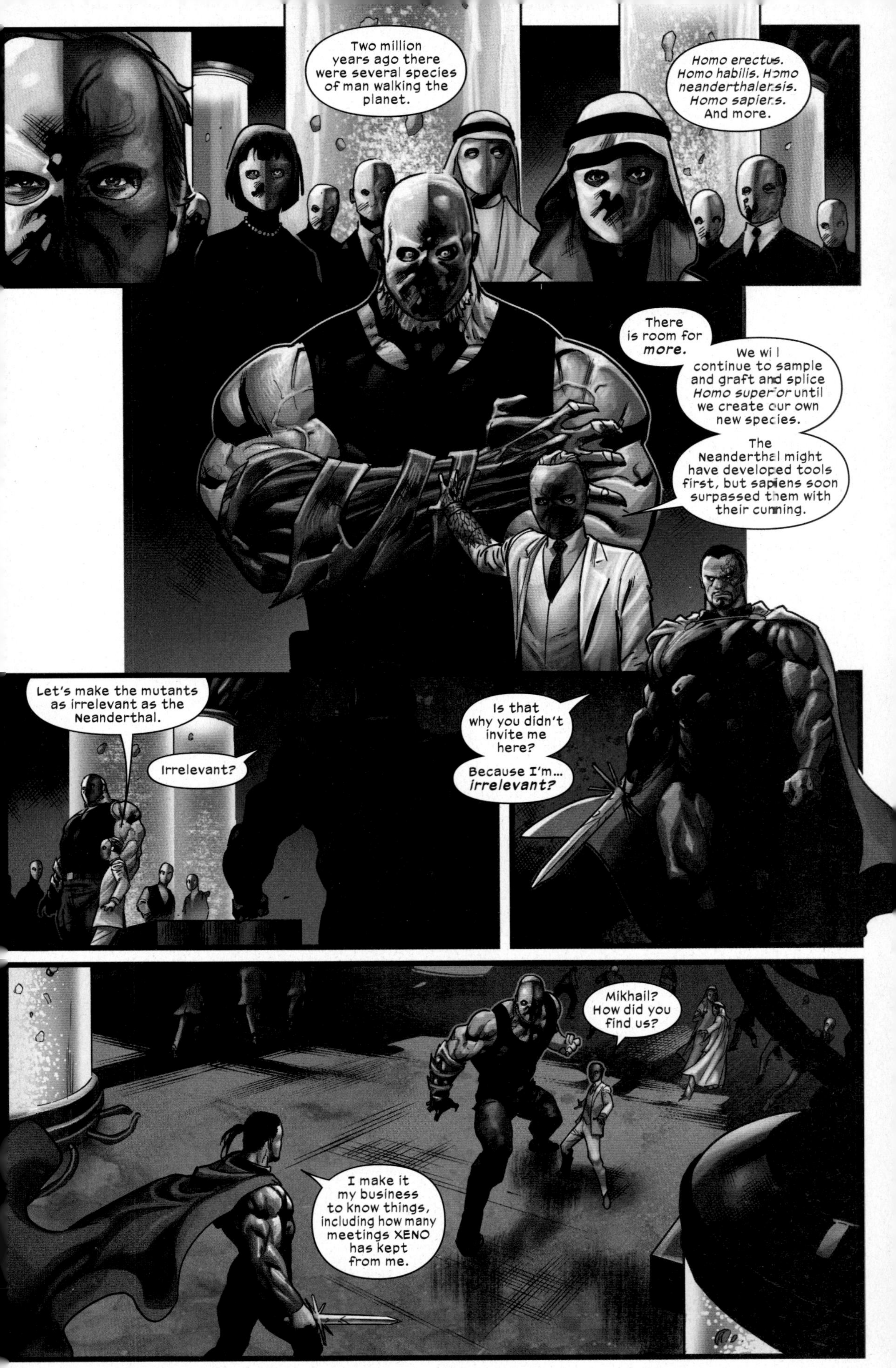
Two million years ago there were several species of man walking the planet.
Homo erectus. Homo habilis. Homo neanderthalensis. Homo sapiens. And more.
There is room for more.
We will continue to sample and graft and splice Homo superior until we create our own new species.
The Neanderthal might have developed tools first, but sapiens soon surpassed them with their cunning.
Let's make the mutants as irrelevant as the Neanderthal.
Irrelevant?
Is that why you didn't invite me here?
Because I'm... irrelevant?
Mikhail? How did you find us?
I make it my business to know things, including how many meetings XENO has kept from me.

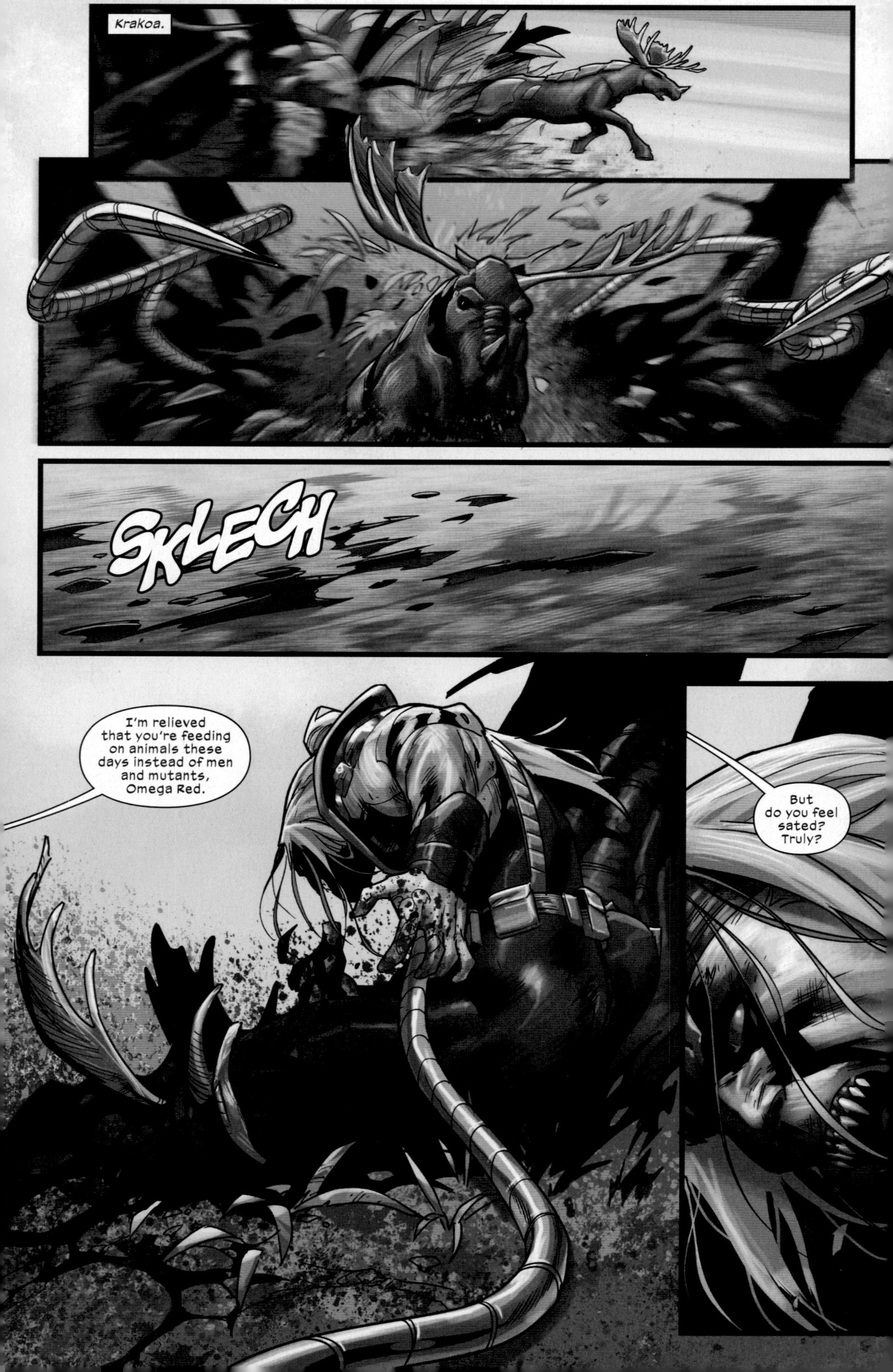
Krakoa.
SKLECH
I'm relieved that you're feeding on animals these days instead of men and mutants, Omega Red.
But do you feel sated? Truly?

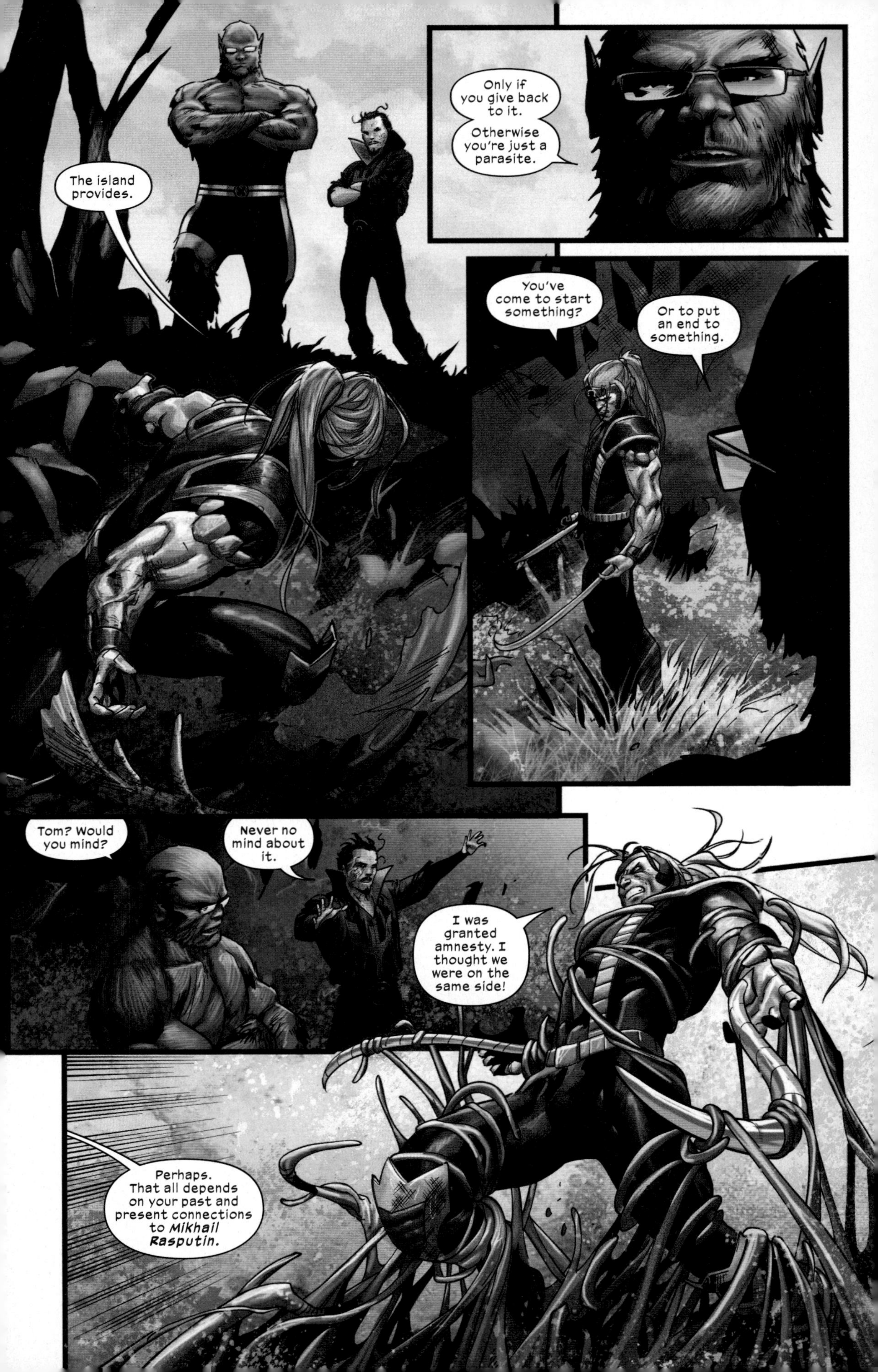
The island provides.
Only if you give back to it.
Otherwise you're just a parasite.
You've come to start something?
Or to put an end to something.
Tom? Would you mind?
Never no mind about it.
I was granted amnesty. I thought we were on the same side!
Perhaps. That all depends on your past and present connections to *Mikhail Rasputin*.

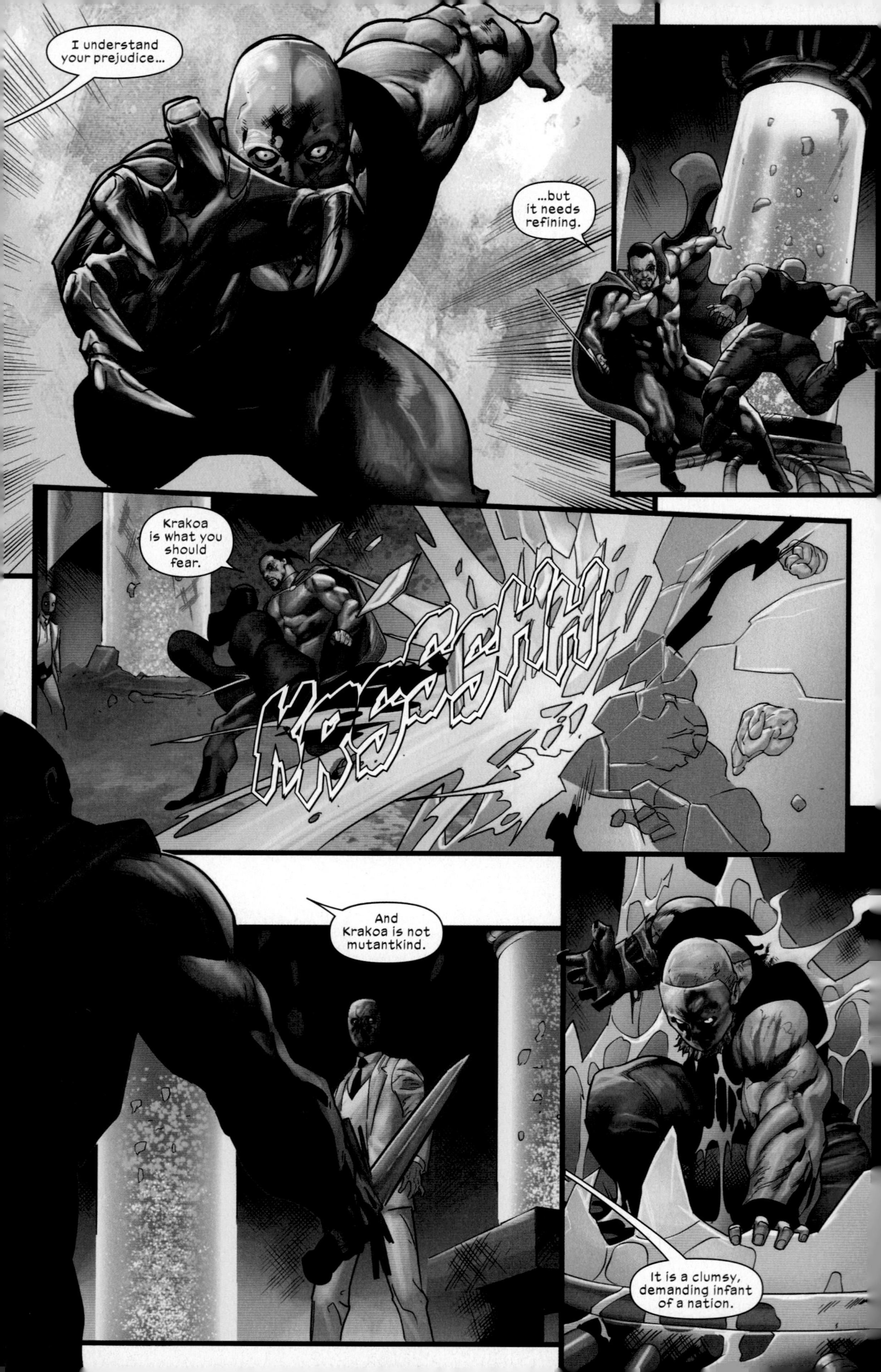
I understand your prejudice...
...but it needs refining.
Krakoa is what you should fear.
KRSSCHH
And Krakoa is not mutantkind.
It is a clumsy, demanding infant of a nation.

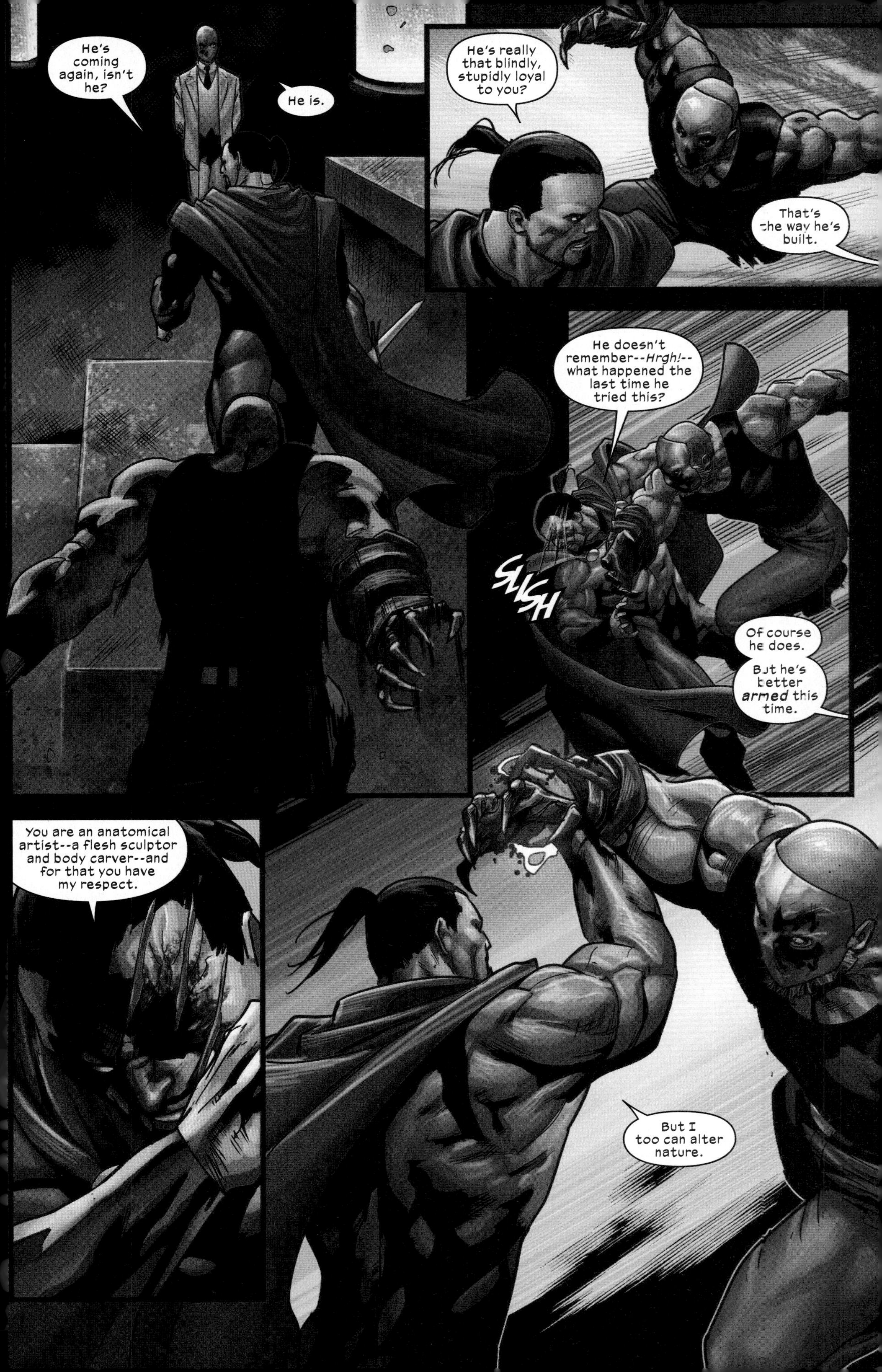
He's coming again, isn't he?
He is.
He's really that blindly, stupidly loyal to you?
That's the way he's built.
He doesn't remember--*Hrgh!*--what happened the last time he tried this?
SLISH
Of course he does.
But he's better *armed* this time.
You are an anatomical artist--a flesh sculptor and body carver--and for that you have my respect.
But I too can alter nature.

And I don't require a scalpel.
KRIKIKIK
As I mentioned before...your prejudice needs refining.
If you really hope to change the world, you need to harness its *powers* and make them your own.
KRINCH
That means working *with* mutants...
...*against* Krakoa.

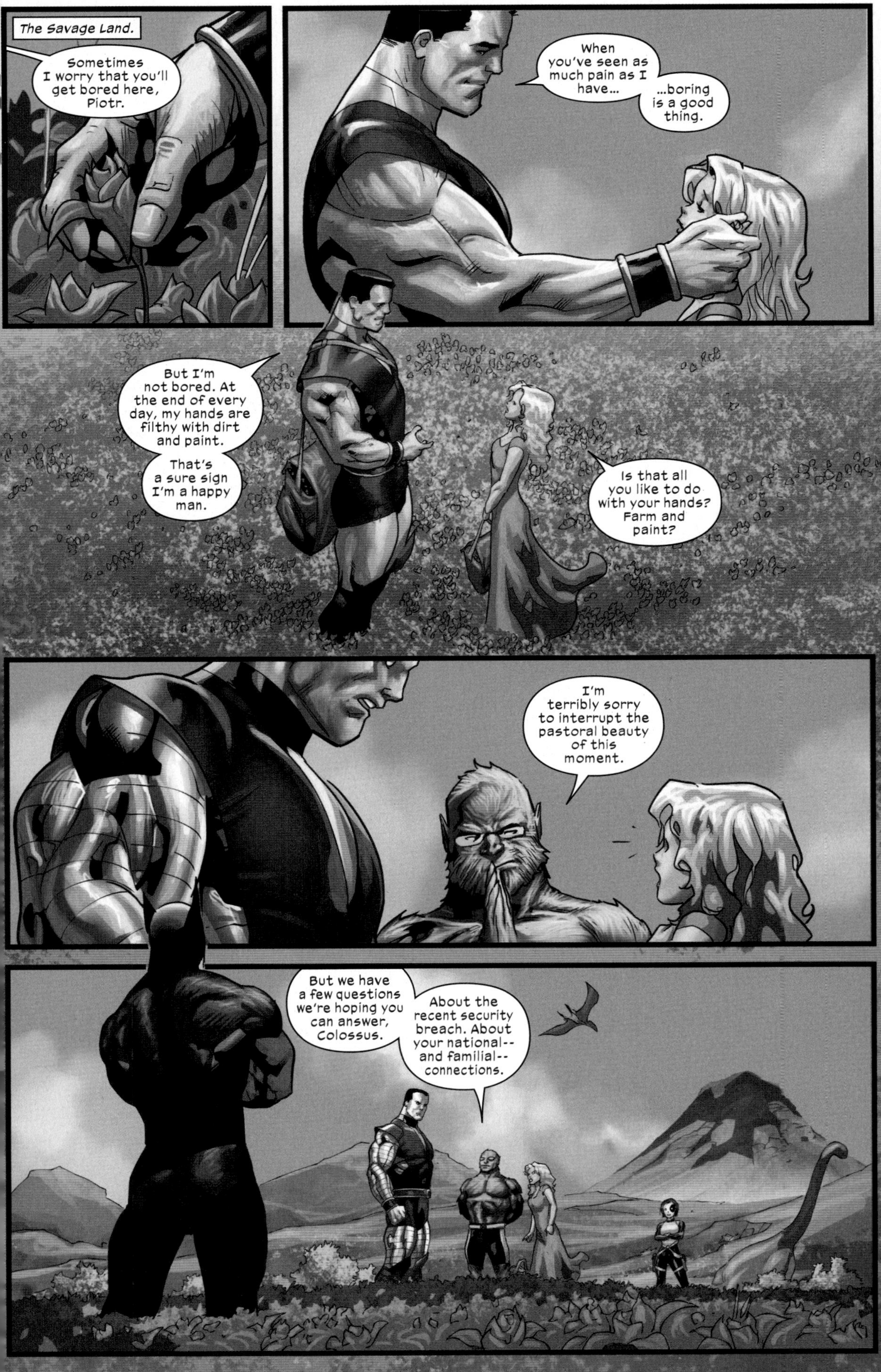
The Savage Land.
Sometimes I worry that you'll get bored here, Piotr.
When you've seen as much pain as I have...
...boring is a good thing.
But I'm not bored. At the end of every day, my hands are filthy with dirt and paint.
That's a sure sign I'm a happy man.
Is that all you like to do with your hands? Farm and paint?
I'm terribly sorry to interrupt the pastoral beauty of this moment.
But we have a few questions we're hoping you can answer, Colossus.
About the recent security breach. About your national--and familial--connections.

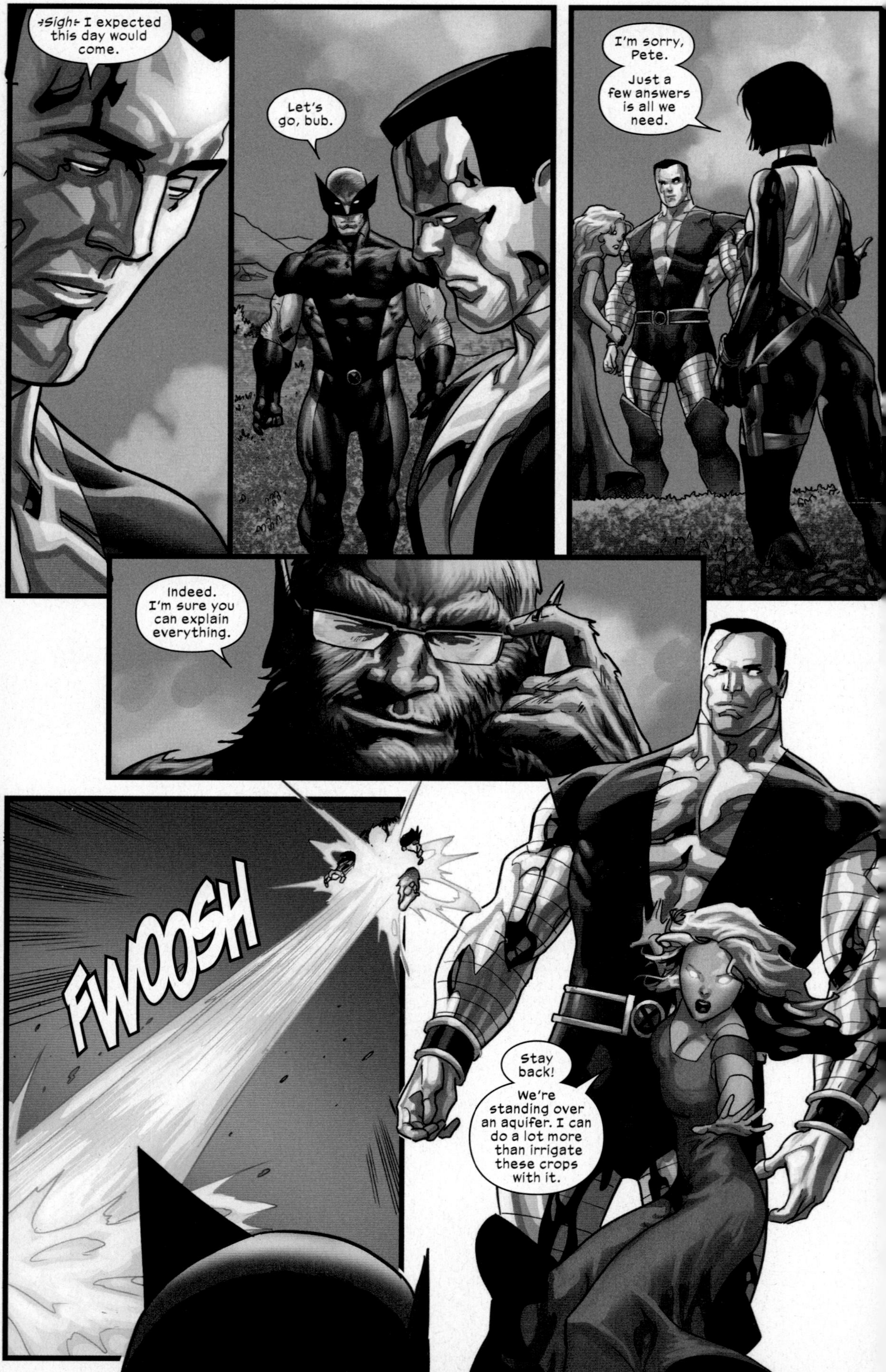

-Sigh- I expected this day would come.
Let's go, bub.
I'm sorry, Pete.
Just a few answers is all we need.
Indeed. I'm sure you can explain everything.
FWOOSH
Stay back!
We're standing over an aquifer. I can do a lot more than irrigate these crops with it.

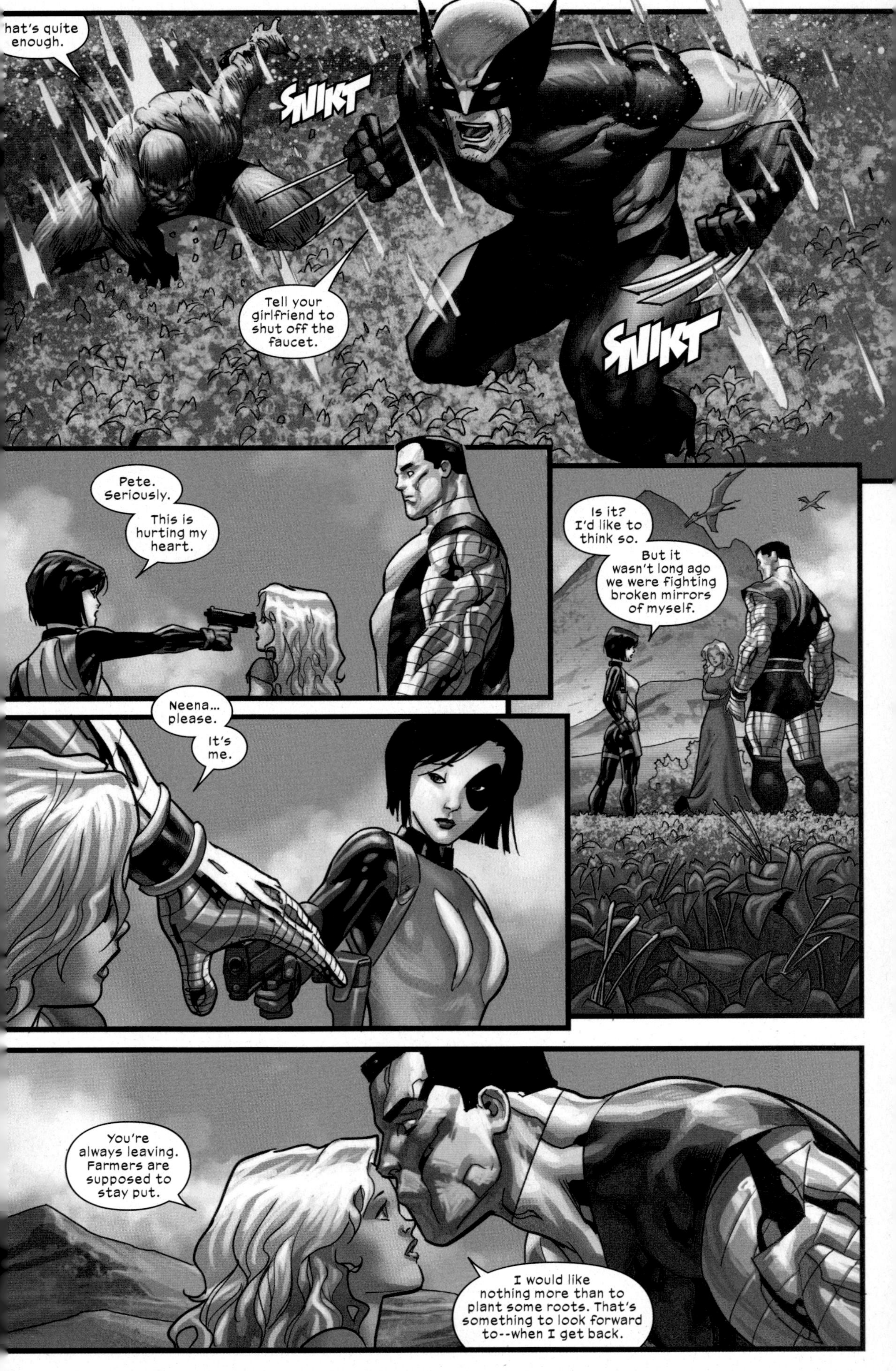
hat's quite enough.
SNIKT
Tell your girlfriend to shut off the faucet.
SNIKT
Pete. Seriously.
This is hurting my heart.
Is it? I'd like to think so.
But it wasn't long ago we were fighting broken mirrors of myself.
Neena... please.
It's me.
You're always leaving. Farmers are supposed to stay put.
I would like nothing more than to plant some roots. That's something to look forward to--when I get back.

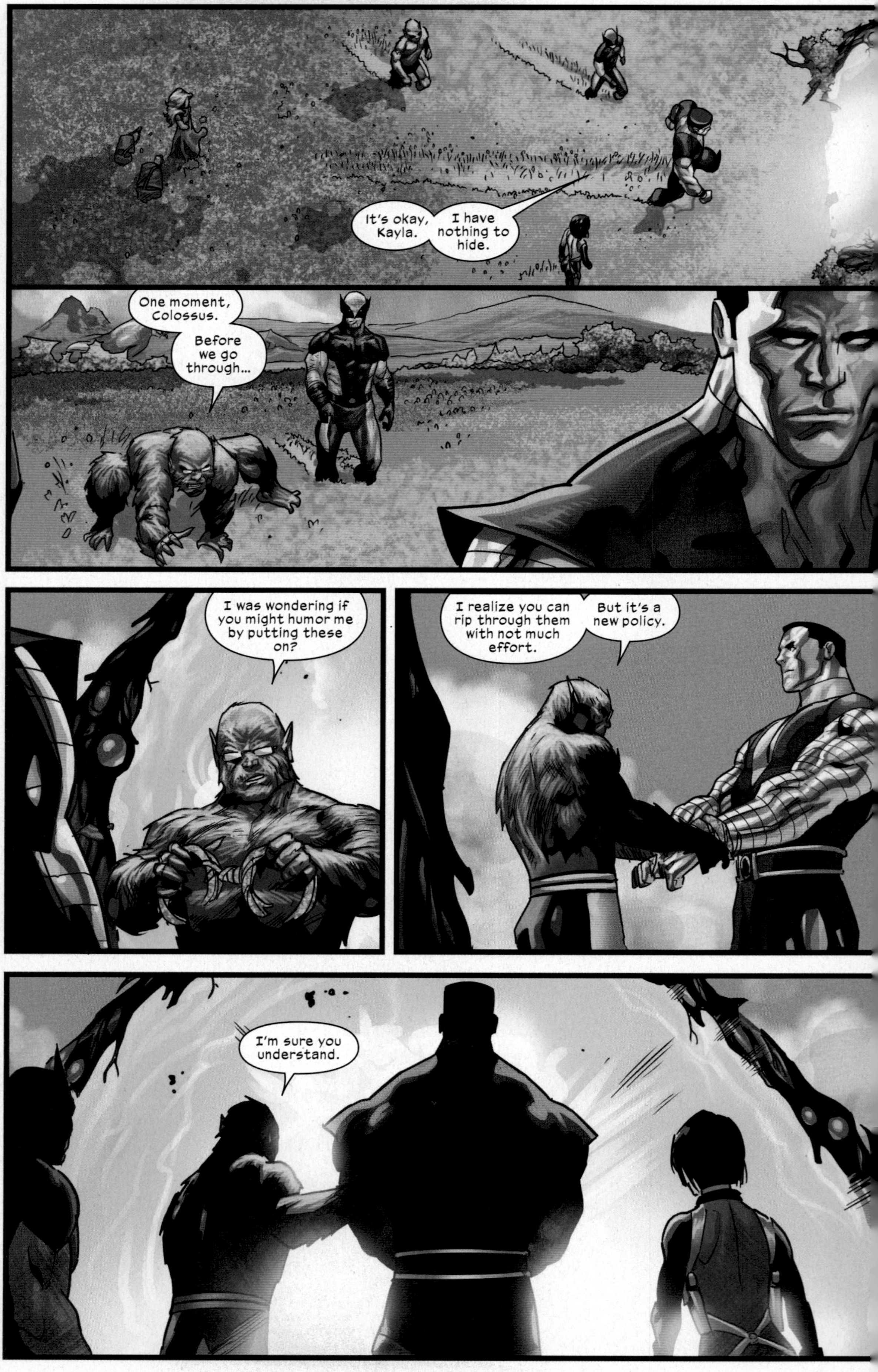
It's okay, Kayla.
I have nothing to hide.
One moment, Colossus.
Before we go through...
I was wondering if you might humor me by putting these on?
I realize you can rip through them with not much effort.
But it's a new policy.
I'm sure you understand.

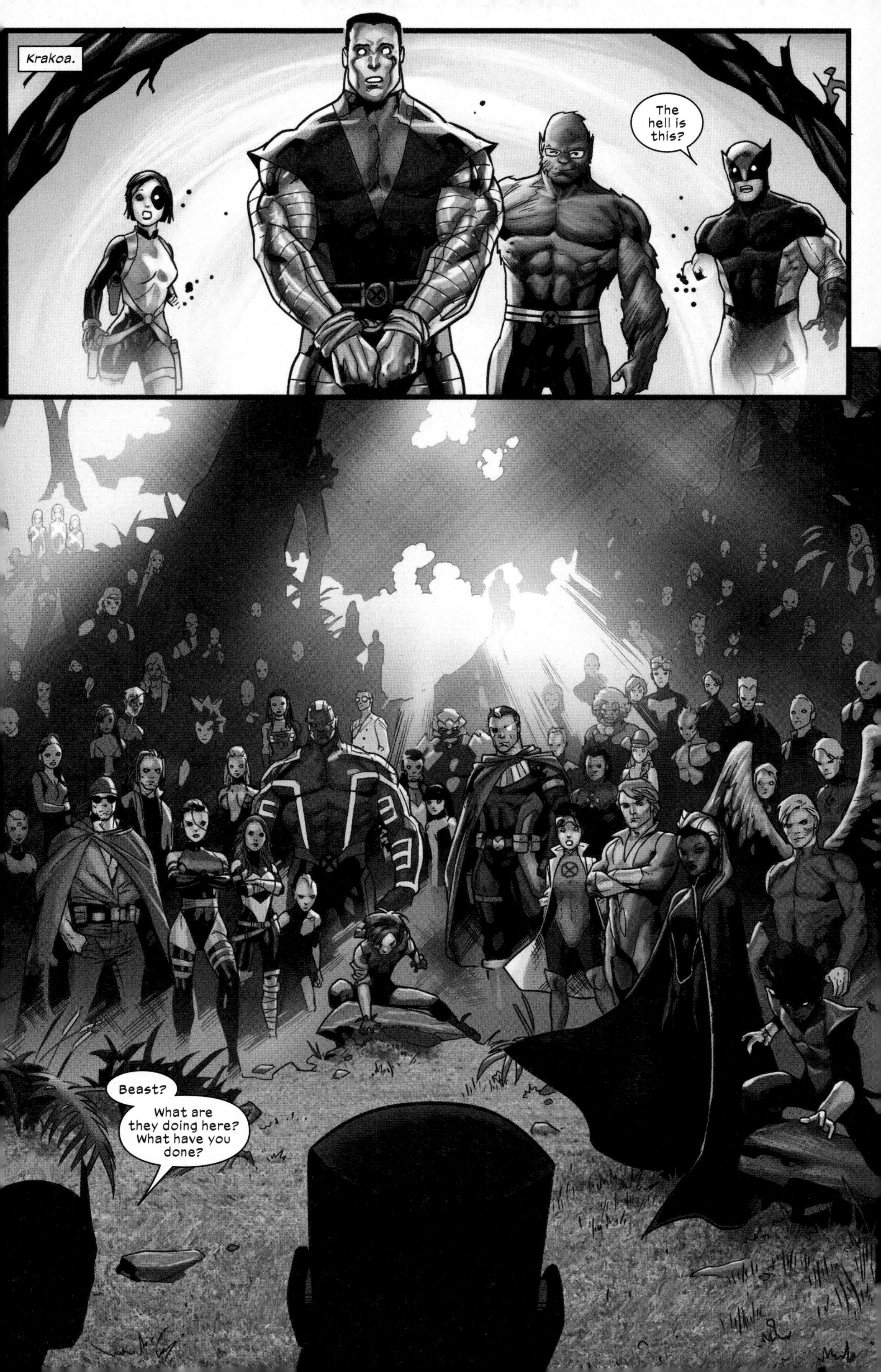

Krakoa.
The hell is this?
Beast?
What are they doing here? What have you done?

BEAST'S LOGBOOK: THE TRAITOR'S PARADE

Our efforts to celebrate mutantkind -- to forgive the sins of our individual histories and build a fresh future as a sovereign society -- is of course commendable.

But I can't help but think it might also be blindly optimistic?

By focusing on the hopeful collective, Xavier's dream ignores the selfish impulses of the individual.

Here are very relevant fears: pollution, incursion, traitorousness.

We are so focused on guarding our gates...that we've neglected to realize what we might have locked ourselves in with.

I have brought this concern up with Xavier several times, but he rebuffs or dismisses or sometimes attempts to placate me by saying things like, "Oh, Beast. Always anxious," and "This is why you're so good at your job."

When I last pressed the issue, this was his response:

"Because I have everyone here," he said and tapped at Cerebro, "I also trust everyone here," at which time he held a hand over his heart.

But we all know this is not a fail-safe. Mind-wipes and mesmerism and telepathic blocks (and, and, and, and -- I'm sure there are many other tricks I haven't even considered) could bypass Cerebro.

Jeremy Bentham's Panopticon was not merely a brilliant design for a prison -- it was a brilliant insight into the philosophy of control. The central guard tower makes the inmates unsure whether they are being observed, and so they behave accordingly. In much the same way, America's crime rates are significantly down due to doorbell cameras, traffic cameras, cell phone cameras. The want to do wrong will always be in us. But the fear of being seen overrides it.

I have a plan, and though it may be controversial and condemned by some, I know it is right. We will detain all mutants with Russian ties. And we will make their detention a spectacle. I don't want to keep this quiet. I want to it to be a parade. I recognize this is unfortunate, but it is also the best possible thing we could do for Krakoa.

A little fear and paranoia keep people safe. It's possible our citizens may come forward with valuable information about their neighbors. It's certain our citizens will know that being watched is the same as being watched over.

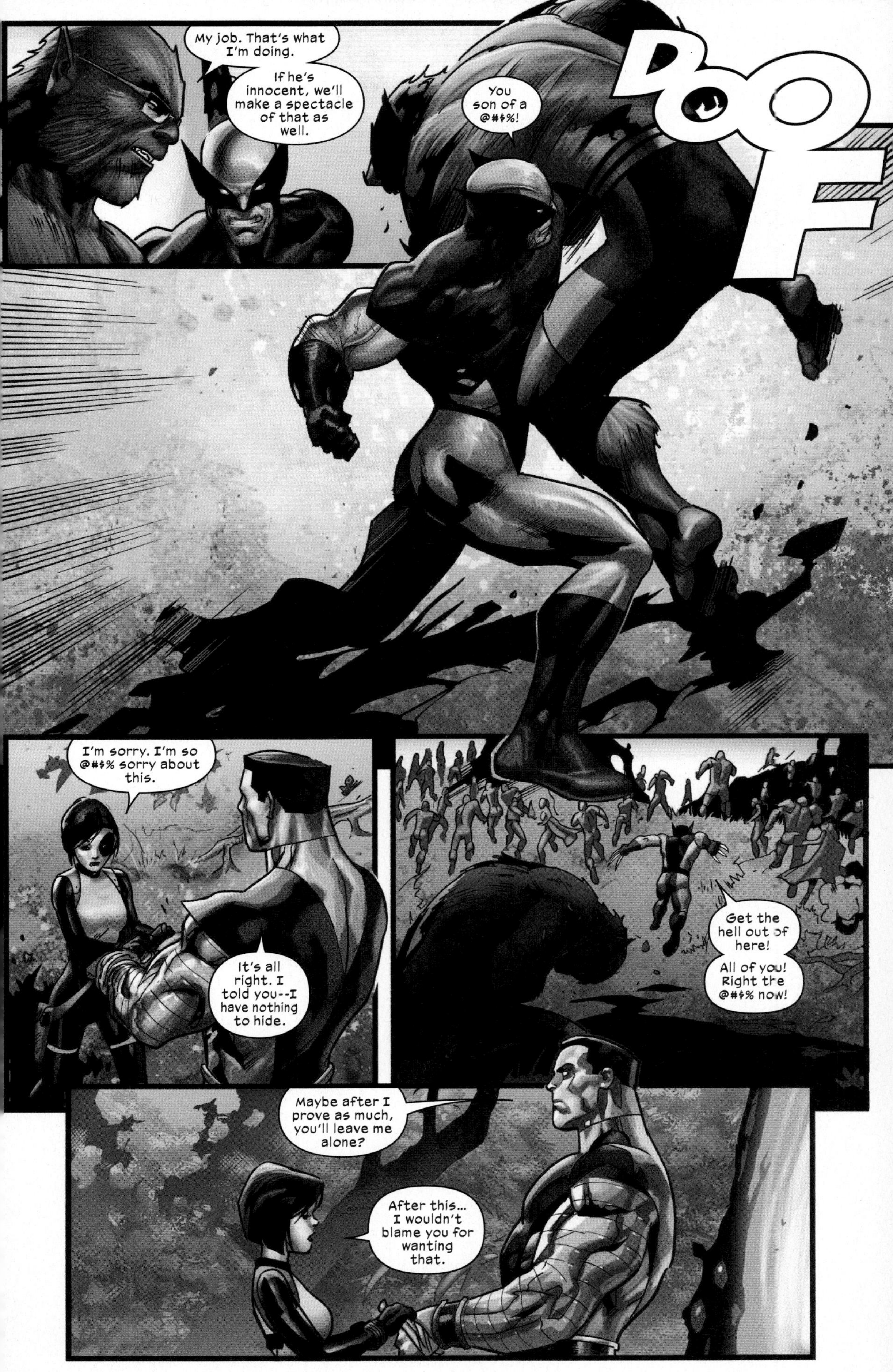

My job. That's what I'm doing.
If he's innocent, we'll make a spectacle of that as well.
You son of a @#$%!
DOOF
I'm sorry. I'm so @#$% sorry about this.
It's all right. I told you--I have nothing to hide.
Get the hell out of here!
All of you! Right the @#$% now!
Maybe after I prove as much, you'll leave me alone?
After this... I wouldn't blame you for wanting that.

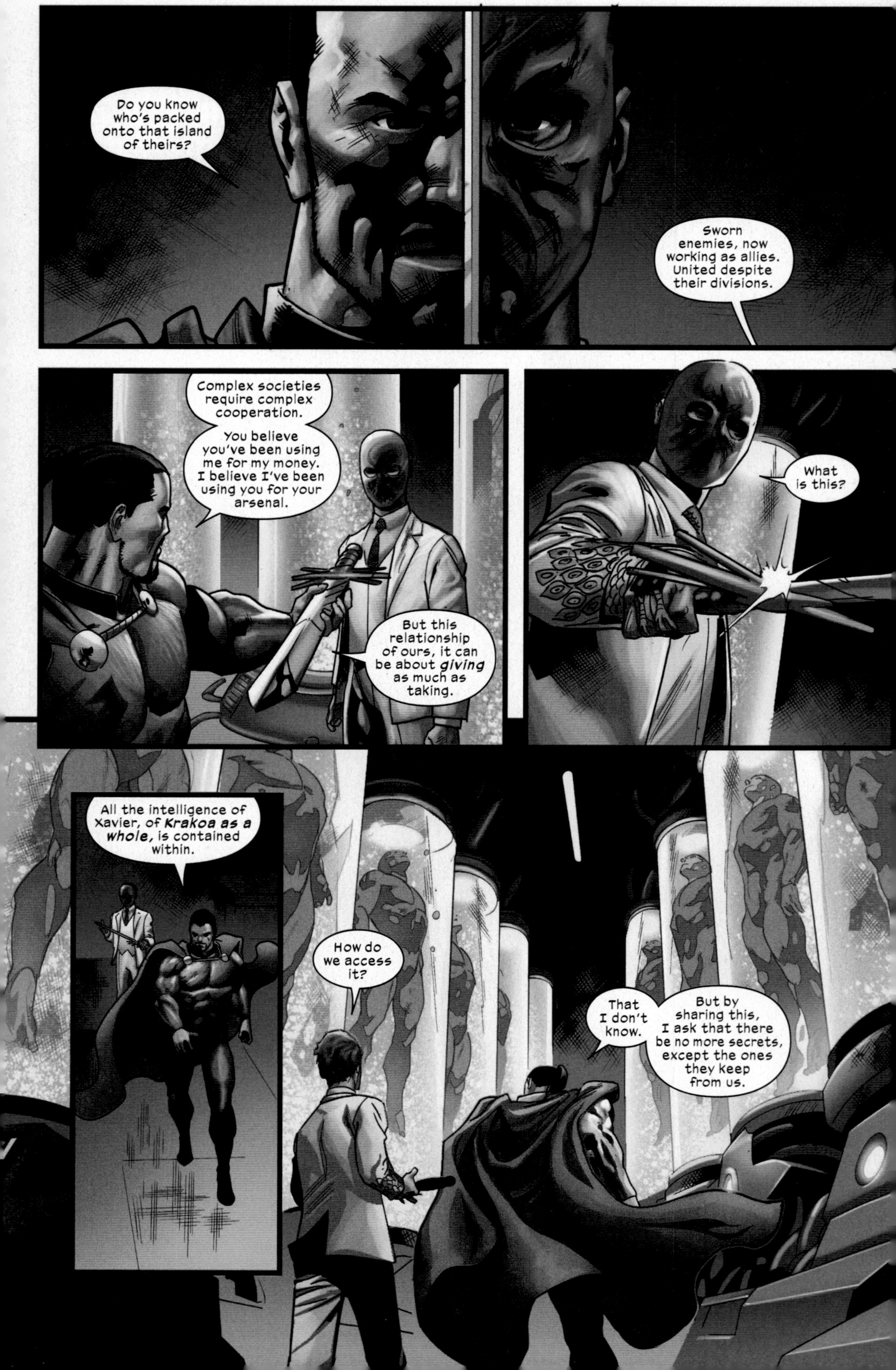
Do you know who's packed onto that island of theirs?
Sworn enemies, now working as allies. United despite their divisions.
Complex societies require complex cooperation.
You believe you've been using me for my money. I believe I've been using you for your arsenal.
But this relationship of ours, it can be about *giving* as much as taking.
What is this?
All the intelligence of Xavier, of ***Krakoa as a whole,*** is contained within.
How do we access it?
That I don't know.
But by sharing this, I ask that there be no more secrets, except the ones they keep from us.

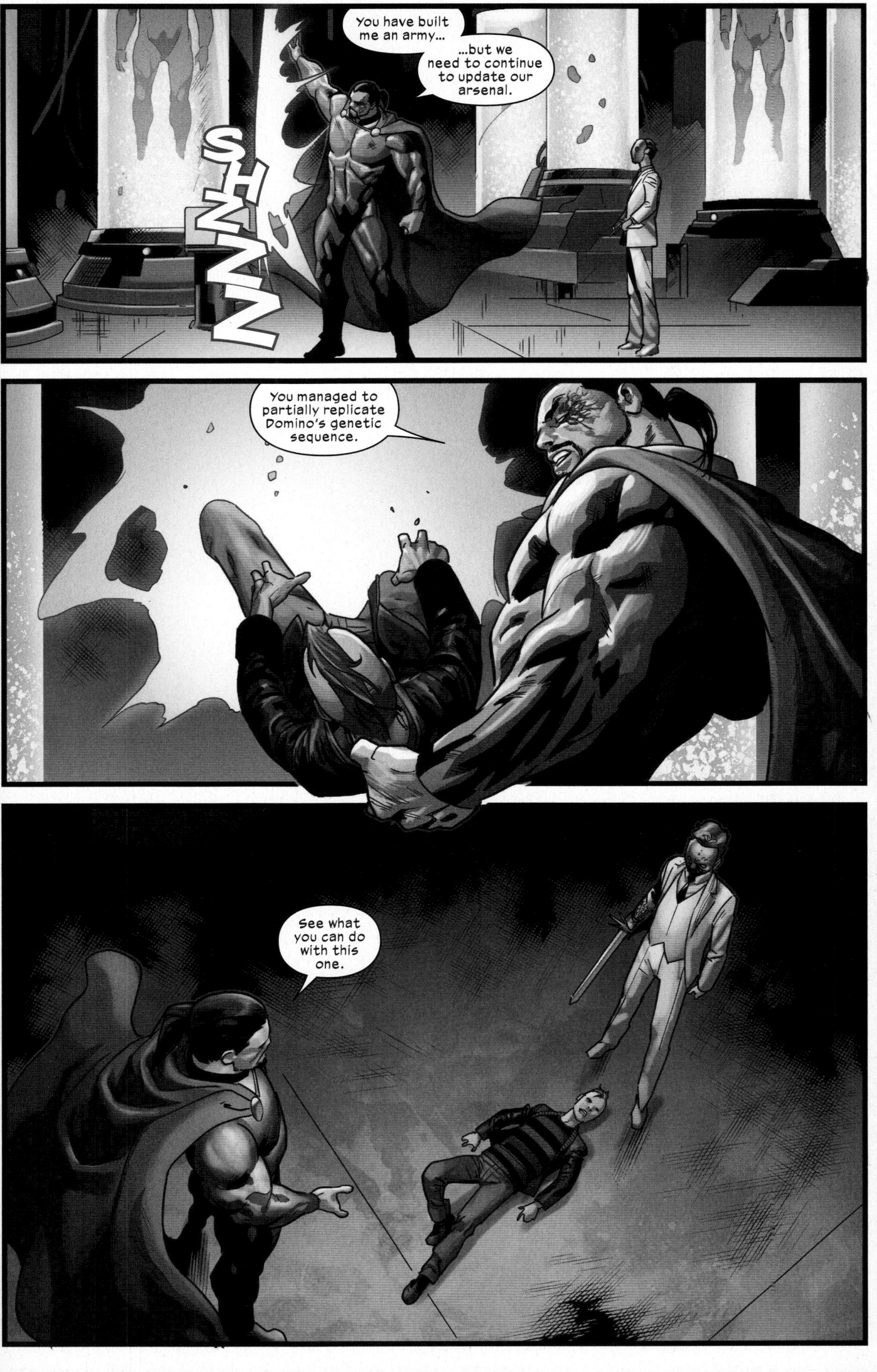
You have built me an army...
...but we need to continue to update our arsenal.
SHZZZ
You managed to partially replicate Domino's genetic sequence.
See what you can do with this one.

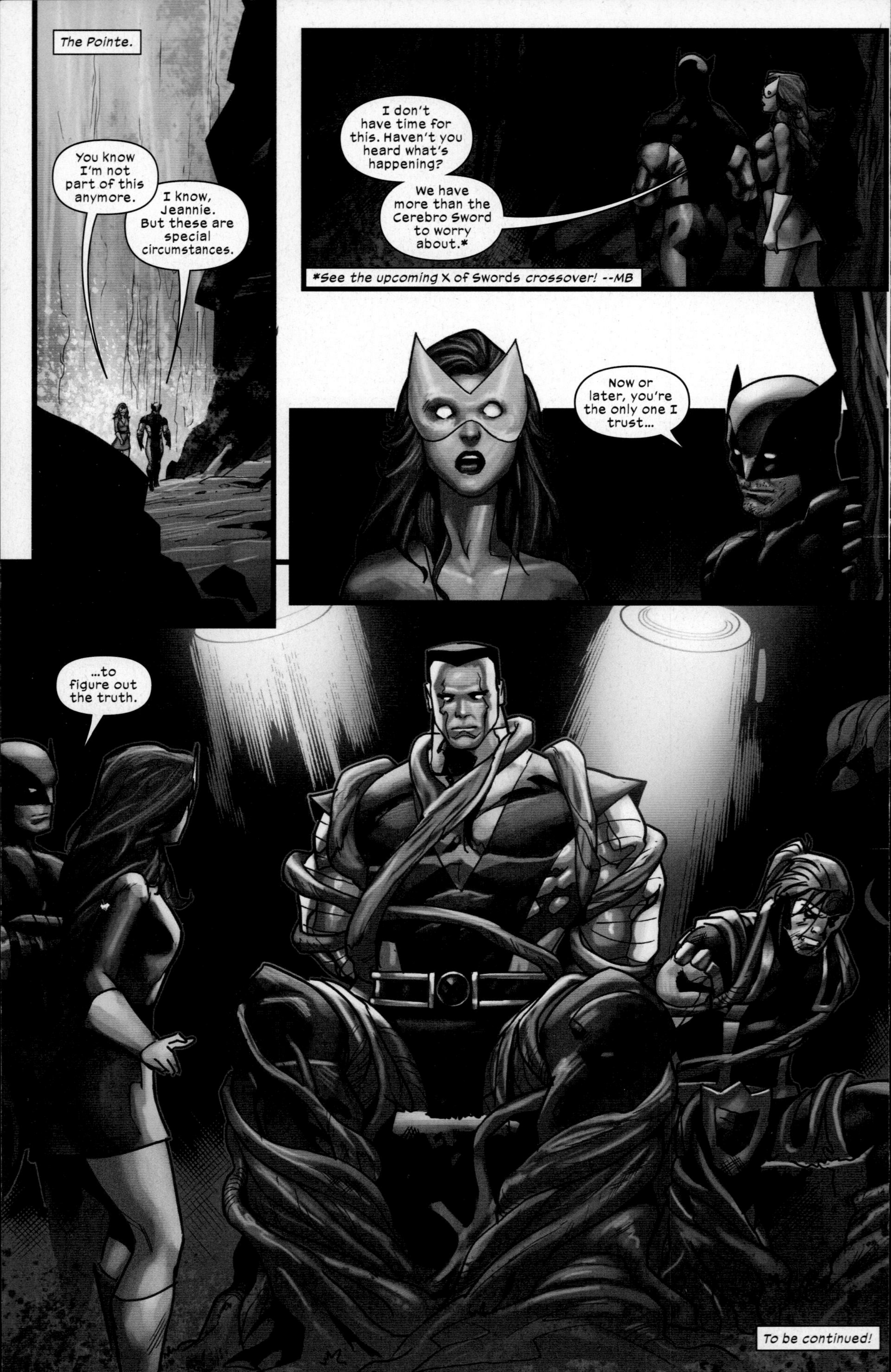

The Pointe.
You know I'm not part of this anymore.
I know, Jeannie. But these are special circumstances.
I don't have time for this. Haven't you heard what's happening?
We have more than the Cerebro Sword to worry about.*
*See the upcoming X of Swords crossover! --MB
Now or later, you're the only one I trust...
...to figure out the truth.
To be continued!

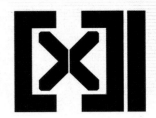

The sun shone in the Savage Land and fields of flowers bloomed brightly. The air was thick with their perfume, and though there was work to do, Piotr could not help but pause in his harvest. Because the pink petals of one breeze-shaken flower had caught his eye, reminding him of a woman swirling her dress as she kicked up her heels in a dance.

Sometimes his hands felt too big and clumsy. If he filled up a glass of water, it sometimes cracked in his grip. If he turned the page of a book, he sometimes tore the spine. But he concentrated now—really concentrated—on pinching off the stem so that he might tuck it gently behind Kayla's ear.

She smiled at him, even her eyes showed her concern. "I'm worried you'll be bored here," she said, and he tried to explain to her how much this place meant to him. As a sanctuary. He liked to put his hands in the dirt in the morning. He liked to dirty his knuckles with paint in the afternoons. He liked to run his fingers through her hair in the evenings. It was easy to forget about pain—the pain of what had come before—when he had so much simple pleasure to focus his attention on.

And then a voice called out to him, saying, "I'm terribly sorry to interrupt the pastoral beauty of this moment."

It was Beast. He smiled with condescension. He held out an arm in invitation. He wanted Piotr to come with him. He wanted to ask questions. He wanted to dredge up everything Piotr had tried to forget, to dig his claws into his still-bruised mind. He wanted to take away this sunlit day, this flower-filled field, this quiet moment with Kayla.

~~Piotr's skin changed—in a flash over silver—as he armored himself. He became something else then. A Colossus. The sun's reflection streamed across his skin when he charged forward. Beast was big, but he was bigger. He seized his old friend and swept him up and slammed him to the ground—once, twice, three times—rag-dolling his body. Beast cried out for him to stop but Colossus' fist met his face with enough force to silence him.~~

~~Blood soaked the ground and the flowers would soon suck the moisture greedily up, reddening their petals.~~

летописец

EXCALIBUR
X-MEN PATH TO X OF SWORDS
BLOOD OF THE CHANGELING!
MAYBAR MW

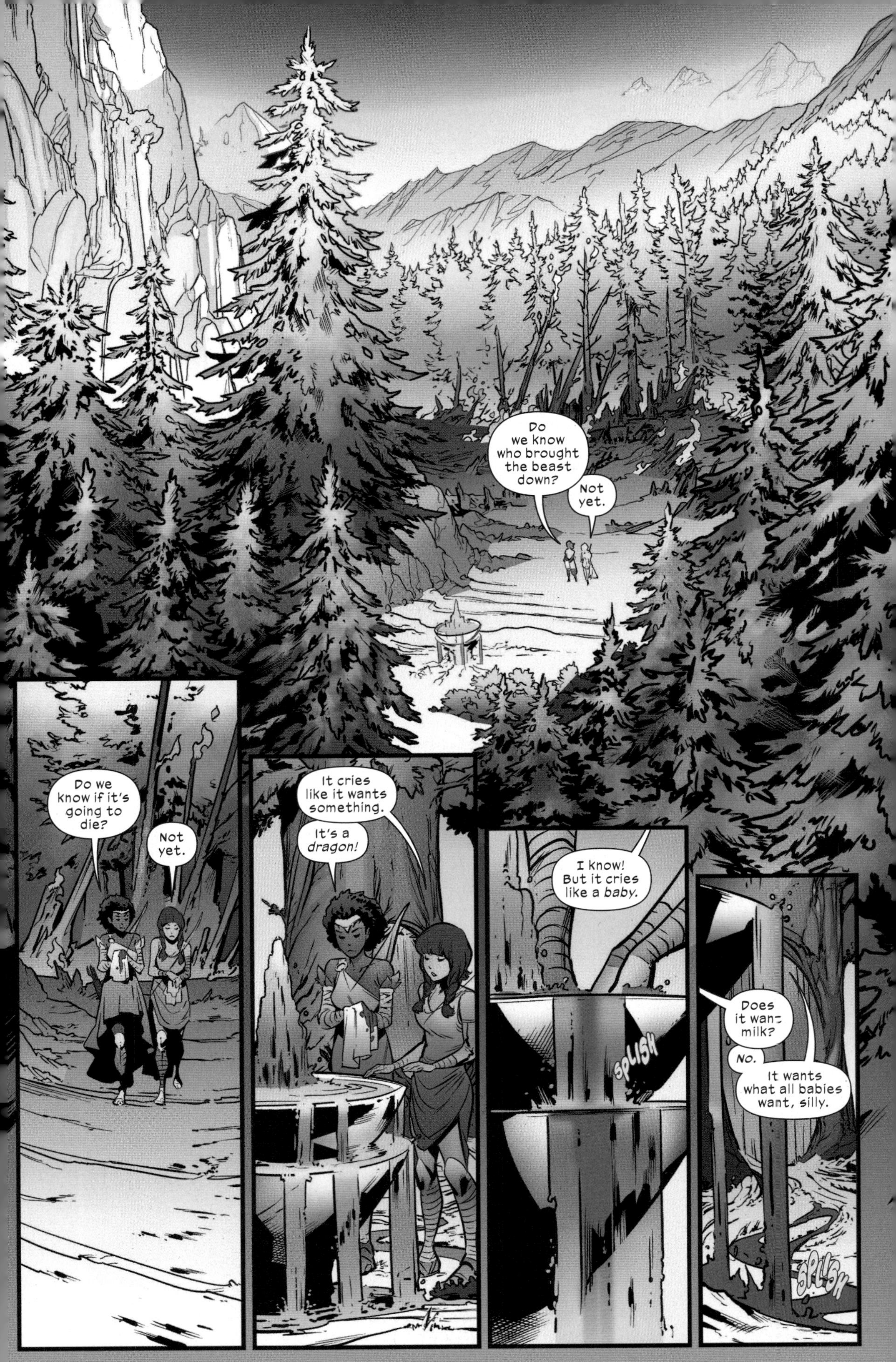
Do we know who brought the beast down?
Not yet.
Do we know if it's going to die?
Not yet.
It cries like it wants something.
It's a *dragon!*
I know! But it cries like a *baby.*
SPLISH
Does it want milk?
No.
It wants what all babies want, silly.
SPLISH

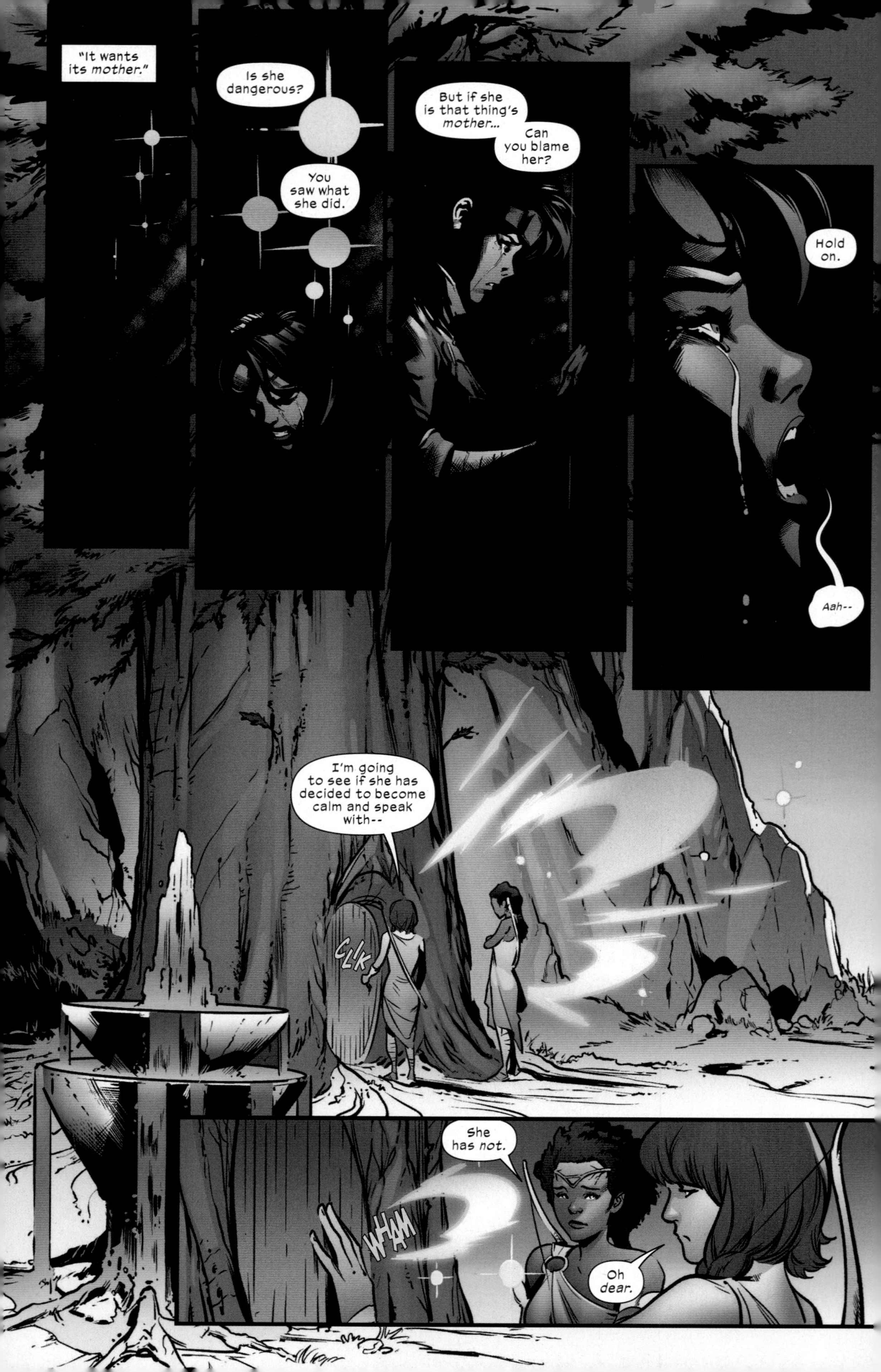
"It wants its *mother.*"
Is she dangerous?
You saw what she did.
But if she is that thing's *mother*...
Can you blame her?
Hold on.
Aah--
I'm going to see if she has decided to become calm and speak with--
CLIK
She has *not.*
WHAM
Oh *dear.*

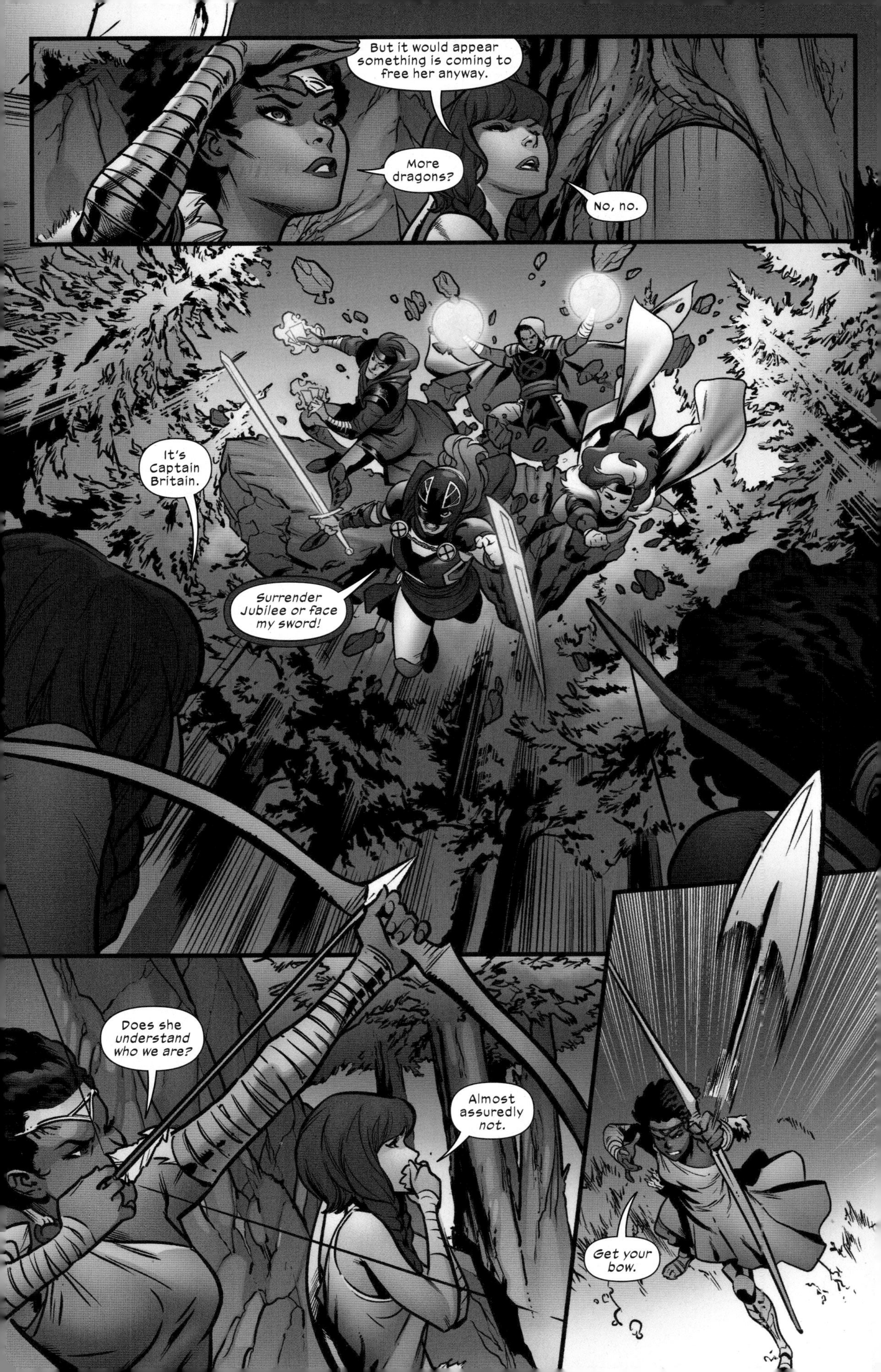
But it would appear something is coming to free her anyway.
More dragons?
No, no.
It's Captain Britain.
Surrender Jubilee or face my sword!
Does she understand who we are?
Almost assuredly not.
Get your bow.

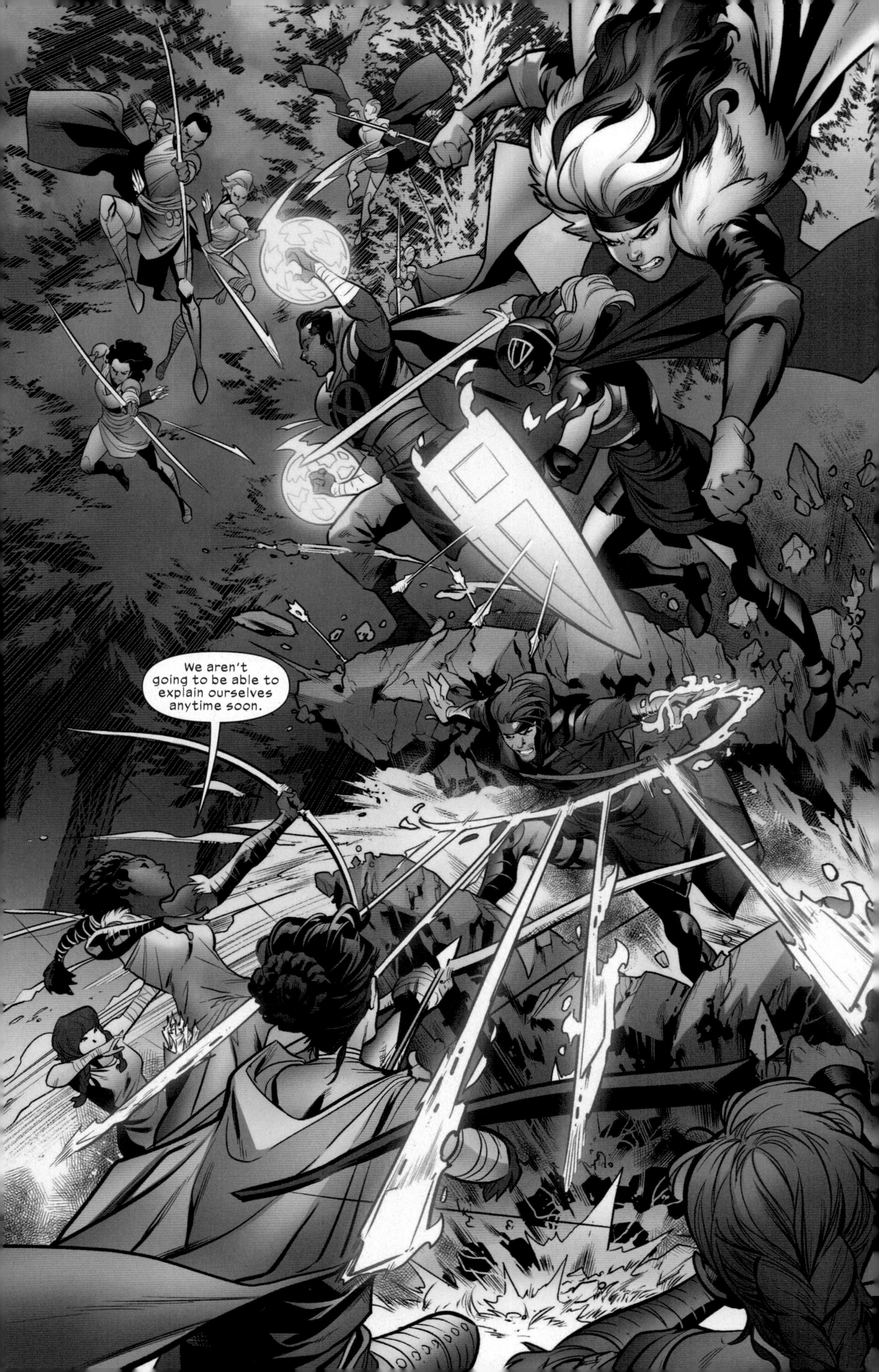
We aren't going to be able to explain ourselves anytime soon.

PRIESTESSES OF OPAL LUNA SATURNYNE

Students and devotees to Saturnyne, the priestesses are organized in two castes -- those of the *White*, who have chosen to live within the walls of the Citadel and the surrounding province, and those of the *Green*, who have taken their training and knowledge to the lands outside of the Citadel and chosen to enact Saturnyne's *intent* rather than her direct *will*. By living alongside the wild thickets that act as buffers between the province of Avalon (or other provinces) and the province of Saturnyne, they are known to act as healers, hunters and keepers of the land.

Priestesses of the White only leave their lady's tower by donning their crescent diadems and taking a nearly faceless form, obscuring their own identity so that they may act in anonymous accordance with Lady Saturnyne's will.

Priestesses of the Green follow Saturnyne's teaching and intent, believing balance to be a nuanced thing that cannot be corrected by distant declaration and requiring attention, action and presence.

Despite their differences, the **Green** are not viewed as heretical; rather, Majestrix allows them, viewing them as a necessary opposition to her own actions, as all things must have opposition.

Occasionally the **White** and the **Green** come into contention when orders given to priestesses for the **White** (ex: "stop Captain Britain and her cohorts," "slay that dragon," etc.) find themselves in conflict with the **Green**'s more *moderate* views, who tend to follow a less draconic code of ethics, such as "if you find a wounded dragon in the woods, nurse it back to health," or "if a woman is causing explosions in the forest, imprison her until she calms down a bit."

Typically the **Green** will fight their enemies, as they say, "only till their sides stitch," meaning until **weariness from battle calms the temper and brings about necessary parlay.**

—

[00_so_below_X]
[00_as_above_X]

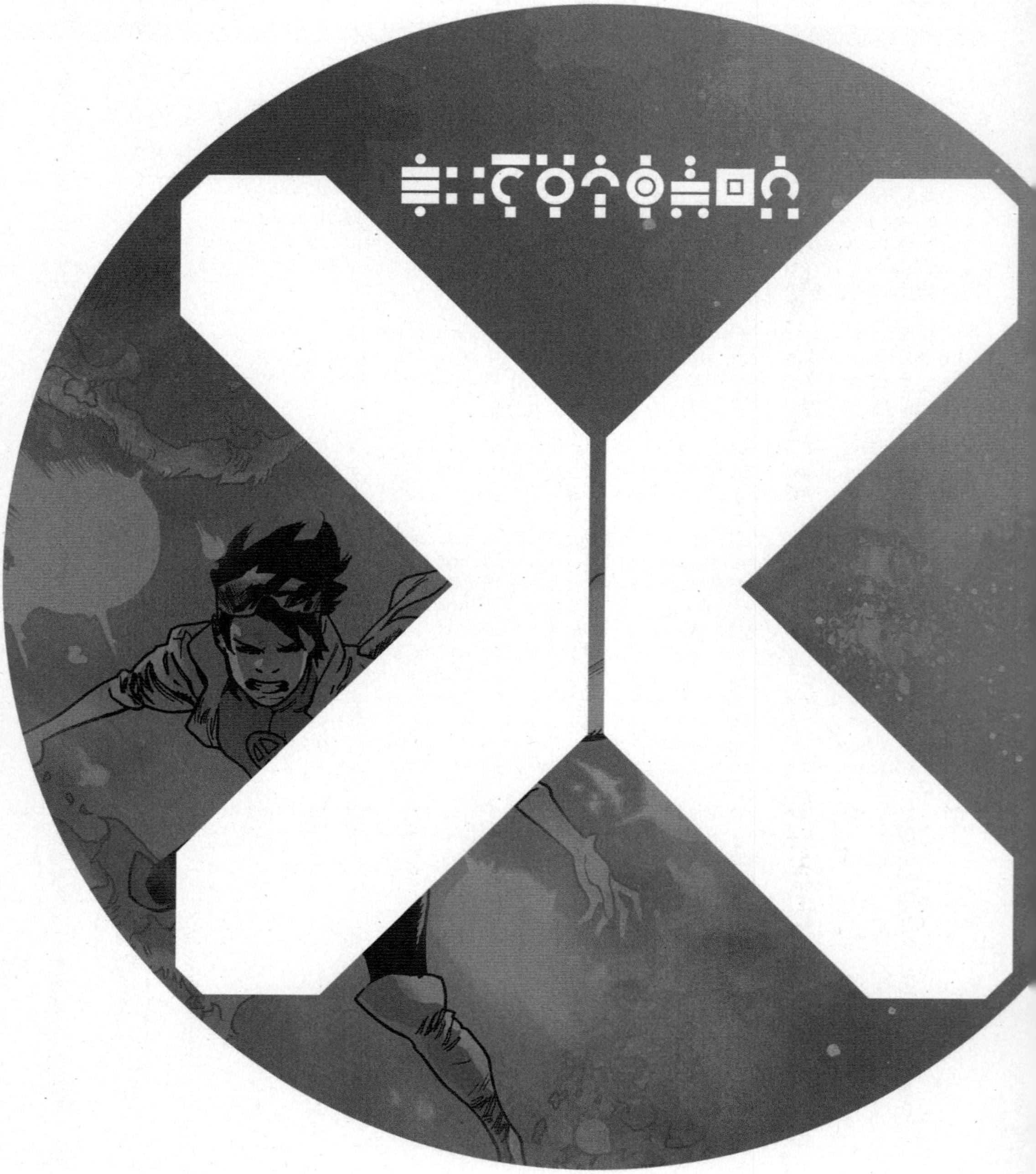

```
TINI HOWARD.....................................[WRITER]
MARCUS TO.......................................[ARTIST]
ERICK ARCINIEGA..........................[COLOR ARTIST]
VC's ARIANA MAHER............................[LETTERER]
TOM MULLER......................................[DESIGN]

MAHMUD ASRAR & MATTHEW WILSON...........[COVER ARTISTS]

NICK RUSSELL...............................[PRODUCTION]

JONATHAN HICKMAN...........................[HEAD OF X]
ANNALISE BISSA......................[ASSISTANT EDITOR]
JORDAN D. WHITE................................[EDITOR]
C.B. CEBULSKI........................[EDITOR IN CHIEF]
```

[11] EXCALIBUR

[ISSUE ELEVEN].....................VERSE XI:
.....................BLOOD OF THE CHANGELING

[00_so_below_X]
[X_above_as_00]

[00_00....00]
[00_00....11]

[00_____the]
[00_realm___]

[00_____of_]

[00_change__]

[ava_[0.11]]
[lon_[0.11]]

[ava_[0.X]]
[lon_[0.X]]

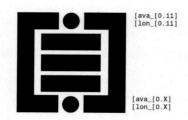

THE GREEN AND THE WHITE

EXCALIBUR seeks to plant a Krakoan gate in Otherworld, as befits a mutant Captain Britain! But their actions have drawn the attention of the Omniversal Majestrix, Opal Luna Saturnyne, and her priestesses, whose attack badly wounded Shogo -- and that simply can't stand.

Gambit

Rogue

Rictor

Jubilee

Apocalypse

Captain Britain

[ava_[0.11]...]
[lon_[0.11]...]

[OMNI..versal.]

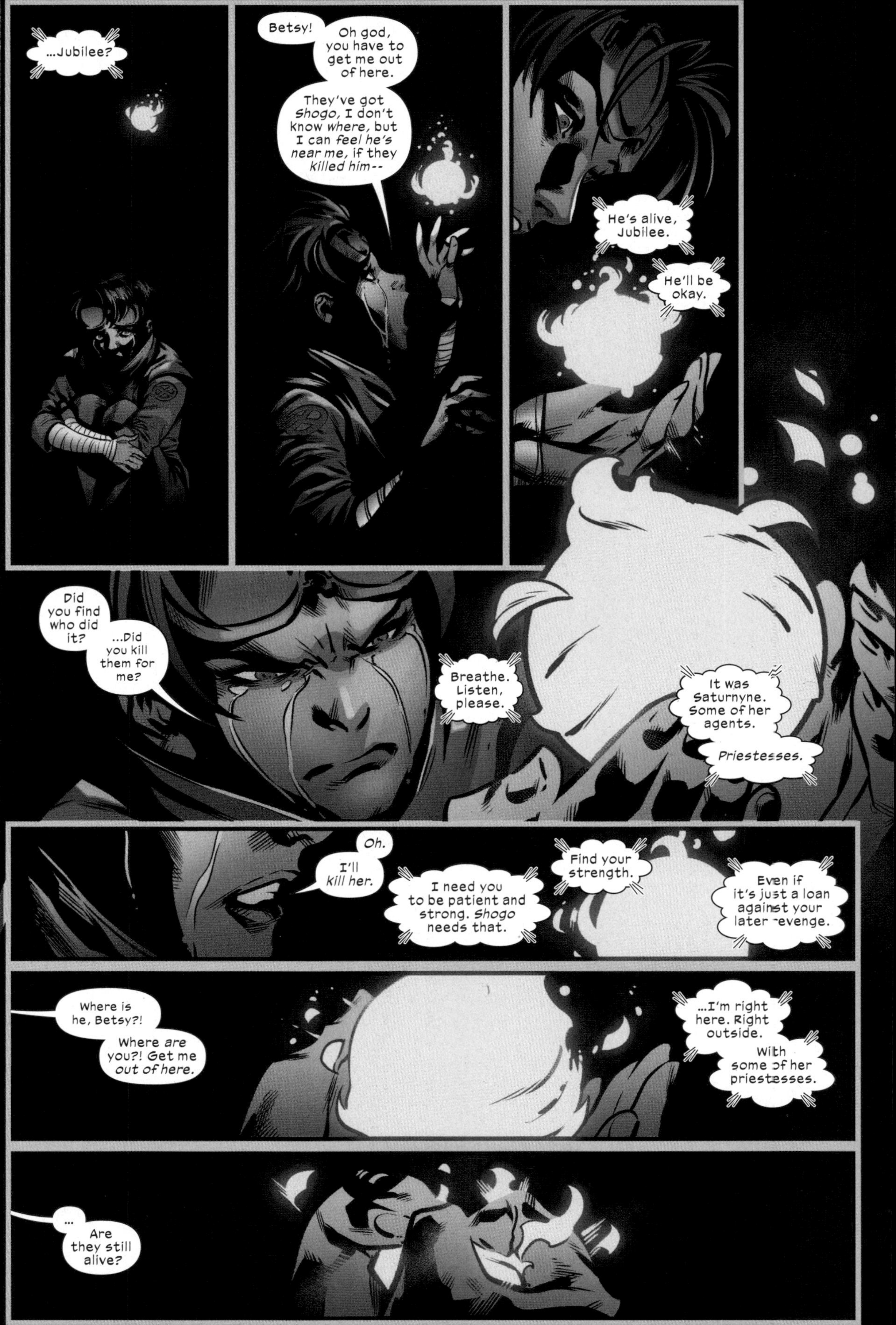
...Jubilee?
Betsy!
Oh god, you have to get me out of here.
They've got *Shogo*, I don't know *where*, but I can *feel* he's *near me*, if they *killed him*--
He's alive, Jubilee.
He'll be okay.
Did you find who did it?
...Did you kill them for me?
Breathe. Listen, please.
It was Saturnyne. Some of her agents.
Priestesses.
Oh.
I'll *kill her.*
I need you to be patient and strong. *Shogo* needs that.
Find your strength.
Even if it's just a loan against your later revenge.
Where is he, Betsy?!
Where *are* you?! Get me *out of here.*
...I'm right here. Right outside.
With some of her priestesses.
...
Are they still alive?

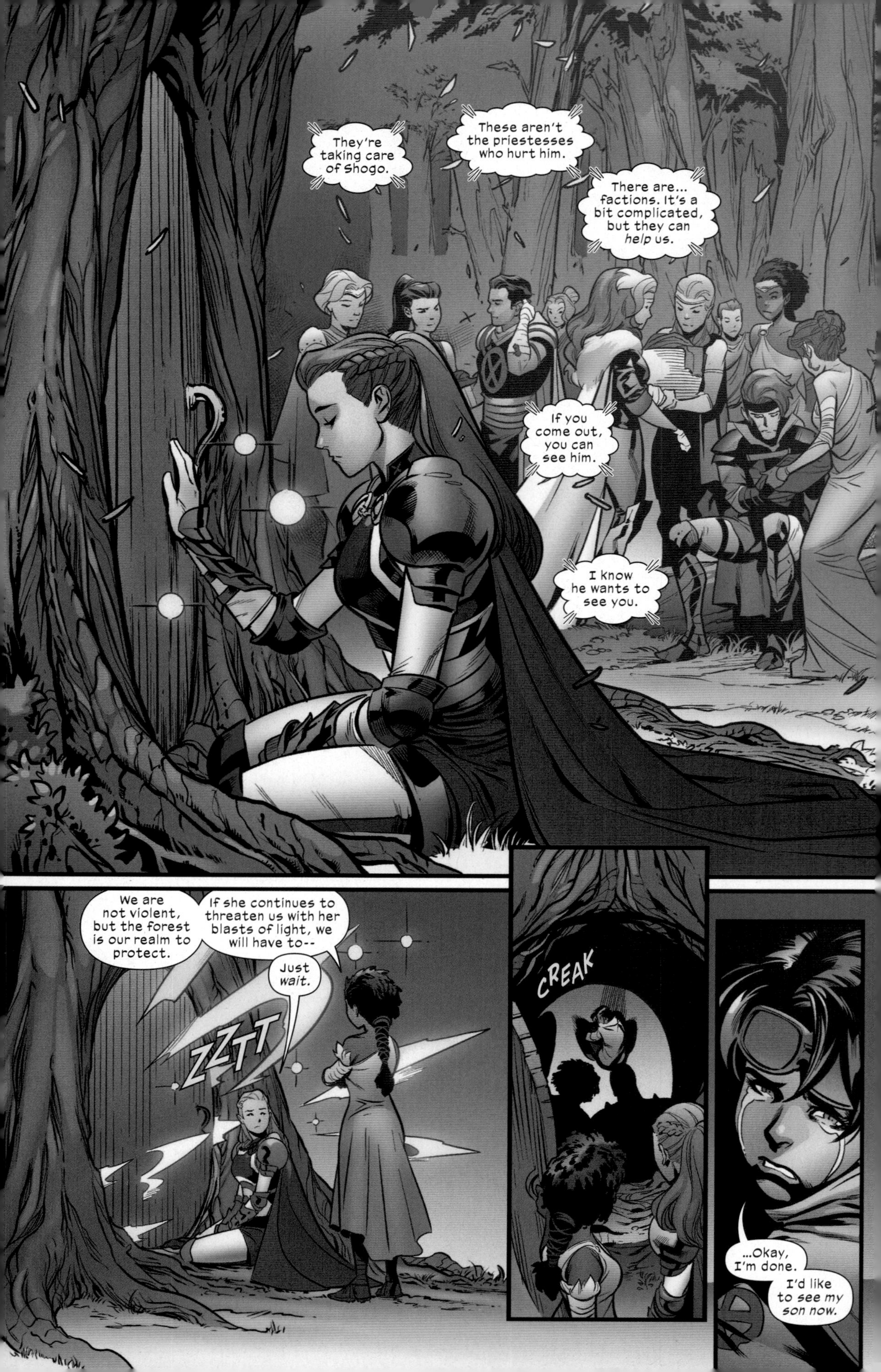
They're taking care of Shogo.
These aren't the priestesses who hurt him.
There are... factions. It's a bit complicated, but they can *help* us.
If you come out, you can see him.
I know he wants to see you.
We are not violent, but the forest is our realm to protect.
If she continues to threaten us with her blasts of light, we will have to--
Just *wait.*
ZZTT
CREAK
...Okay, I'm done.
I'd like to see my *son now.*

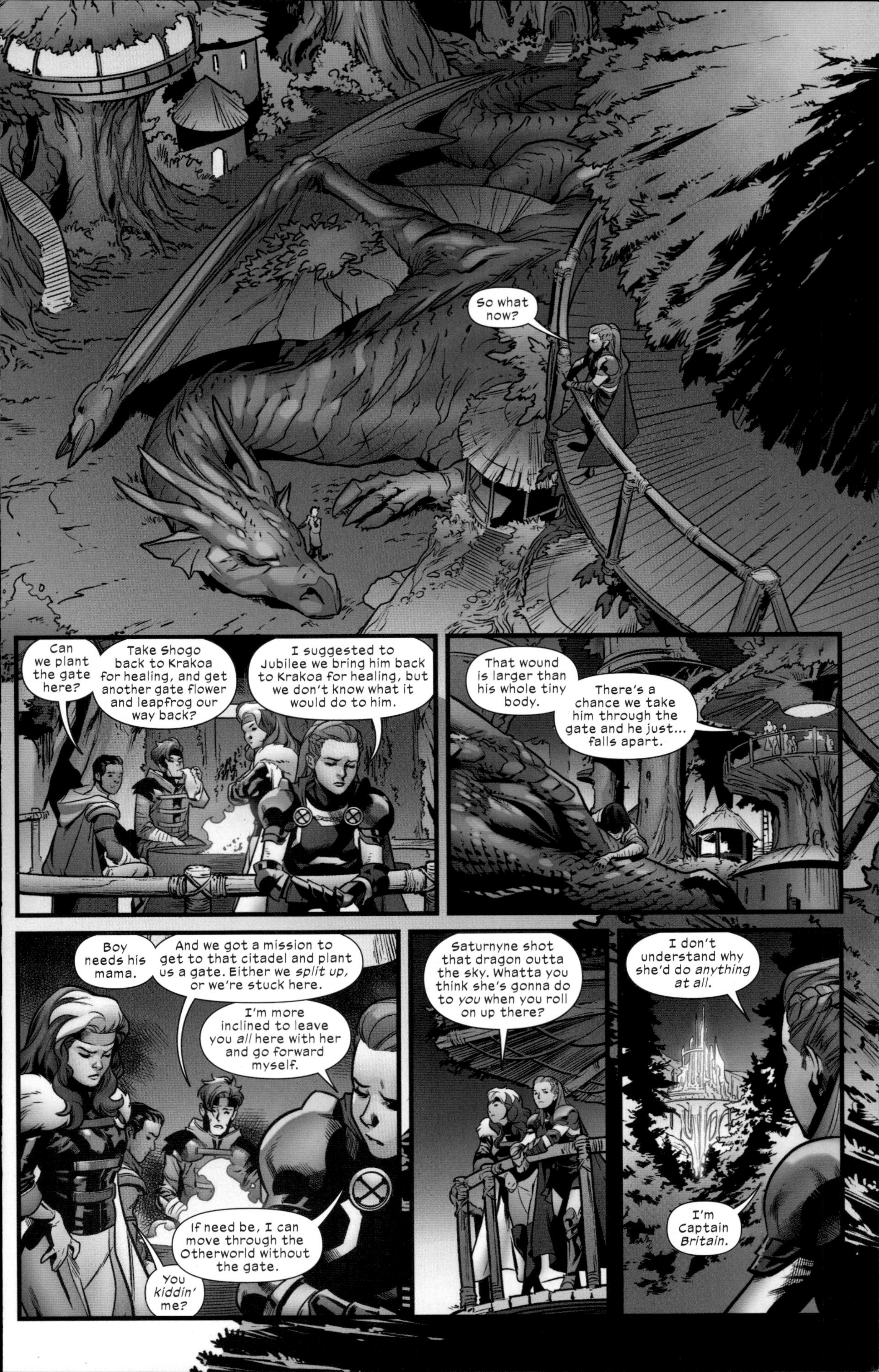
So what now?
Can we plant the gate here?
Take Shogo back to Krakoa for healing, and get another gate flower and leapfrog our way back?
I suggested to Jubilee we bring him back to Krakoa for healing, but we don't know what it would do to him.
That wound is larger than his whole tiny body.
There's a chance we take him through the gate and he just... falls apart.
Boy needs his mama.
And we got a mission to get to that citadel and plant us a gate. Either we split up, or we're stuck here.
I'm more inclined to leave you all here with her and go forward myself.
If need be, I can move through the Otherworld without the gate.
You kiddin' me?
Saturnyne shot that dragon outta the sky. Whatta you think she's gonna do to you when you roll on up there?
I don't understand why she'd do anything at all.
I'm Captain Britain.

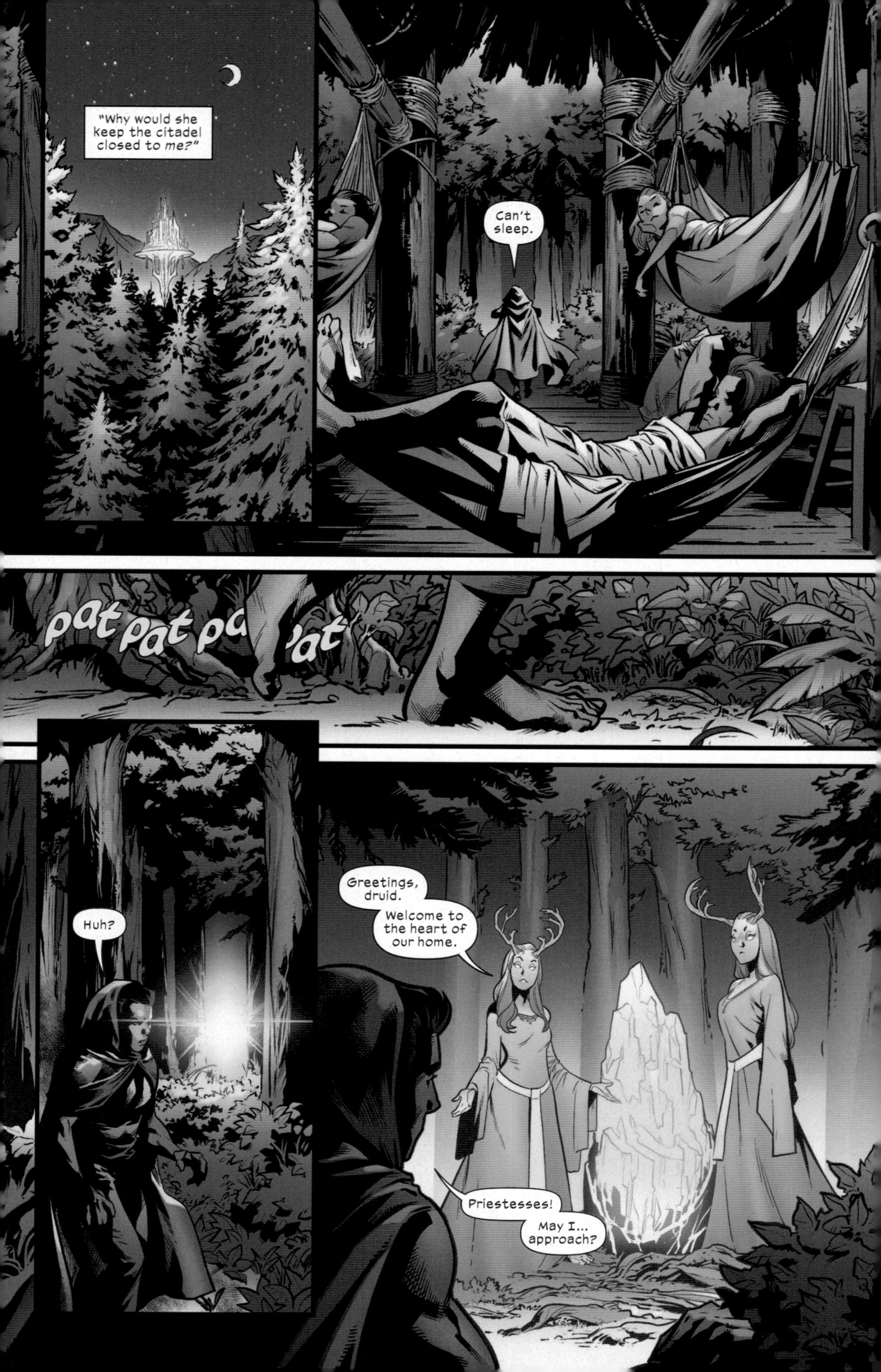
"Why would she keep the citadel closed to me?"
Can't sleep.
pat pat pa pat
Huh?
Greetings, druid.
Welcome to the heart of our home.
Priestesses!
May I... approach?

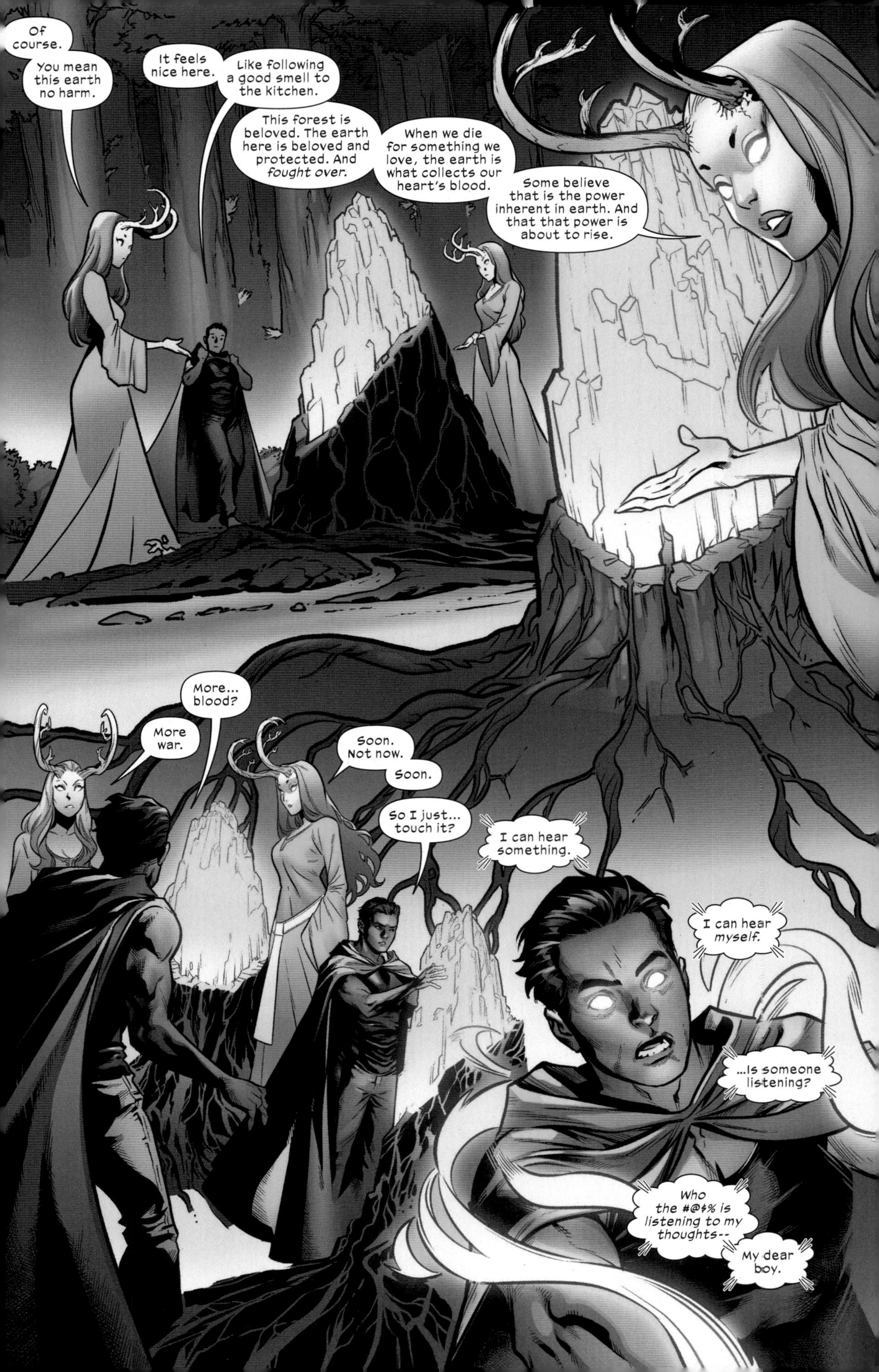
Of course.
You mean this earth no harm.
It feels nice here.
Like following a good smell to the kitchen.
This forest is beloved. The earth here is beloved and protected. And *fought over.*
When we die for something we love, the earth is what collects our heart's blood.
Some believe that is the power inherent in earth. And that that power is about to rise.
More... blood?
More war.
Soon. Not now.
Soon.
So I just... touch it?
I can hear something.
I can hear *myself.*
...Is someone listening?
Who the #@$% is listening to my thoughts--
My dear boy.

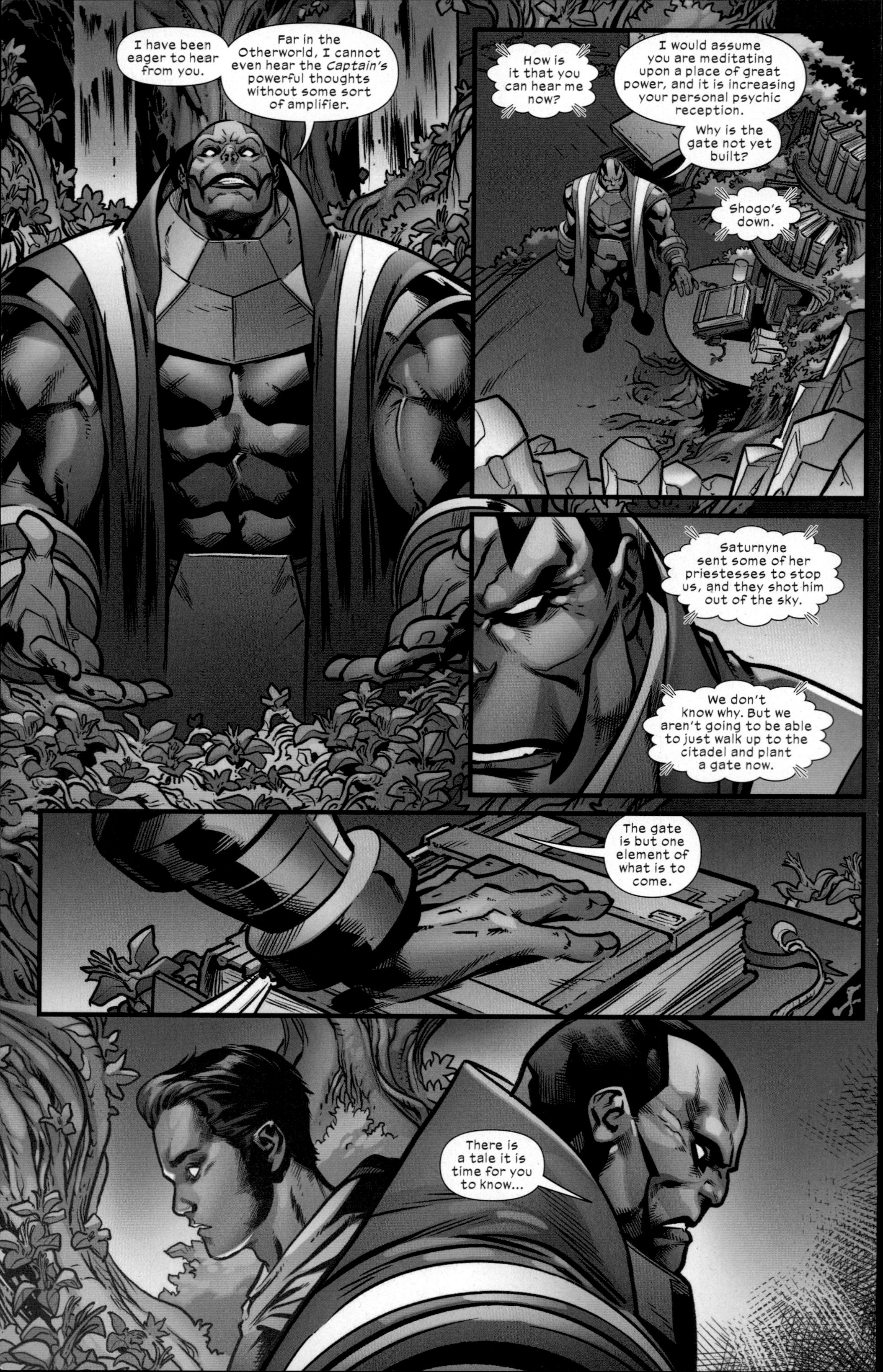
I have been eager to hear from you.
Far in the Otherworld, I cannot even hear the *Captain's* powerful thoughts without some sort of amplifier.
How is it that you can hear me now?
I would assume you are meditating upon a place of great power, and it is increasing your personal psychic reception.
Why is the gate not yet built?
Shogo's down.
Saturnyne sent some of her priestesses to stop us, and they shot him out of the sky.
We don't know why. But we aren't going to be able to just walk up to the citadel and plant a gate now.
The gate is but one element of what is to come.
There is a tale it is time for you to know...

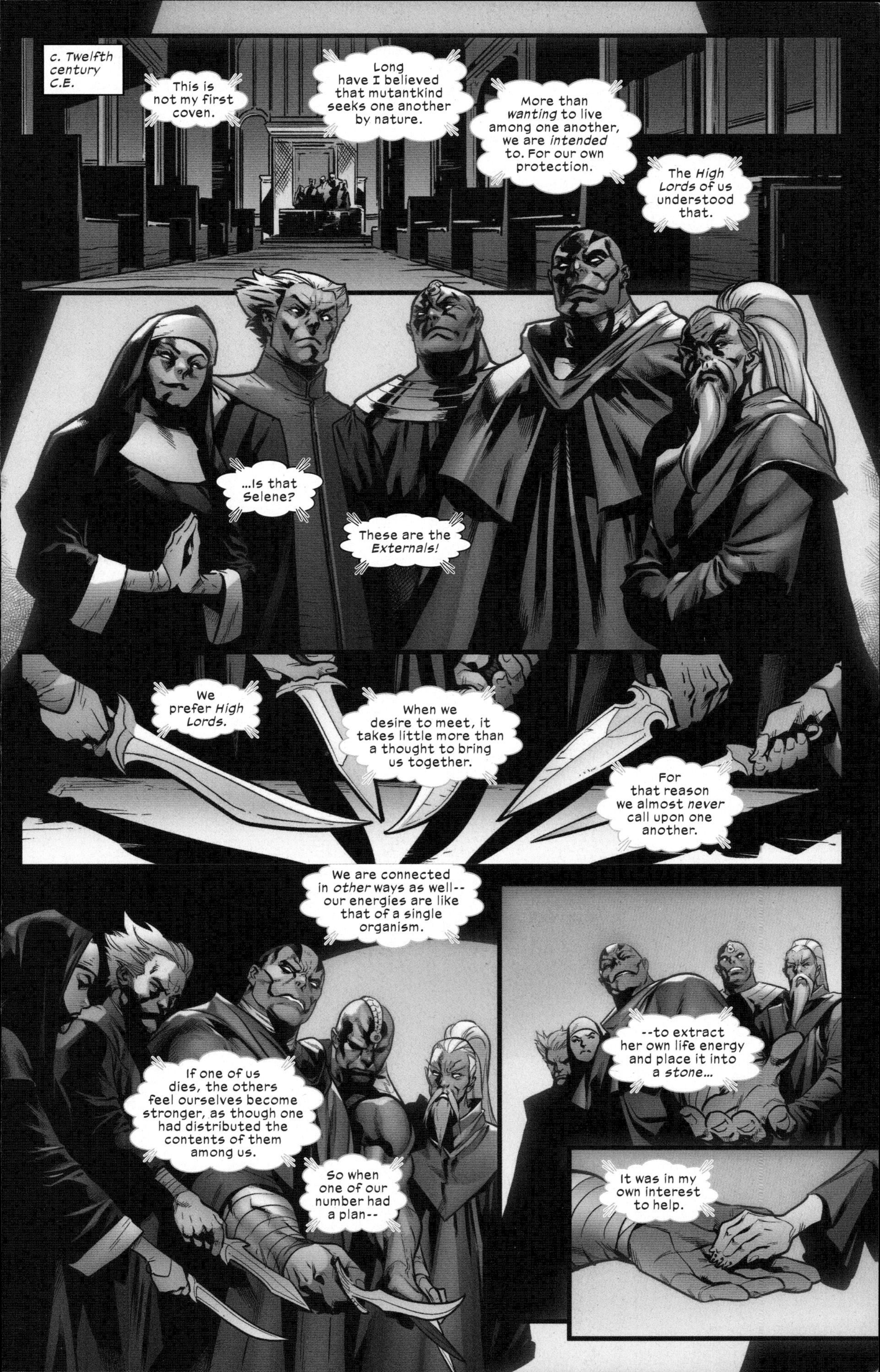

c. Twelfth century C.E.
This is not my first coven.
Long have I believed that mutantkind seeks one another by nature.
More than *wanting* to live among one another, we are *intended* to. For our own protection.
The *High Lords* of us understood that.
...Is that Selene?
These are the *Externals!*
We prefer *High Lords.*
When we desire to meet, it takes little more than a thought to bring us together.
For that reason we almost *never* call upon one another.
We are connected in *other* ways as well-- our energies are like that of a single organism.
If one of us dies, the others feel ourselves become stronger, as though one had distributed the contents of them among us.
So when one of our number had a plan--
--to extract her own life energy and place it into a *stone*...
It was in my own interest to help.

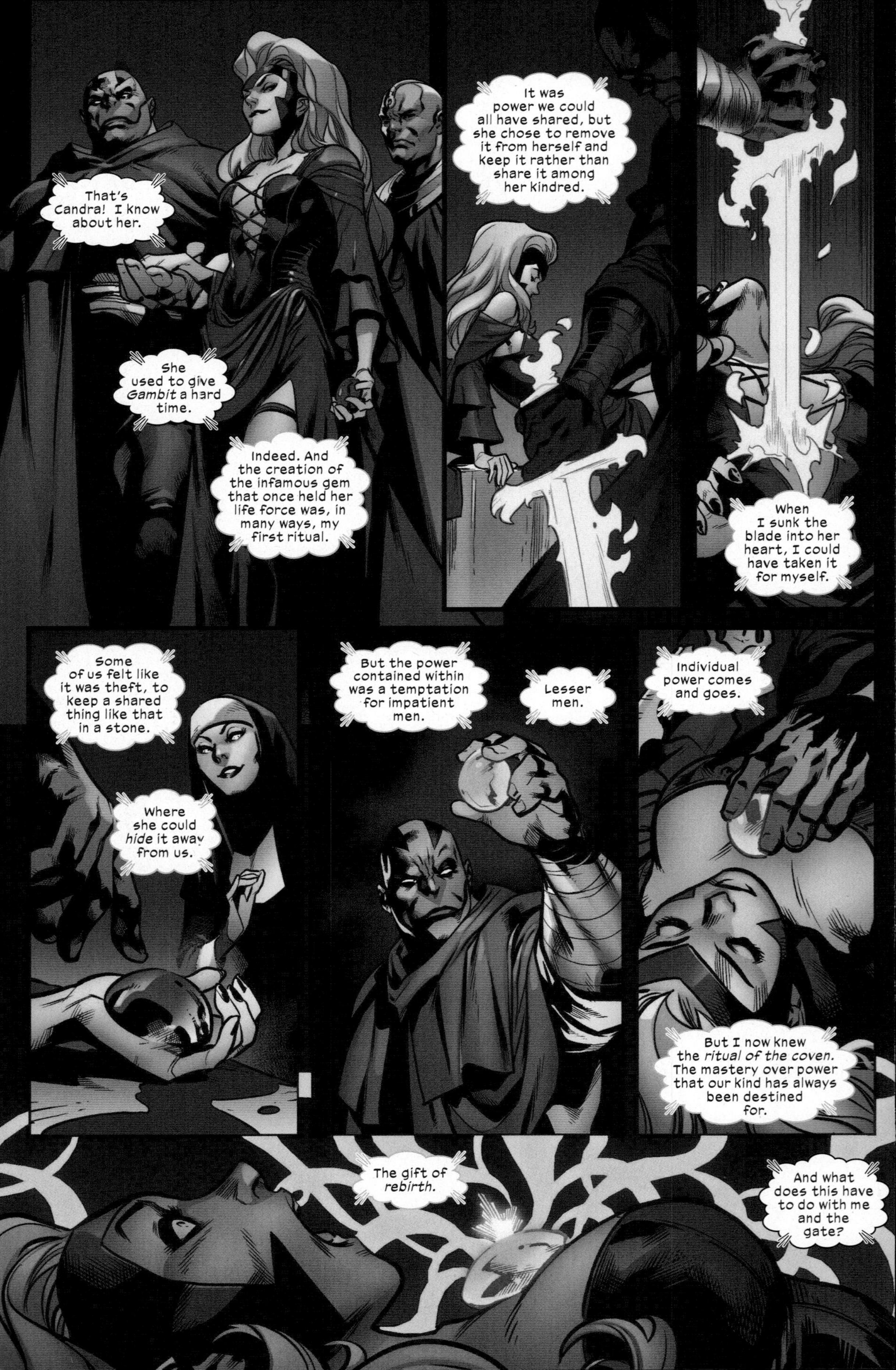
That's Candra! I know about her.
She used to give *Gambit* a hard time.
Indeed. And the creation of the infamous gem that once held her life force was, in many ways, my first ritual.
It was power we could all have shared, but she chose to remove it from herself and keep it rather than share it among her kindred.
When I sunk the blade into her heart, I could have taken it for myself.
Some of us felt like it was theft, to keep a shared thing like that in a stone.
Where she could *hide* it away from us.
But the power contained within was a temptation for impatient men.
Lesser men.
Individual power comes and goes.
But I now knew the *ritual of the coven.* The mastery over power that our kind has always been destined for.
The gift of *rebirth.*
And what does this have to do with me and the gate?

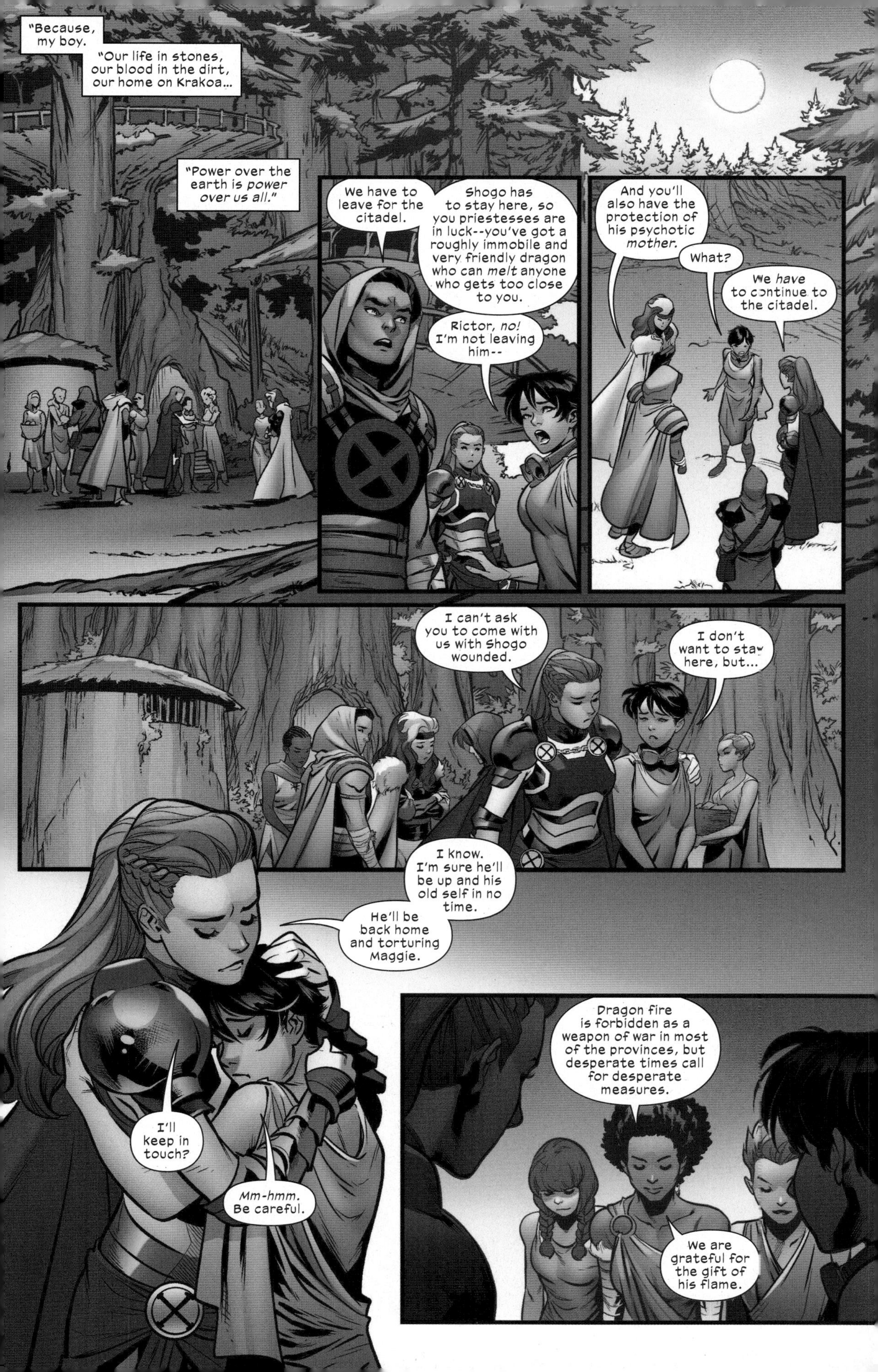
"Because, my boy.
"Our life in stones, our blood in the dirt, our home on Krakoa...
"Power over the earth is *power over us all.*"
We have to leave for the citadel.
Shogo has to stay here, so you priestesses are in luck--you've got a roughly immobile and very friendly dragon who can *melt* anyone who gets too close to you.
Rictor, *no!* I'm not leaving him--
And you'll also have the protection of his psychotic *mother.*
What?
We *have* to continue to the citadel.
I can't ask you to come with us with Shogo wounded.
I don't want to stay here, but...
I know. I'm sure he'll be up and his old self in no time.
He'll be back home and torturing Maggie.
I'll keep in touch?
Mm-hmm. Be careful.
Dragon fire is forbidden as a weapon of war in most of the provinces, but desperate times call for desperate measures.
We are grateful for the gift of his flame.

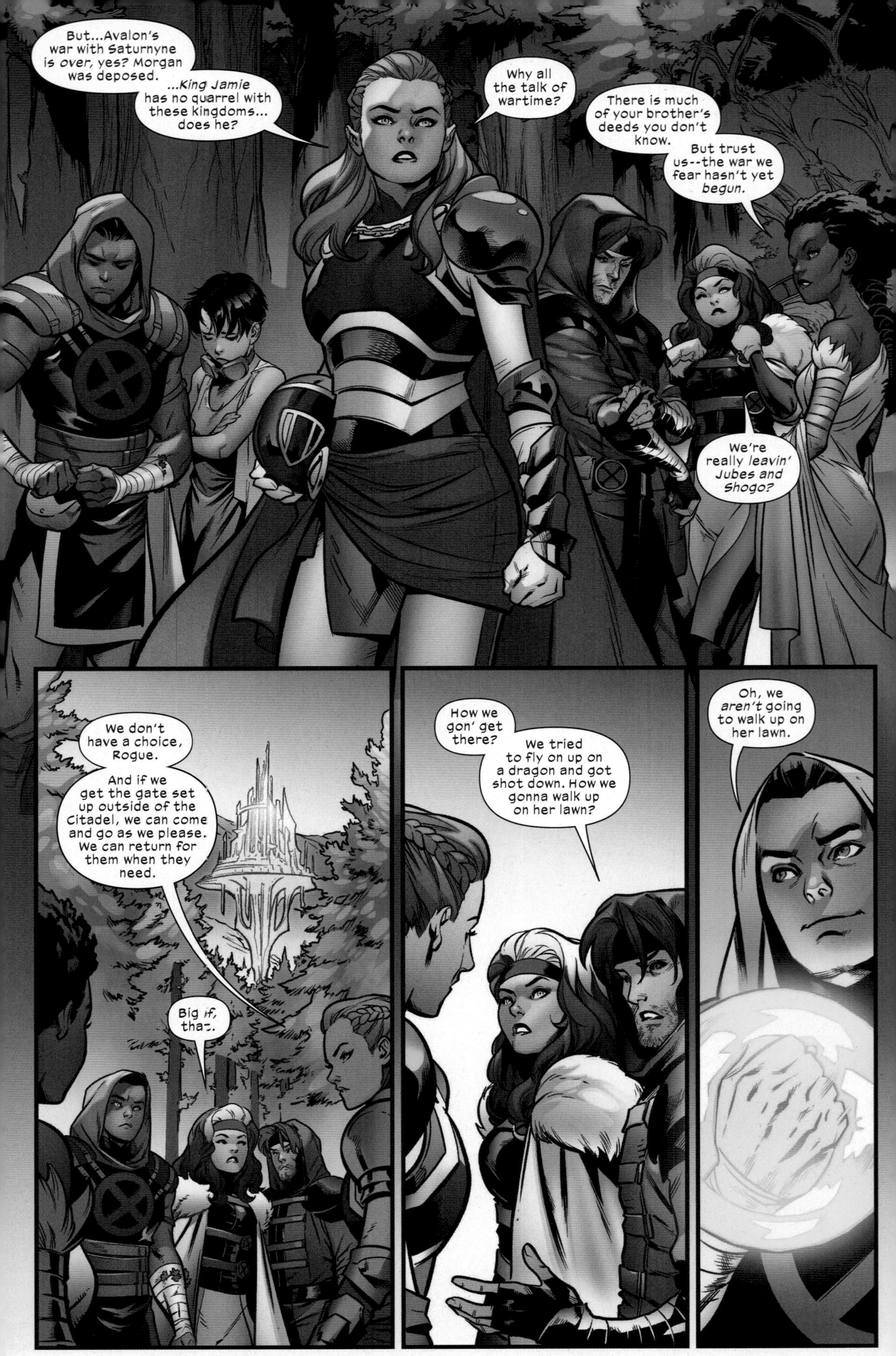
But...Avalon's war with Saturnyne is over, yes? Morgan was deposed.
...King Jamie has no quarrel with these kingdoms... does he?
Why all the talk of wartime?
There is much of your brother's deeds you don't know.
But trust us--the war we fear hasn't yet begun.
We're really leavin' Jubes and Shogo?
We don't have a choice, Rogue.
And if we get the gate set up outside of the Citadel, we can come and go as we please. We can return for them when they need.
Big if, that.
How we gon' get there?
We tried to fly on up on a dragon and got shot down. How we gonna walk up on her lawn?
Oh, we aren't going to walk up on her lawn.

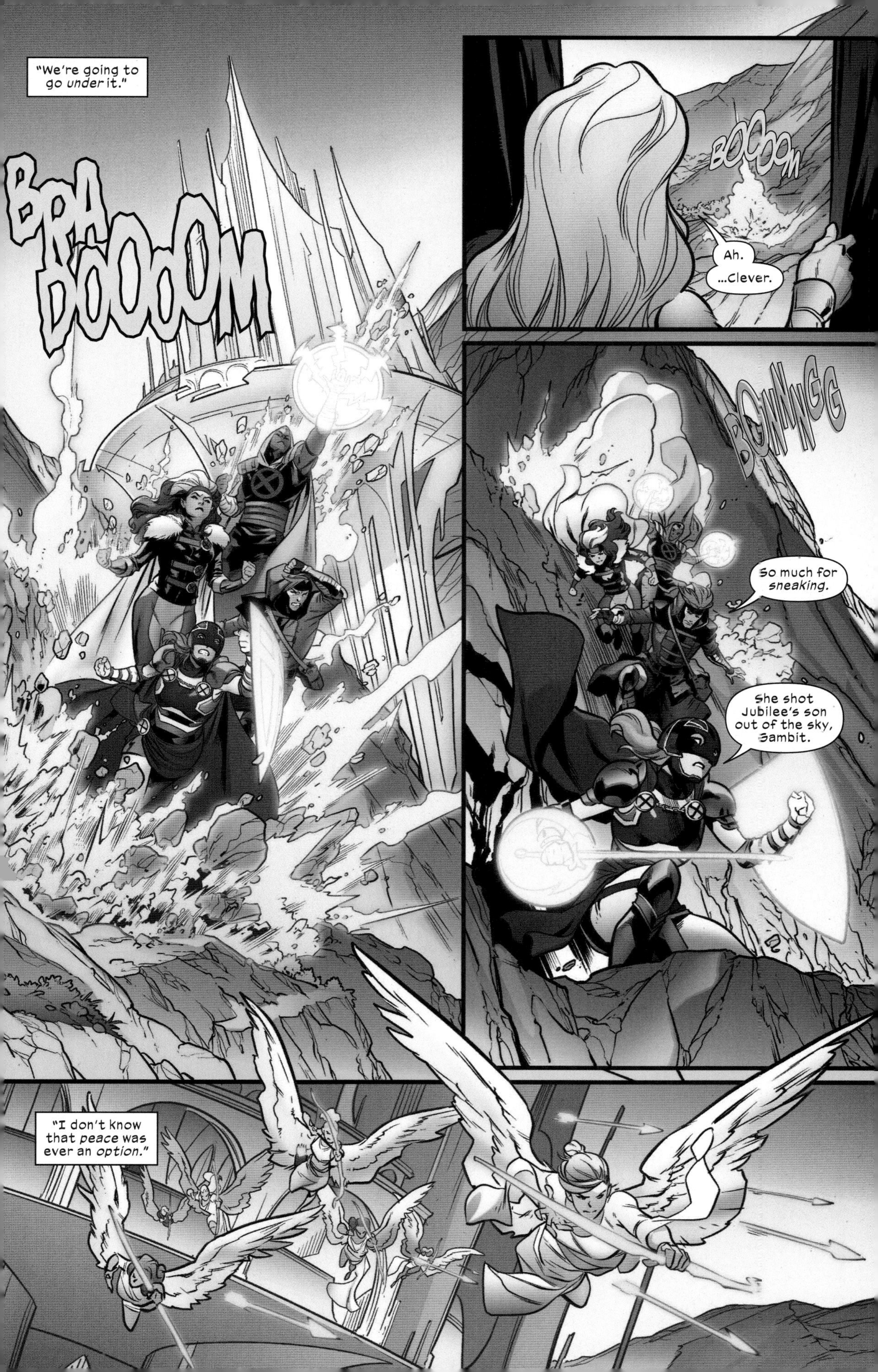
"We're going to go *under* it."
BRA BOOOOOM
BOOOOOM
Ah.
...Clever.
BOINNNGG
So much for *sneaking.*
She shot Jubilee's son out of the sky, Gambit.
"I don't know that *peace* was ever an *option.*"

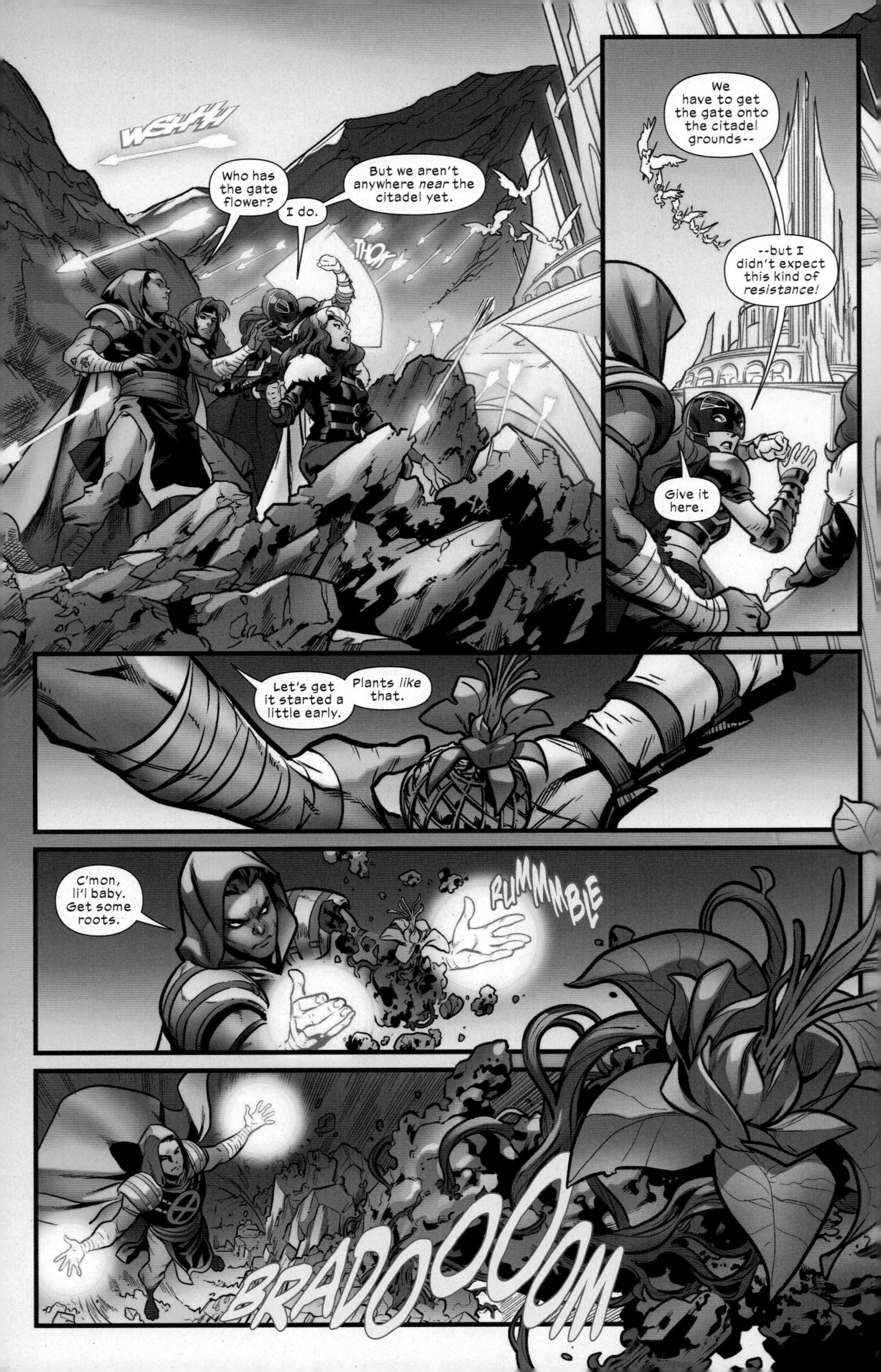
WSHHH
Who has the gate flower?
I do.
But we aren't anywhere *near* the citadel yet.
THOK
We have to get the gate onto the citadel grounds--
--but I didn't expect this kind of *resistance!*
Give it here.
Let's get it started a little early.
Plants *like* that.
C'mon, li'l baby. Get some roots.
RUMMMMBLE
BRADOOOOM

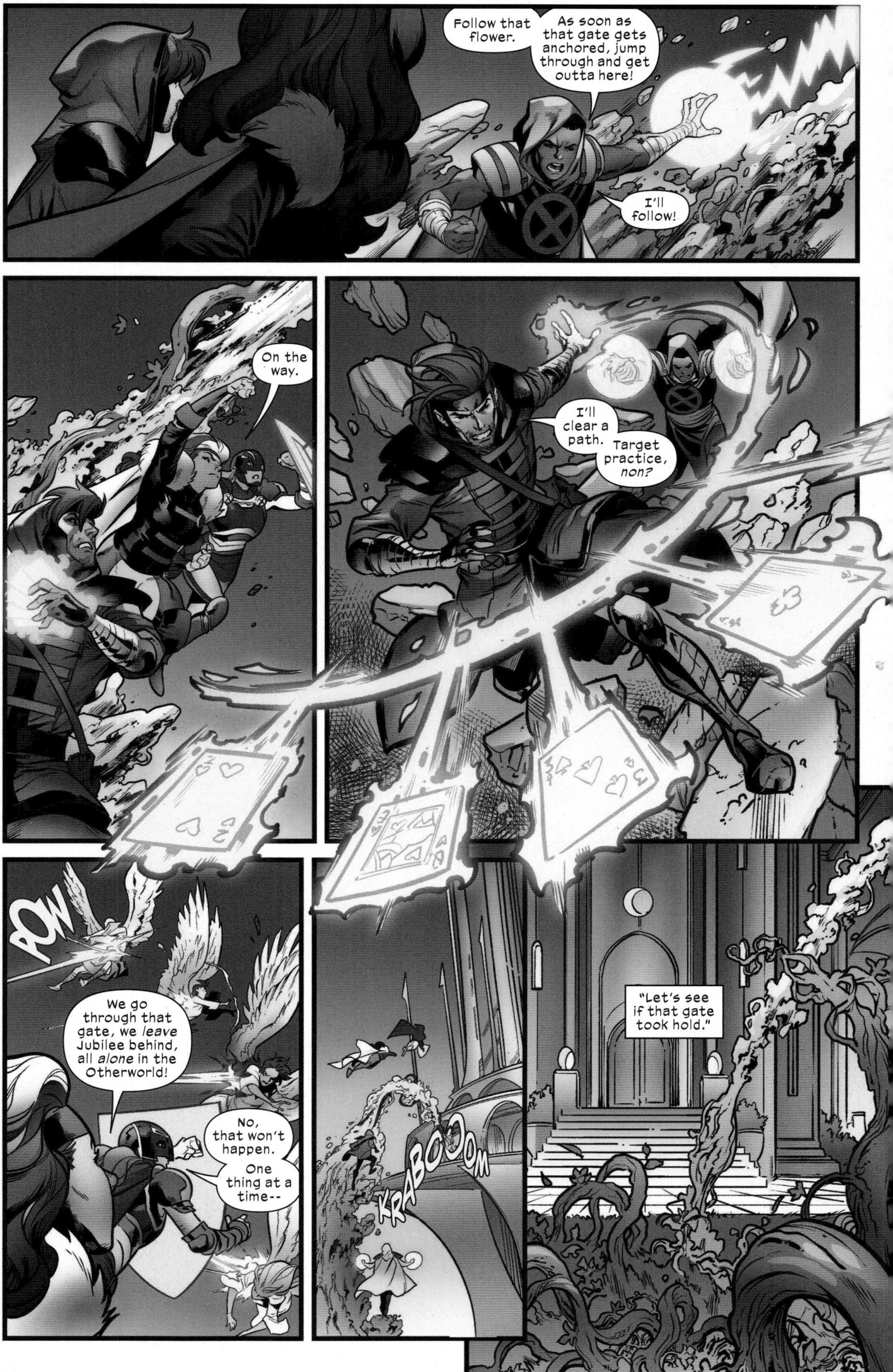

Follow that flower.
As soon as that gate gets anchored, jump through and get outta here!
I'll follow!
On the way.
I'll clear a path.
Target practice, *non?*
POW
We go through that gate, we *leave* Jubilee behind, all *alone* in the Otherworld!
No, that won't happen.
One thing at a time--
KRABOOOM
"Let's see if that gate took hold."

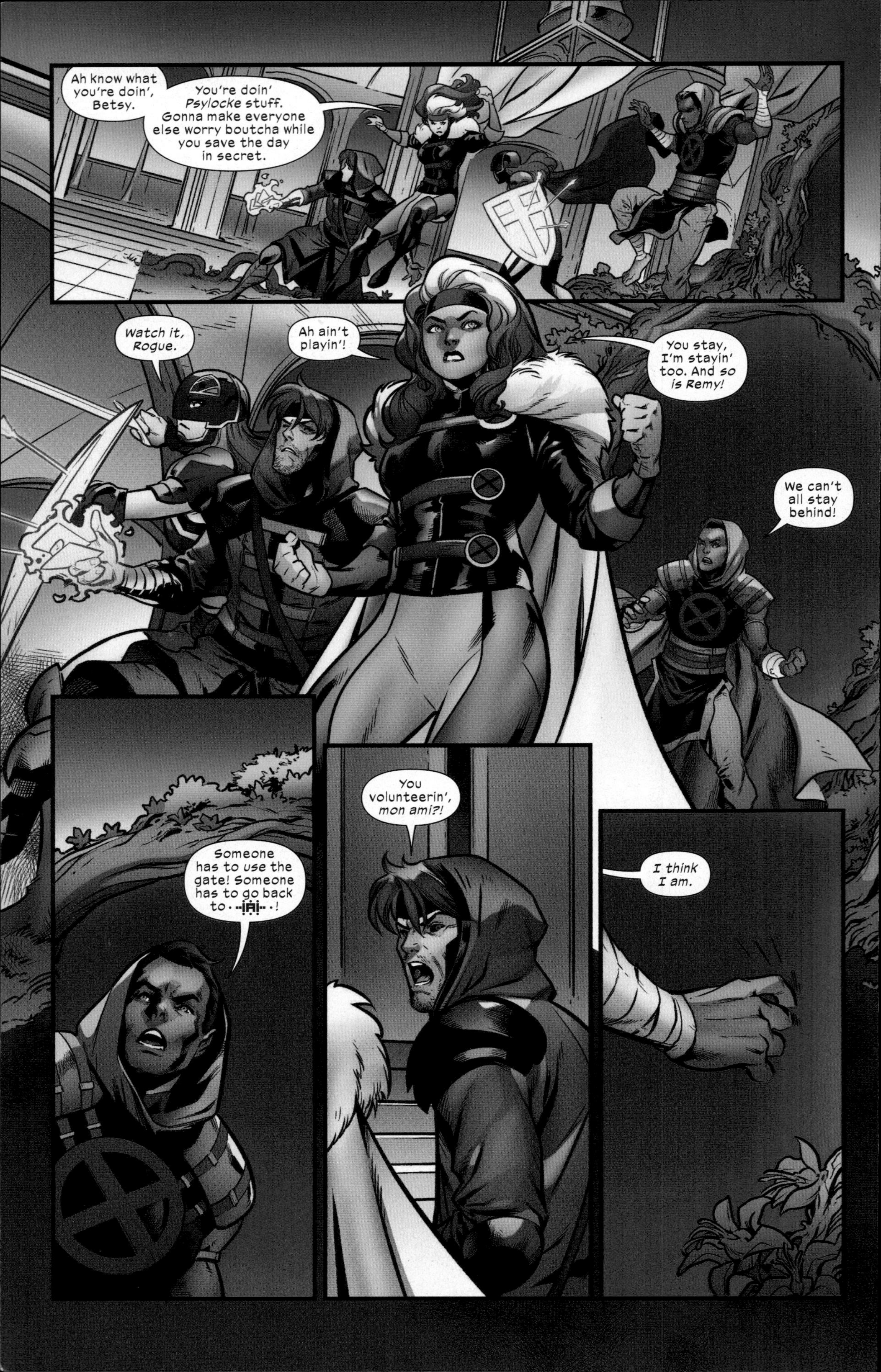
Ah know what you're doin', Betsy.
You're doin' *Psylocke* stuff. Gonna make everyone else worry boutcha while you save the day in secret.
Watch it, Rogue.
Ah ain't *playin'*!
You stay, I'm stayin' too. And so is *Remy!*
We can't all stay behind!
Someone has to *use* the gate! Someone has to go back to ...!
You *volunteerin'*, *mon ami?!*
I think I am.

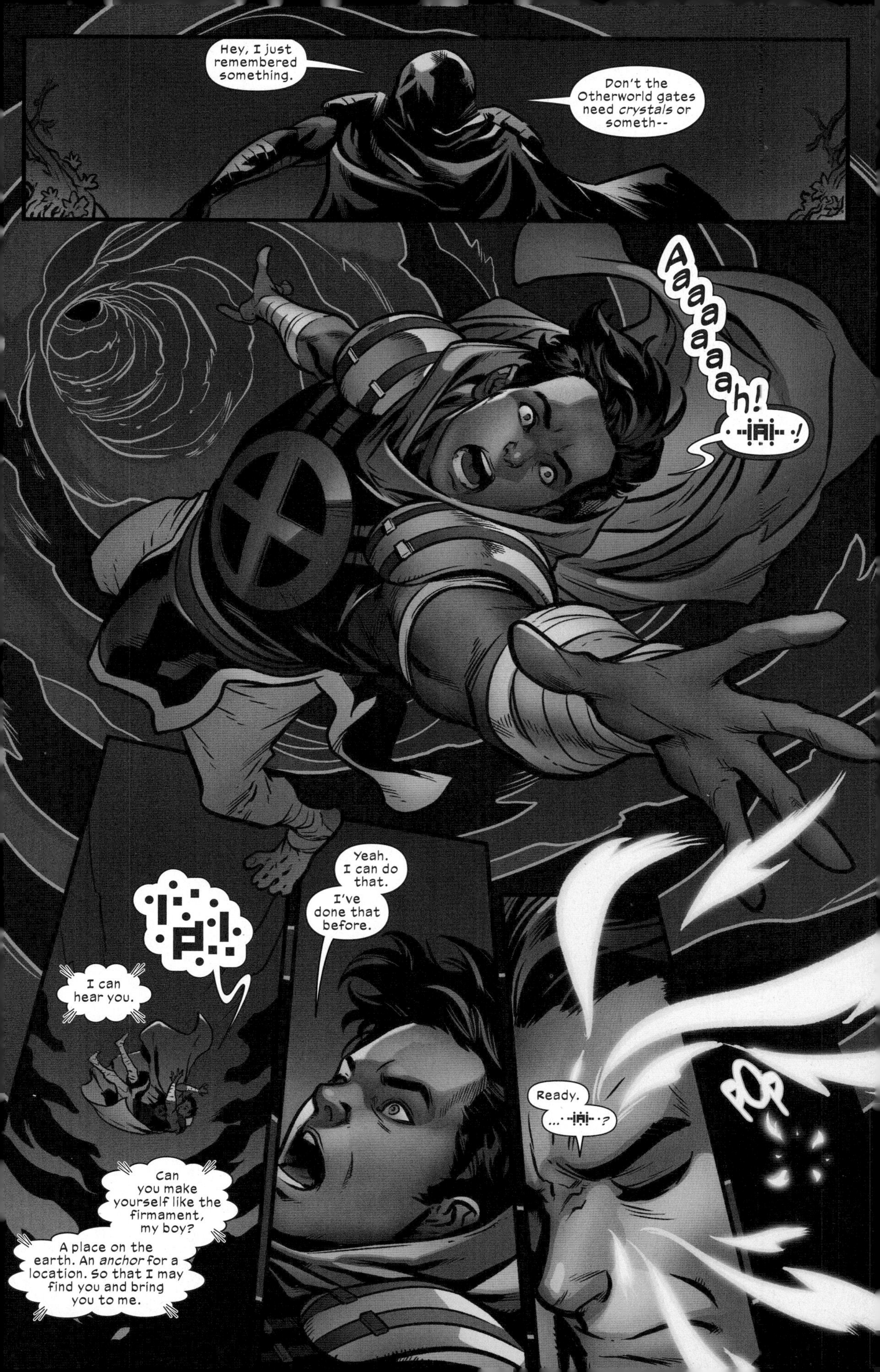
Hey, I just remembered something.
Don't the Otherworld gates need *crystals* or someth--
Aaaaaaah!
I can hear you.
Yeah. I can do that.
I've done that before.
Can you make yourself like the firmament, my boy?
A place on the earth. An *anchor* for a location. So that I may find you and bring you to me.
Ready.
POP

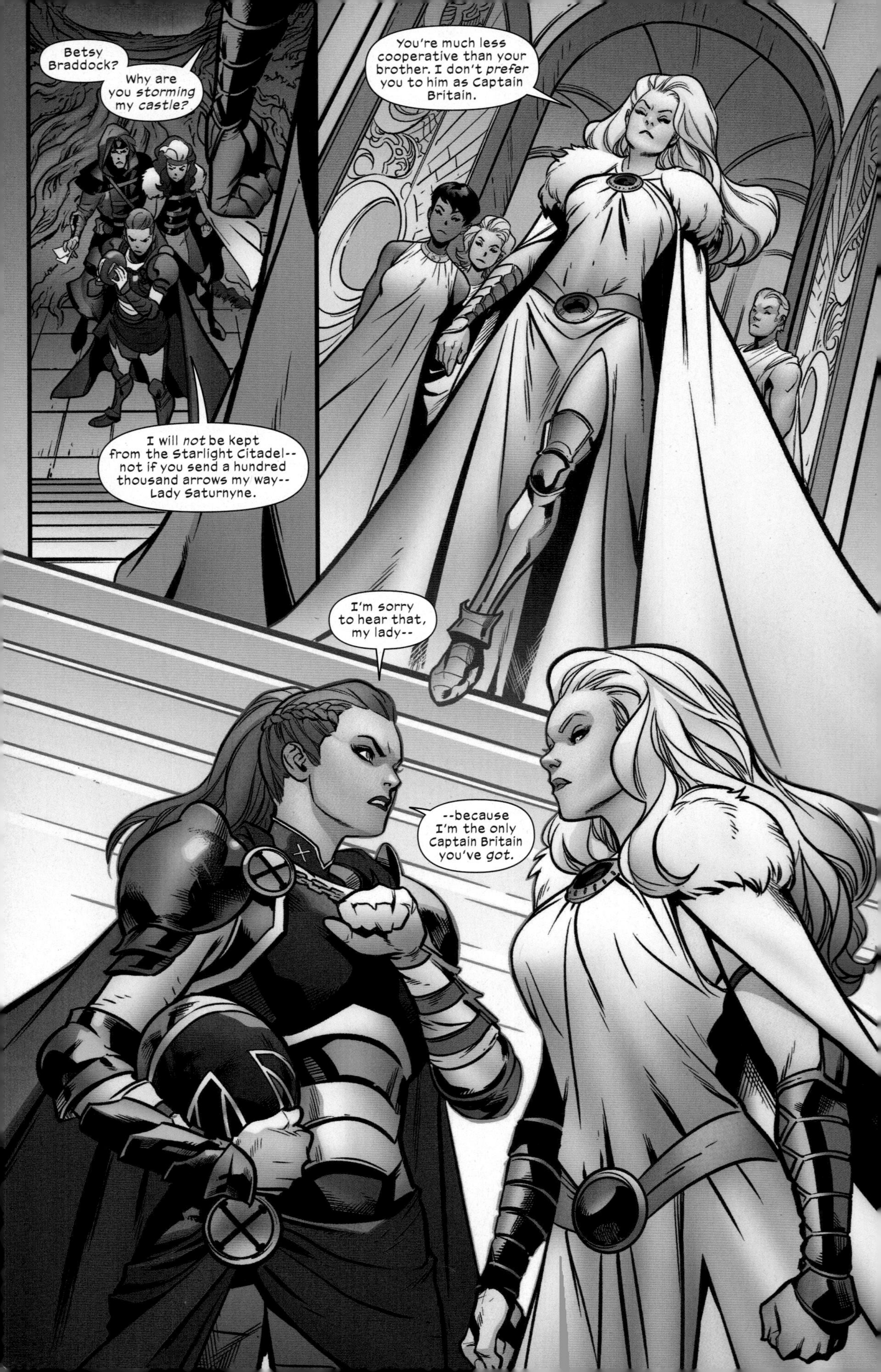

Betsy Braddock?
Why are you *storming* my *castle?*
I will *not* be kept from the Starlight Citadel-- not if you send a hundred thousand arrows my way-- Lady Saturnyne.
You're much less cooperative than your brother. I don't *prefer* you to him as Captain Britain.
I'm sorry to hear that, my lady--
--because I'm the only Captain Britain you've *got.*

[dawn_of_x]

[kra_]
[koa_]

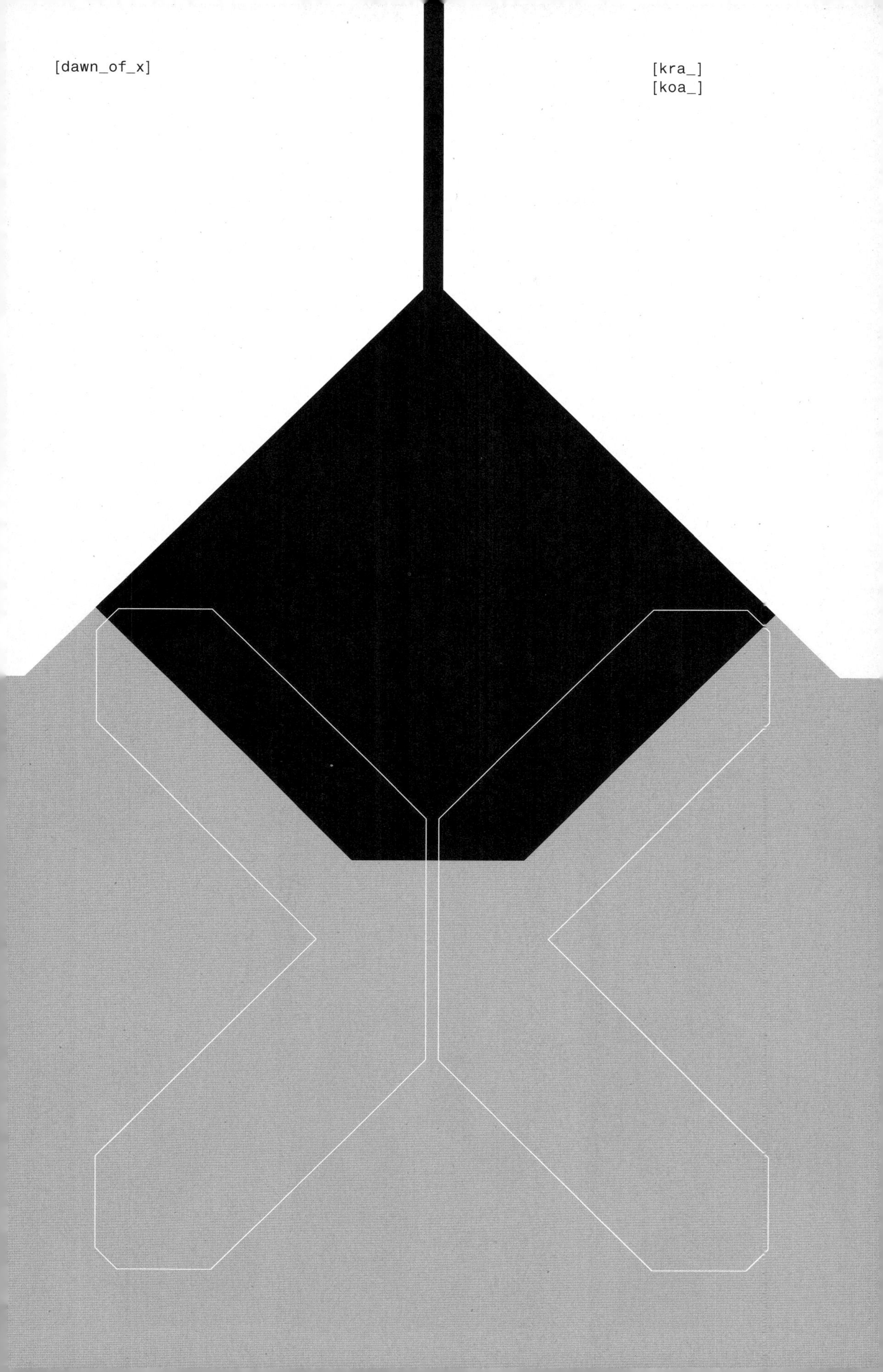

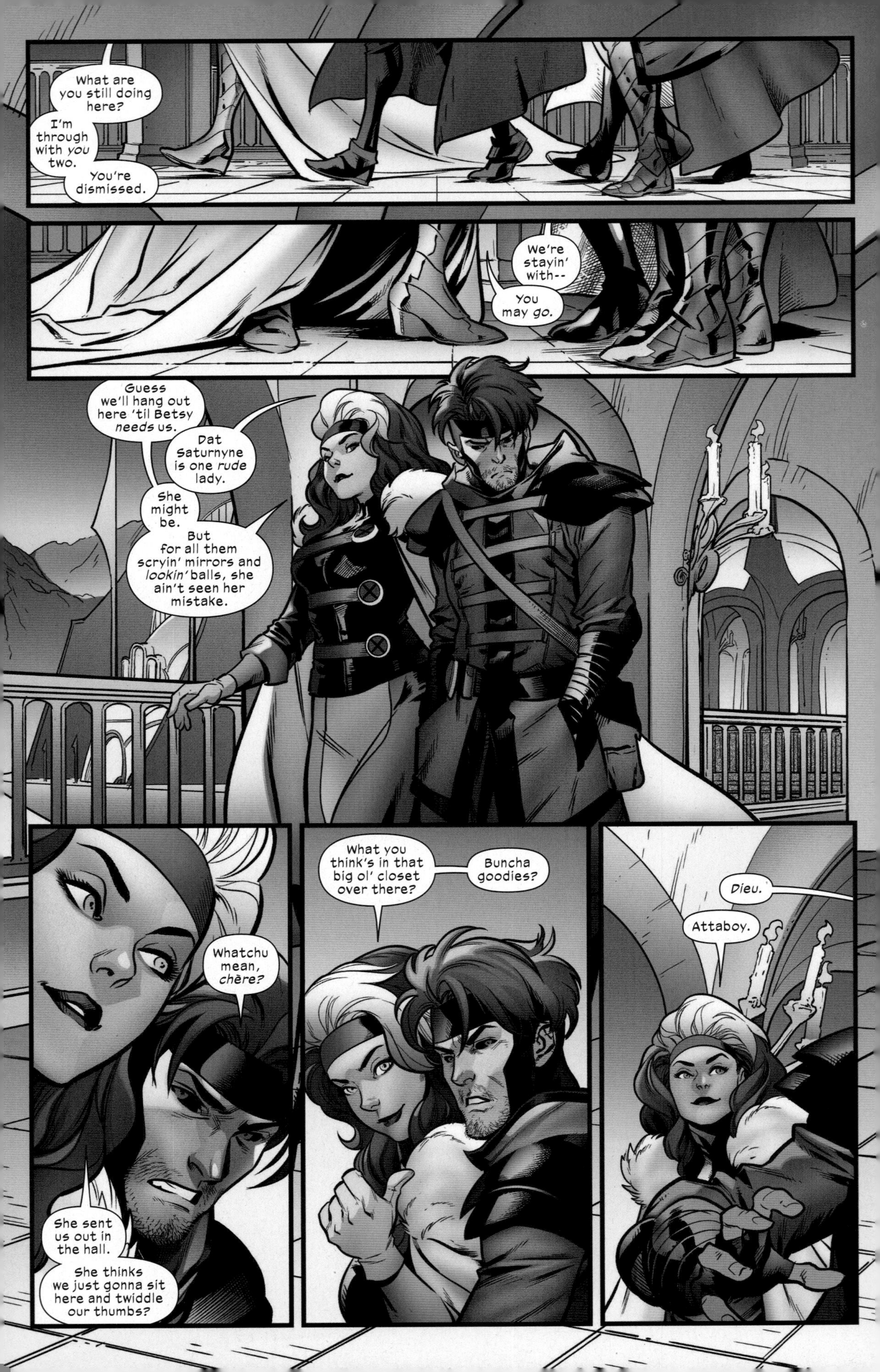
What are you still doing here?
I'm through with *you* two.
You're dismissed.
We're stayin' with--
You may *go*.
Guess we'll hang out here 'til Betsy *needs* us.
Dat Saturnyne is one *rude* lady.
She might be.
But for all them scryin' mirrors and *lookin'* balls, she ain't seen her mistake.
Whatchu mean, *chère?*
She sent us out in the hall.
She thinks we just gonna sit here and twiddle our thumbs?
What you think's in that big ol' closet over there?
Buncha goodies?
Dieu.
Attaboy.

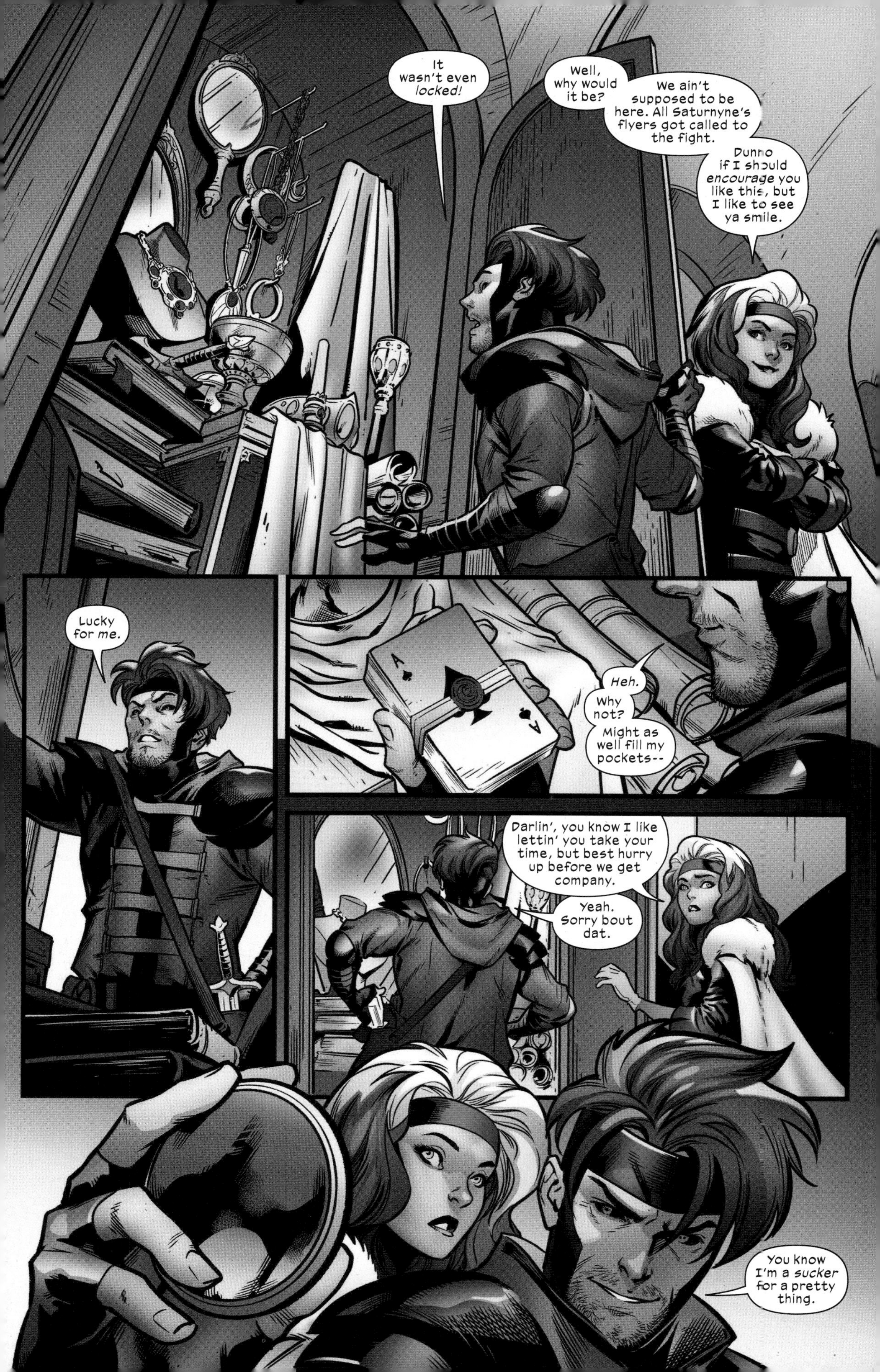
It wasn't even *locked!*
Well, why would it be?
We ain't supposed to be here. All Saturnyne's flyers got called to the fight.
Dunno if I should *encourage* you like this, but I like to see ya smile.
Lucky for me.
Heh.
Why not?
Might as well fill my pockets--
Darlin', you know I like lettin' you take your time, but best hurry up before we get company.
Yeah. Sorry bout dat.
You know I'm a *sucker* for a pretty thing.

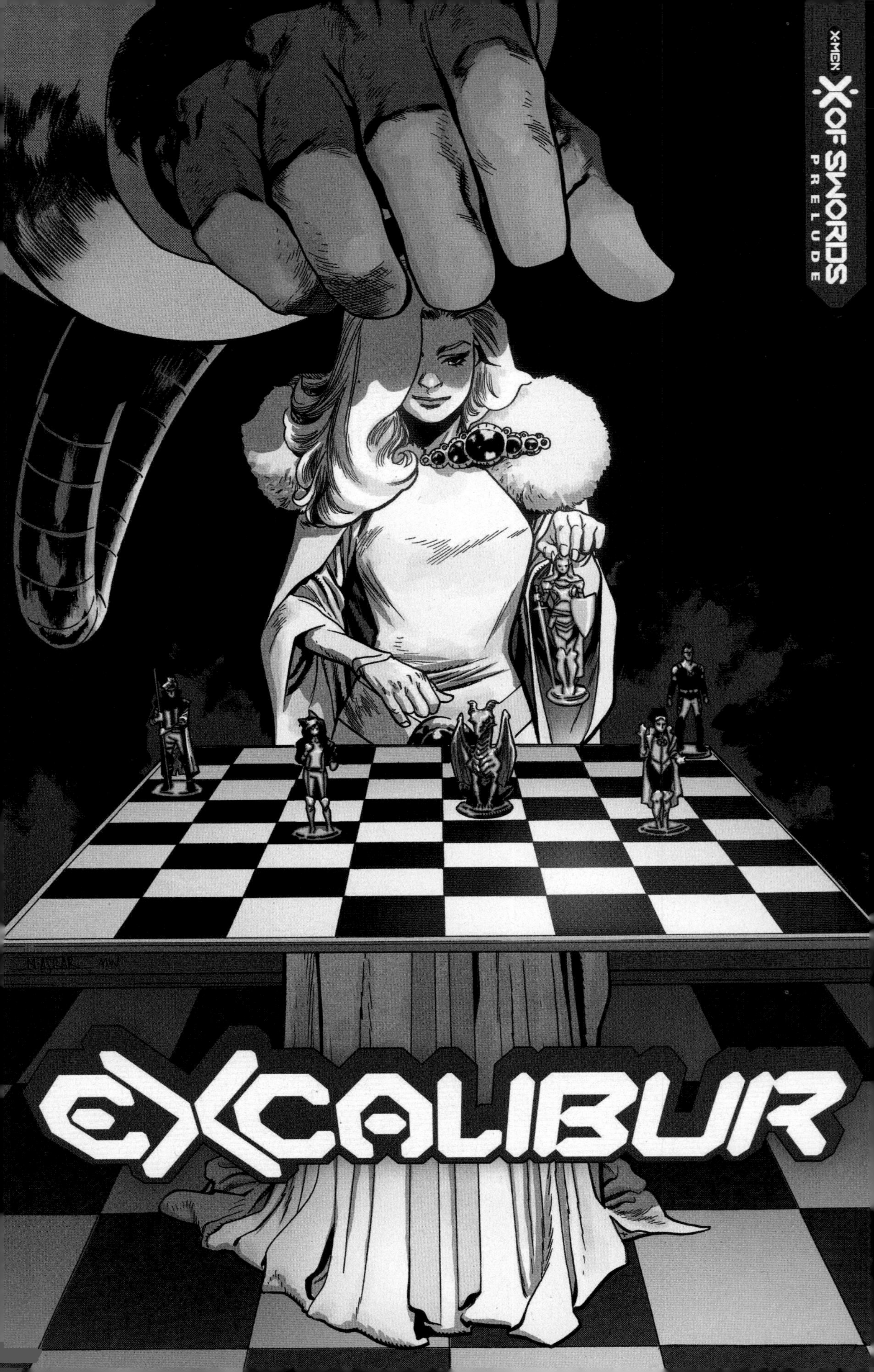
X-MEN X OF SWORDS PRELUDE
EXCALIBUR

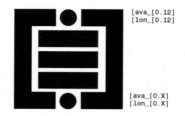

[ava_[0.12]
[lon_[0.12]

[ava_[0.X]
[lon_[0.X]

EXTERNAL FORCES

EXCALIBUR's quest to plant a permanent Krakoan gate into Otherworld led them directly to Opal Luna Saturnyne, the Omniversal Majestrix, who was none too happy with their meddling in her affairs. Her priestesses attacked the team as they approached the Starlight Citadel, and in the midst of the confrontation, Rictor jumped through an incomplete Krakoan gate.

With Rictor's fate unknown and Rogue and Gambit getting into trouble elsewhere in the Citadel, Captain Britain now faces an infuriated Saturnyne...

Apocalypse

Gambit

Rogue

Rictor

Captain
Britain

Saturnyne

[ava_[0.12]...]
[lon_[0.12]...]

[OMNI..versal]

[00_so_below_X]
[00_as_above_X]

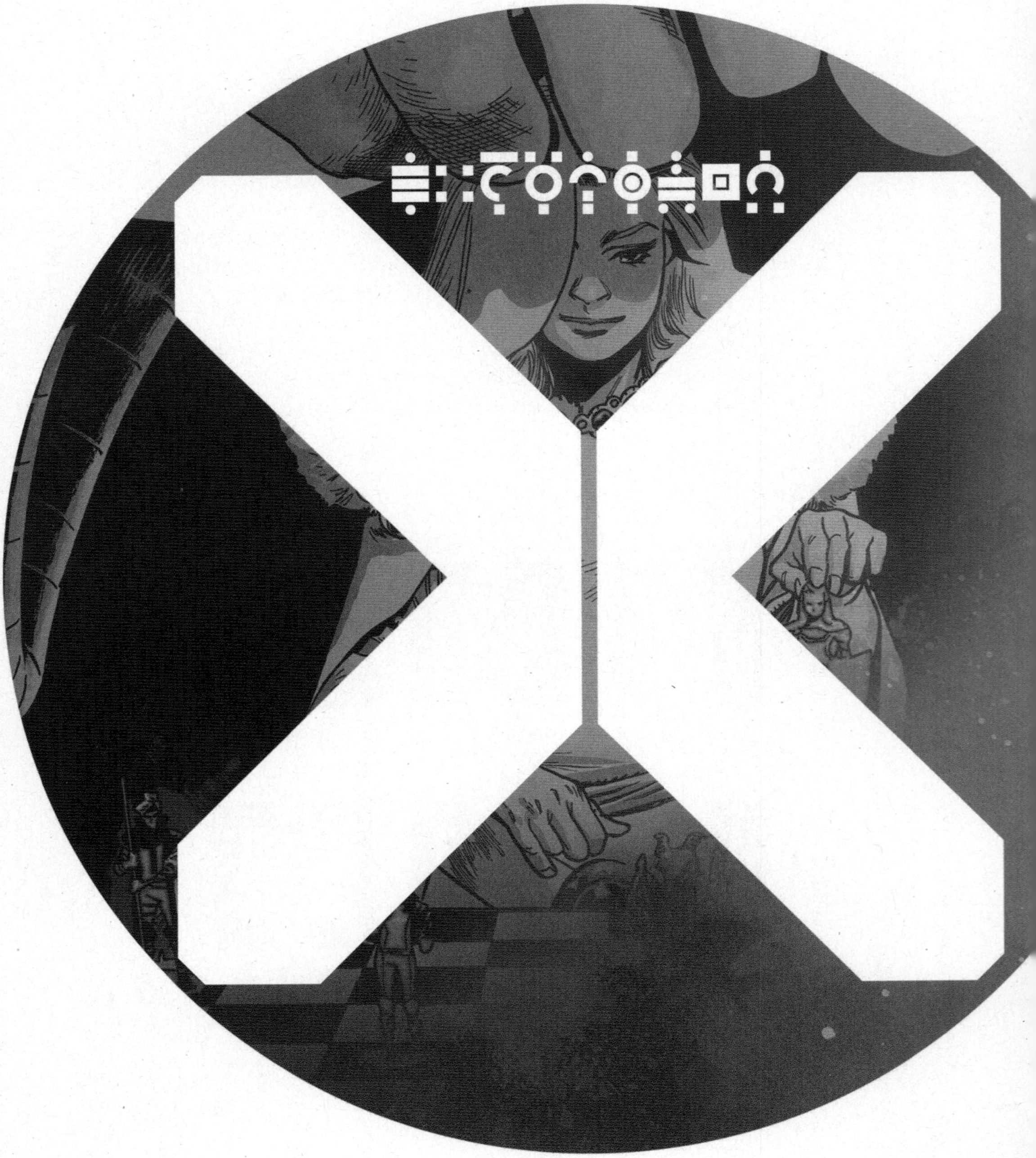

TINI HOWARD....................................[WRITER]
MARCUS TO......................................[ARTIST]
ERICK ARCINIEGA..........................[COLOR ARTIST]
VC's ARIANA MAHER...........................[LETTERER]
TOM MULLER.....................................[DESIGN]

MAHMUD ASRAR & MATTHEW WILSON............[COVER ARTISTS]

ANTHONY GAMBINO............................[PRODUCTION]

JONATHAN HICKMAN............................[HEAD OF X]
ANNALISE BISSA......................[ASSISTANT EDITOR]
JORDAN D. WHITE................................[EDITOR]
C.B. CEBULSKI........................[EDITOR IN CHIEF]

[12] EXCALIBUR

[ISSUE TWELVE].................VERSE XII:
..........................THE BEGINNING

[00_so_below_X]
[X_above_as_00]

[00_00....00]
[00_00....12]

[00_____the]
[00_realm___]

[00_____of_]

[00_change__]

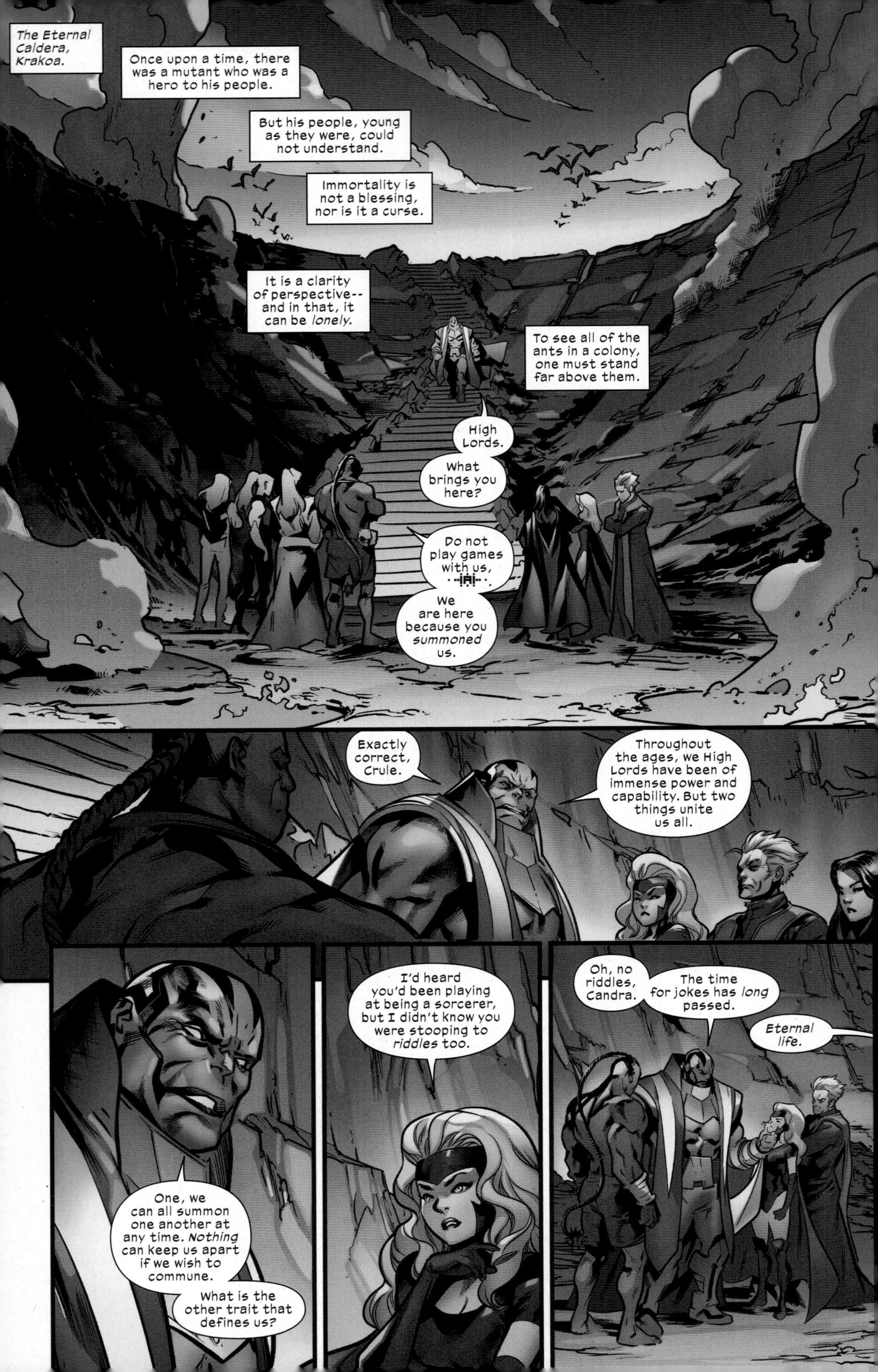
The Eternal Caldera, Krakoa.
Once upon a time, there was a mutant who was a hero to his people.
But his people, young as they were, could not understand.
Immortality is not a blessing, nor is it a curse.
It is a clarity of perspective--and in that, it can be *lonely*.
To see all of the ants in a colony, one must stand far above them.
High Lords.
What brings you here?
Do not play games with us,
We are here because you *summoned* us.
Exactly correct, Crule.
Throughout the ages, we High Lords have been of immense power and capability. But two things unite us all.
One, we can all summon one another at any time. *Nothing* can keep us apart if we wish to commune.
What is the other trait that defines us?
I'd heard you'd been playing at being a sorcerer, but I didn't know you were stooping to *riddles* too.
Oh, no riddles, Candra.
The time for jokes has *long* passed.
Eternal life.

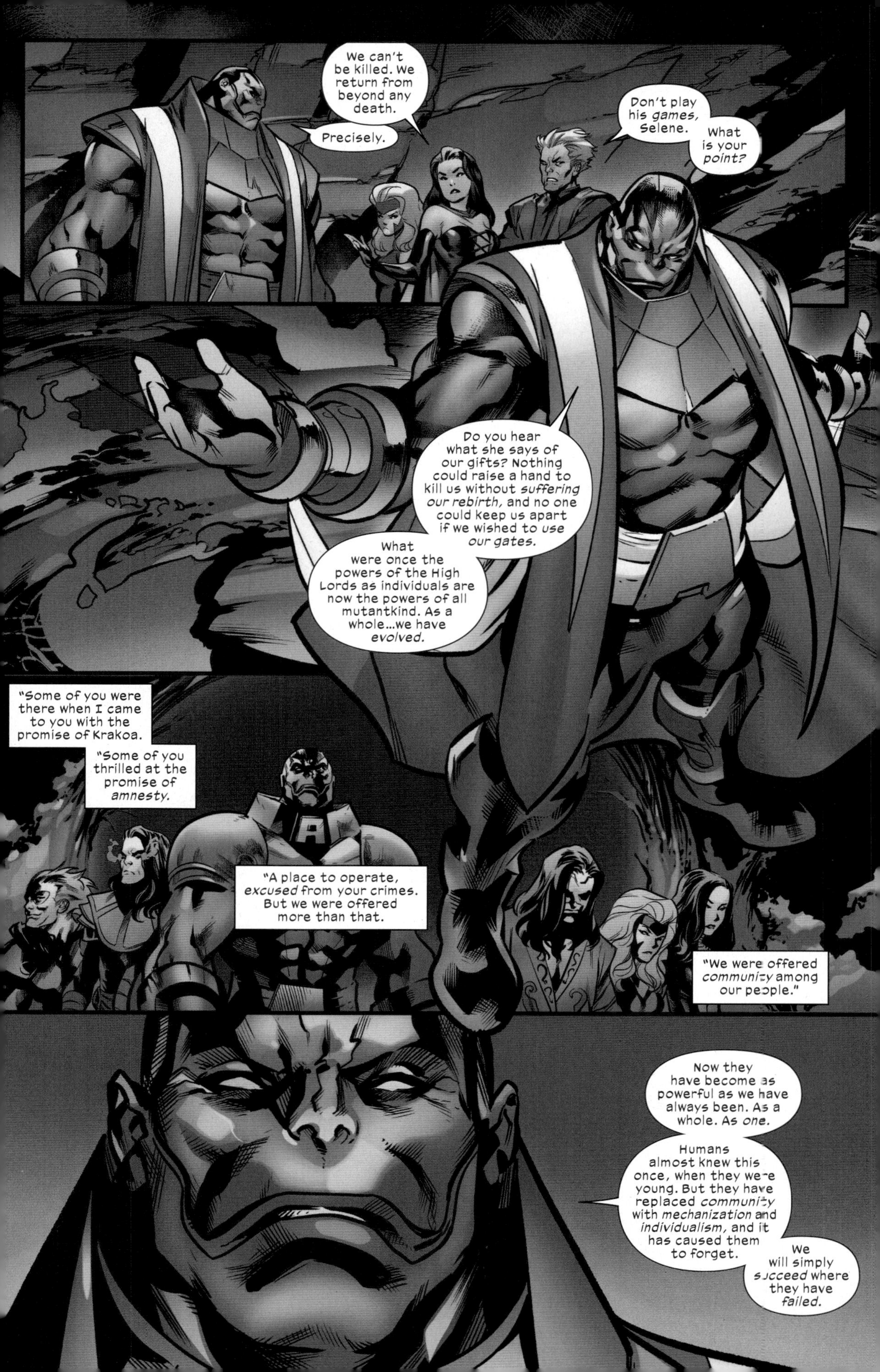
We can't be killed. We return from beyond any death.
Precisely.
Don't play his *games*, Selene.
What is your *point?*
Do you hear what she says of our gifts? Nothing could raise a hand to kill us without *suffering our rebirth,* and no one could keep us apart if we wished to *use our gates.*
What were once the powers of the High Lords as individuals are now the powers of all mutantkind. As a whole...we have *evolved.*
"Some of you were there when I came to you with the promise of Krakoa.
"Some of you thrilled at the promise of *amnesty.*
"A place to operate, *excused* from your crimes. But we were offered more than that.
"We were offered *community* among our people."
Now they have become as powerful as we have always been. As a whole. As *one.*
Humans almost knew this once, when they were young. But they have replaced *community* with *mechanization* and *individualism,* and it has caused them to forget.
We will simply *succeed* where they have *failed.*

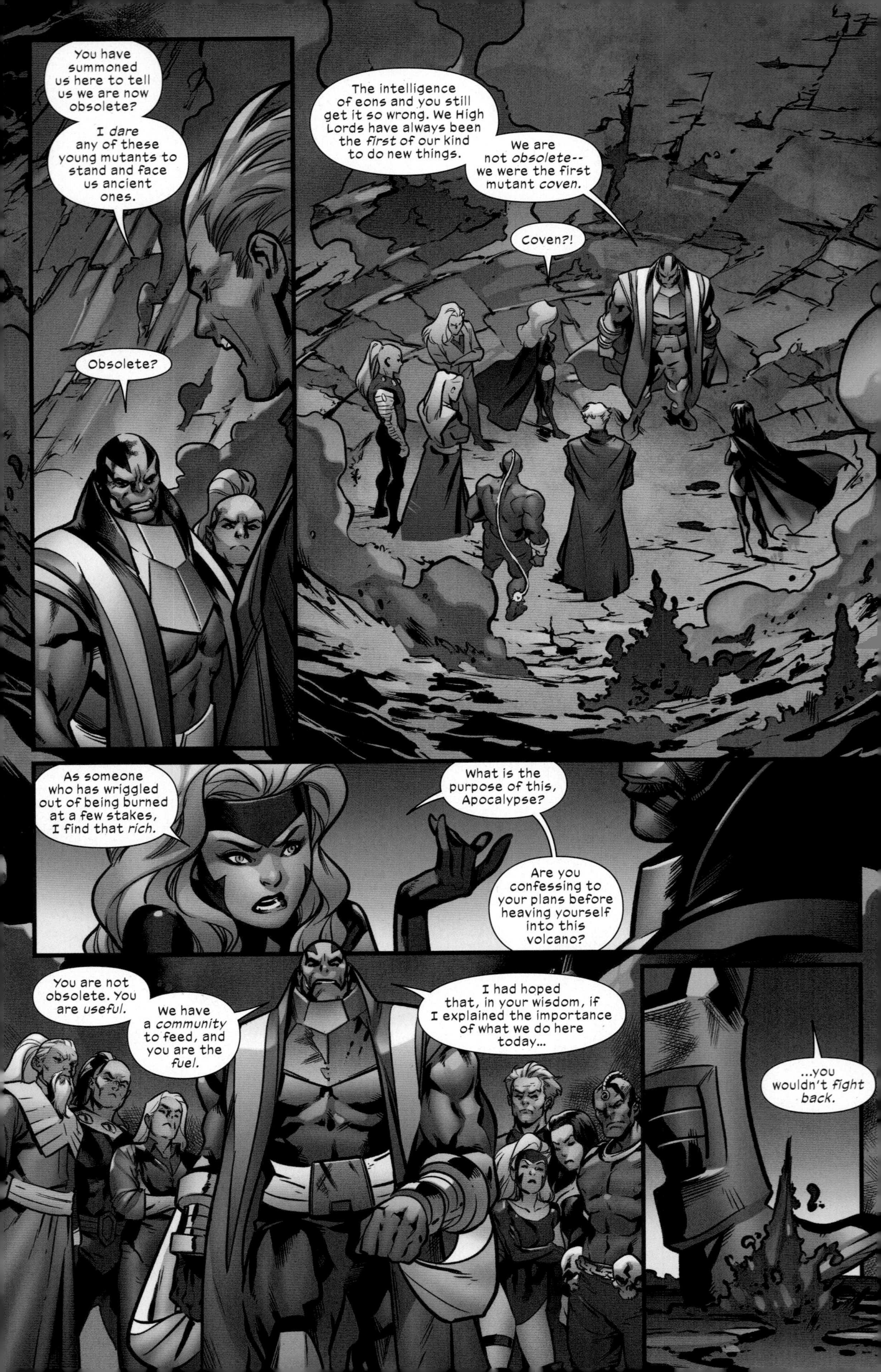
You have summoned us here to tell us we are now obsolete?
I *dare* any of these young mutants to stand and face us ancient ones.
Obsolete?
The intelligence of eons and you still get it so wrong. We High Lords have always been the *first* of our kind to do new things.
We are not *obsolete*-- we were the first mutant *coven.*
Coven?!
As someone who has wriggled out of being burned at a few stakes, I find that *rich.*
What is the purpose of this, Apocalypse?
Are you confessing to your plans before heaving yourself into this volcano?
You are not obsolete. You are *useful.*
We have a *community* to feed, and you are the *fuel.*
I had hoped that, in your wisdom, if I explained the importance of what we do here today...
...you wouldn't *fight* back.

THE HIGH LORDS

THE EXTERNALS

At times believed to be a subspecies or evolved offshoot of mutantdom, it is now believed that the so-called "High Lords" were perhaps an early tendency toward the eventual gifts that mutantkind would come to possess during the pax Krakoa. Much has been supposed of their origin, limitations, and abilities, but it largely remains in the realm of theory. What is not theoretical is their long-term involvement in human politics, finance, and law - they have oft been seen as a sort of "mutant Illuminati."

In addition to the abilities of very old, powerful mutants, their additional External gifts included:

1:: RESURRECTION. High Lords of Mutantdom can be killed, but most possess rapid healing traits, and all return (occasionally in a different form) if they meet true death. Mutants suspected to have External traits have indeed been tested with death, returning, at times, several years later.

2:: COMMUNION. High Lords are always aware of one another, can communicate across great distances, and can come together at will. They are known to possess a shared life force - when one External kills another, their ancient energy is dispersed within the remaining Externals. Additionally, their life force can be contained within a gem, which has been shown to keep it out of the shared energetic loop.

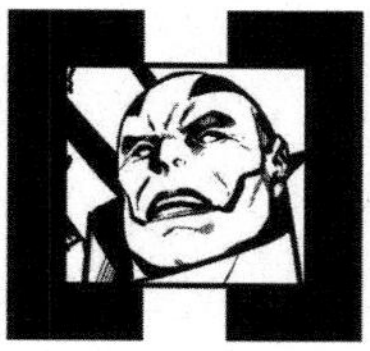

Apocalypse

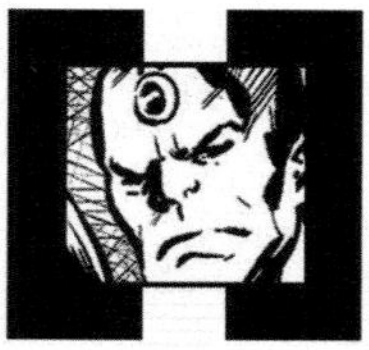

Crule

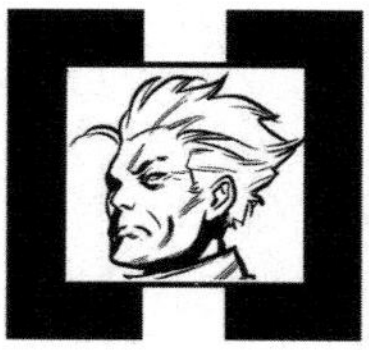

Nicodemus

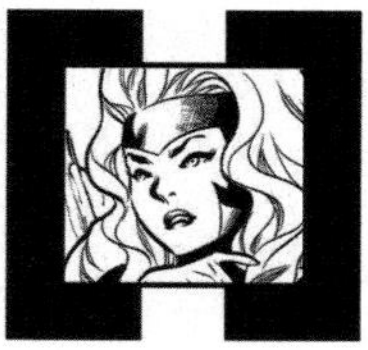

Candra

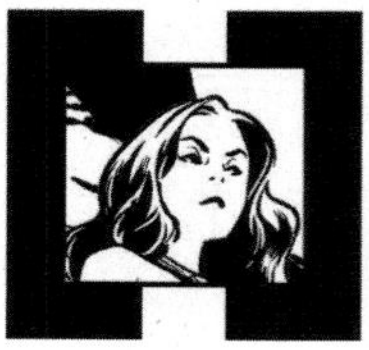

Selene

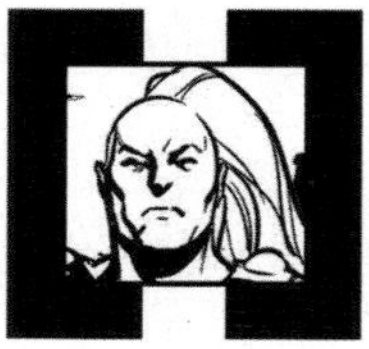

Gideon

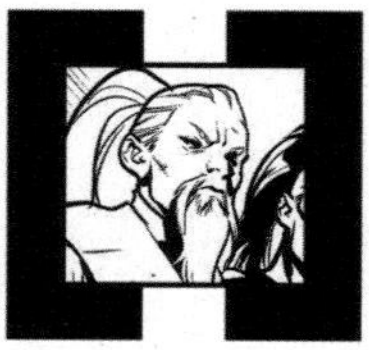

Saul

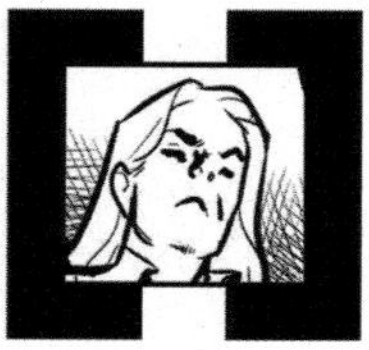

Absolom

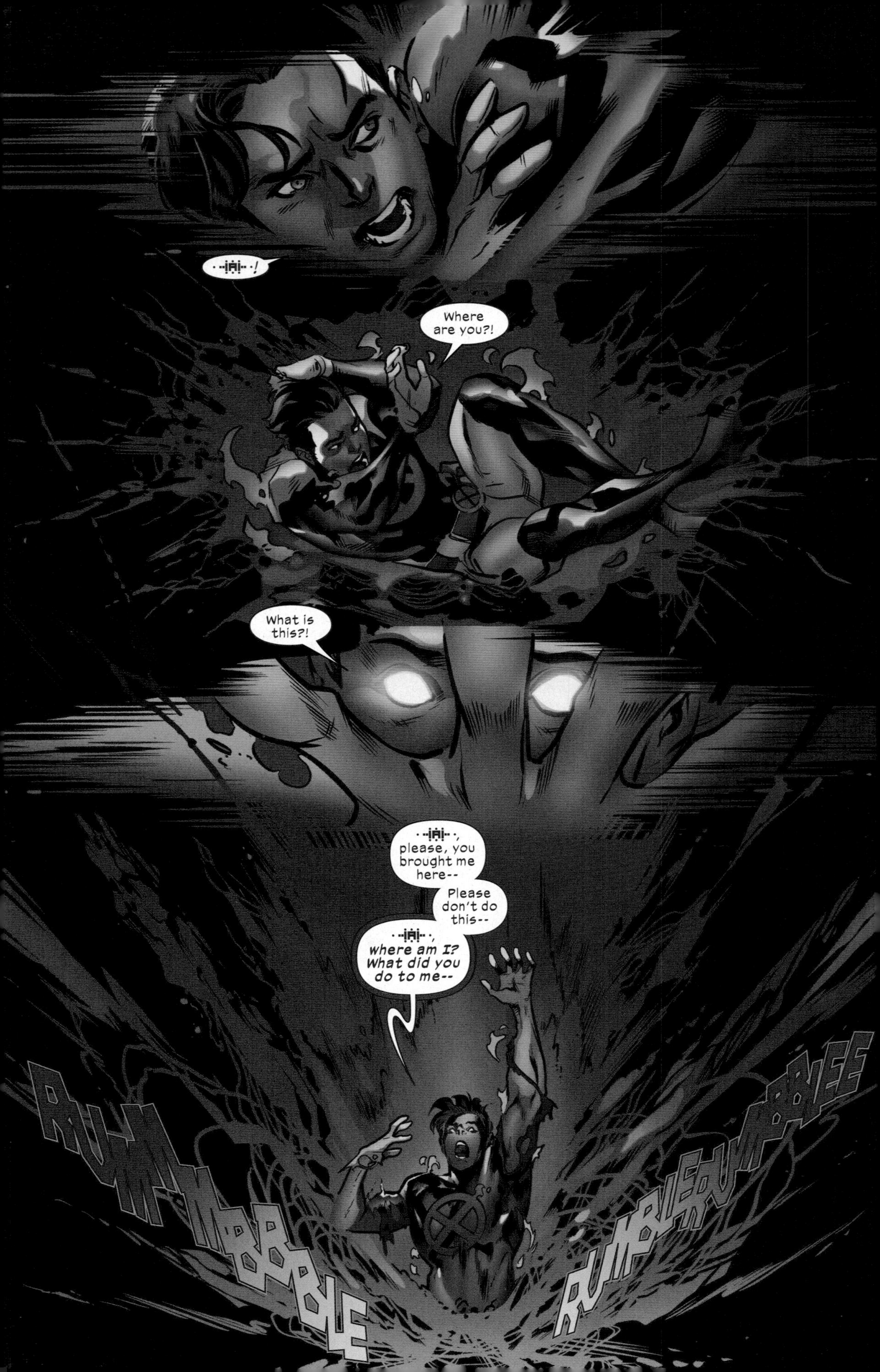
Where are you?!
What is this?!
please, you brought me here--
Please don't do this--
where am I? What did you do to me--

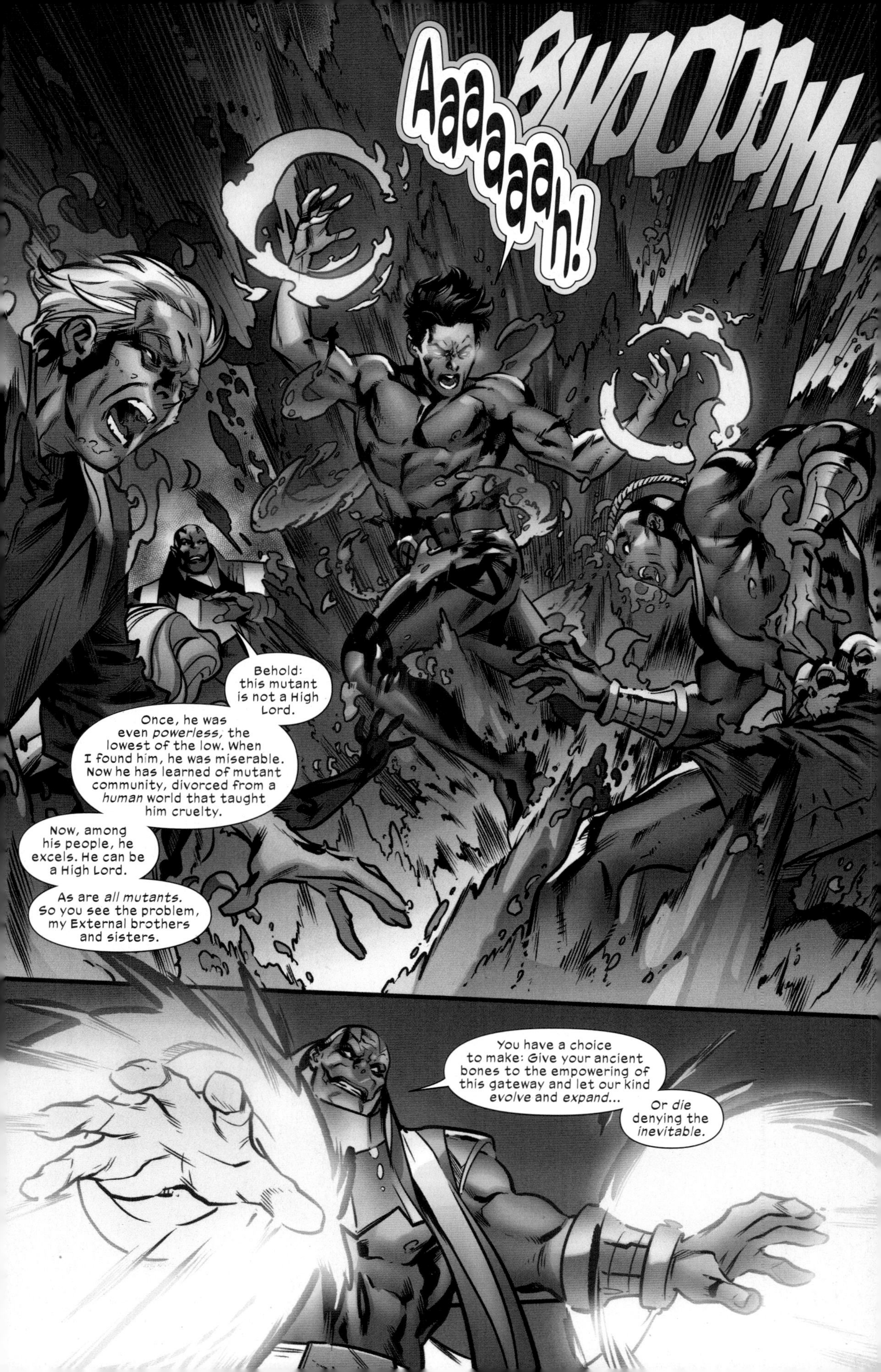
Aaaaaaah!
BWOOOOMM
Behold: this mutant is not a High Lord.
Once, he was even *powerless,* the lowest of the low. When I found him, he was miserable. Now he has learned of mutant community, divorced from a *human* world that taught him cruelty.
Now, among his people, he excels. He can be a High Lord.
As are *all mutants.* So you see the problem, my External brothers and sisters.
You have a choice to make: Give your ancient bones to the empowering of this gateway and let our kind *evolve* and *expand*...
Or *die* denying the *inevitable.*

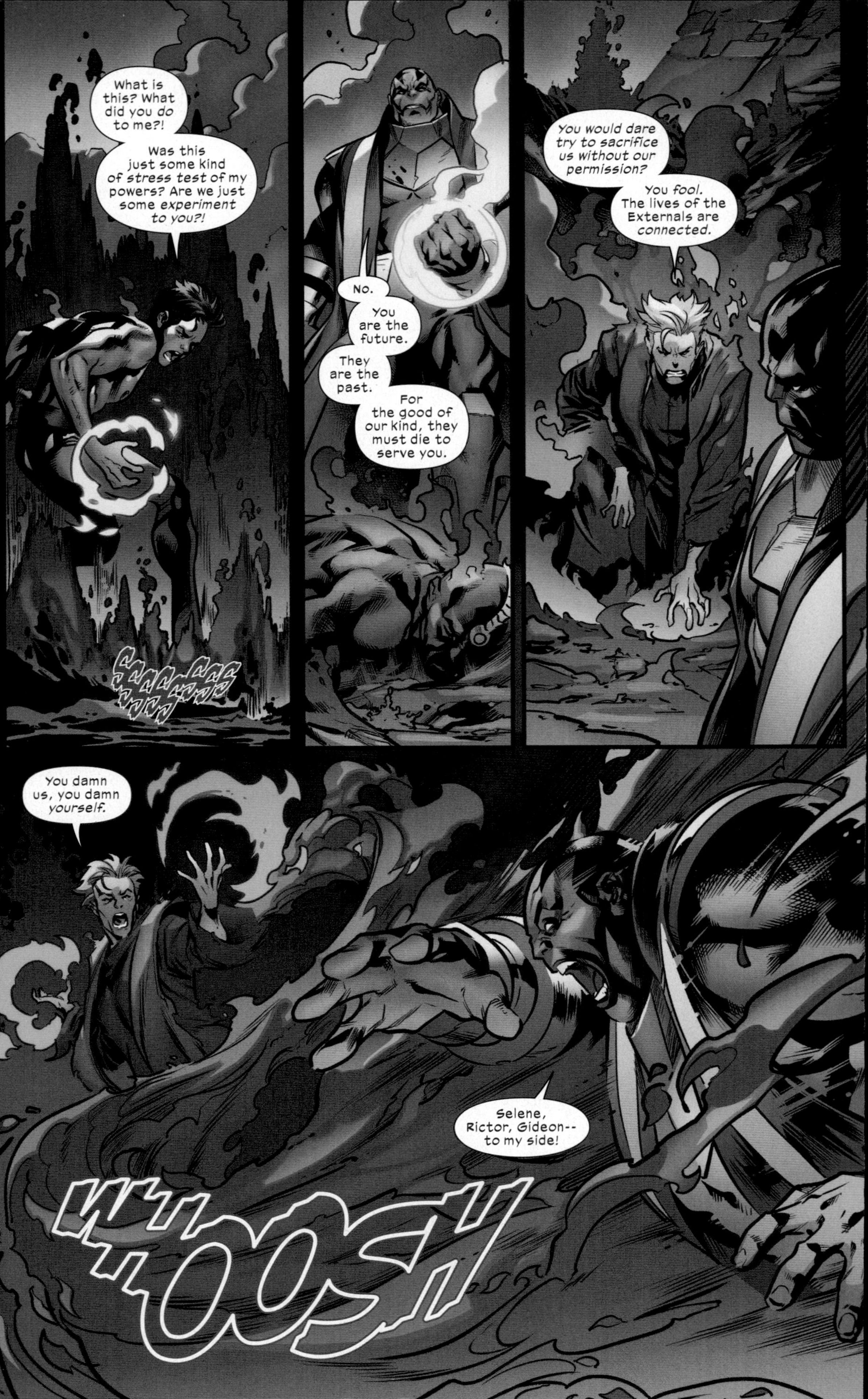

What is this? What did you do to me?!
Was this just some kind of *stress test* of my powers? Are we just some *experiment* to you?!
SSSSSSS
No.
You are the future.
They are the past.
For the good of our kind, they must die to serve you.
You would dare try to sacrifice us without our permission?
You *fool.* The lives of the Externals are *connected.*
You damn us, you damn *yourself.*
Selene, Rictor, Gideon-- to my side!
WHOOSH

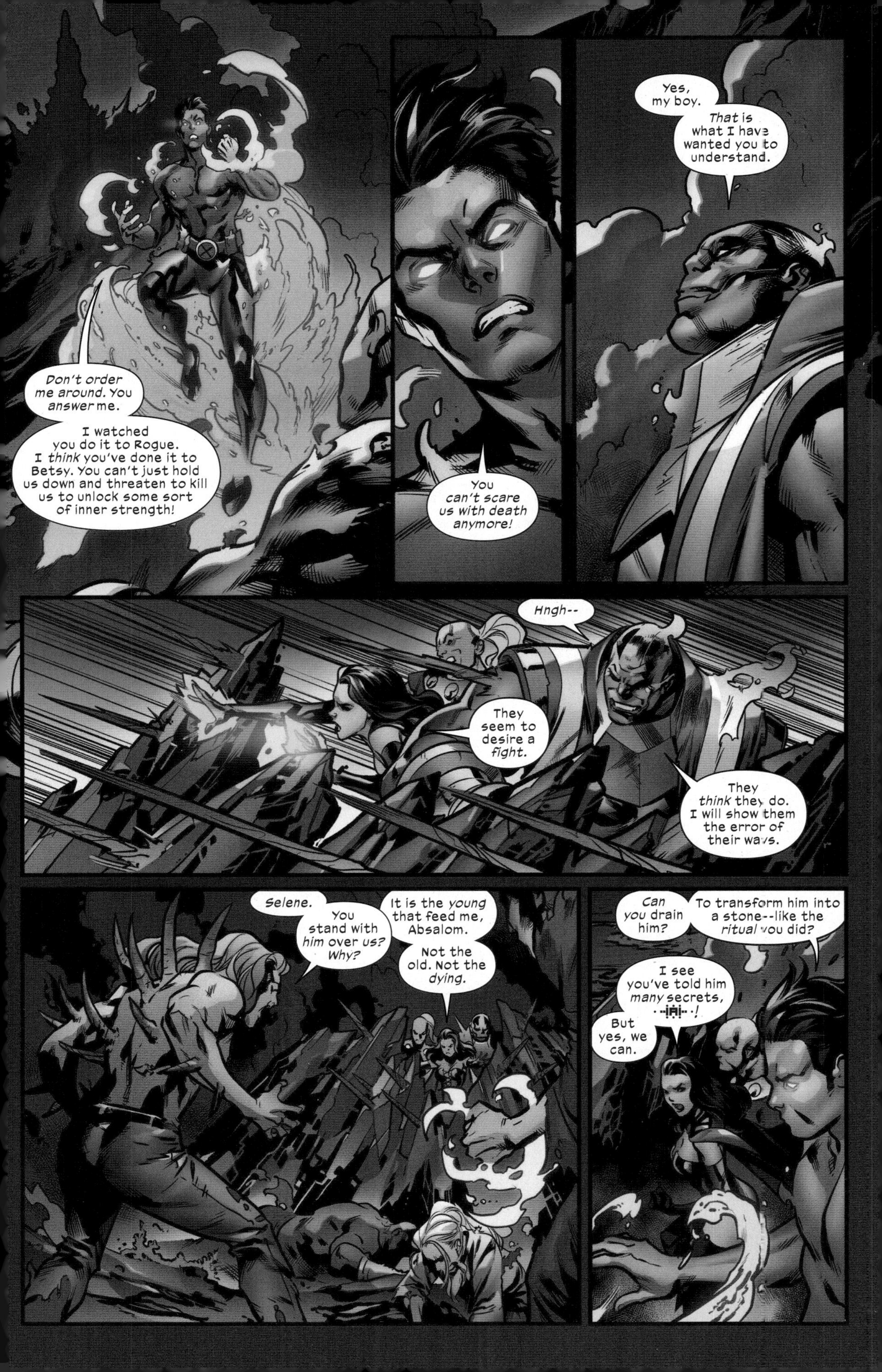

Don't order me around. You answer me.
I watched you do it to Rogue. I think you've done it to Betsy. You can't just hold us down and threaten to kill us to unlock some sort of inner strength!
You can't scare us with death anymore!
Yes, my boy.
That is what I have wanted you to understand.
Hngh--
They seem to desire a fight.
They think they do. I will show them the error of their ways.
Selene.
You stand with him over us? Why?
It is the young that feed me, Absalom.
Not the old. Not the dying.
Can you drain him?
To transform him into a stone--like the ritual you did?
I see you've told him many secrets,
But yes, we can.

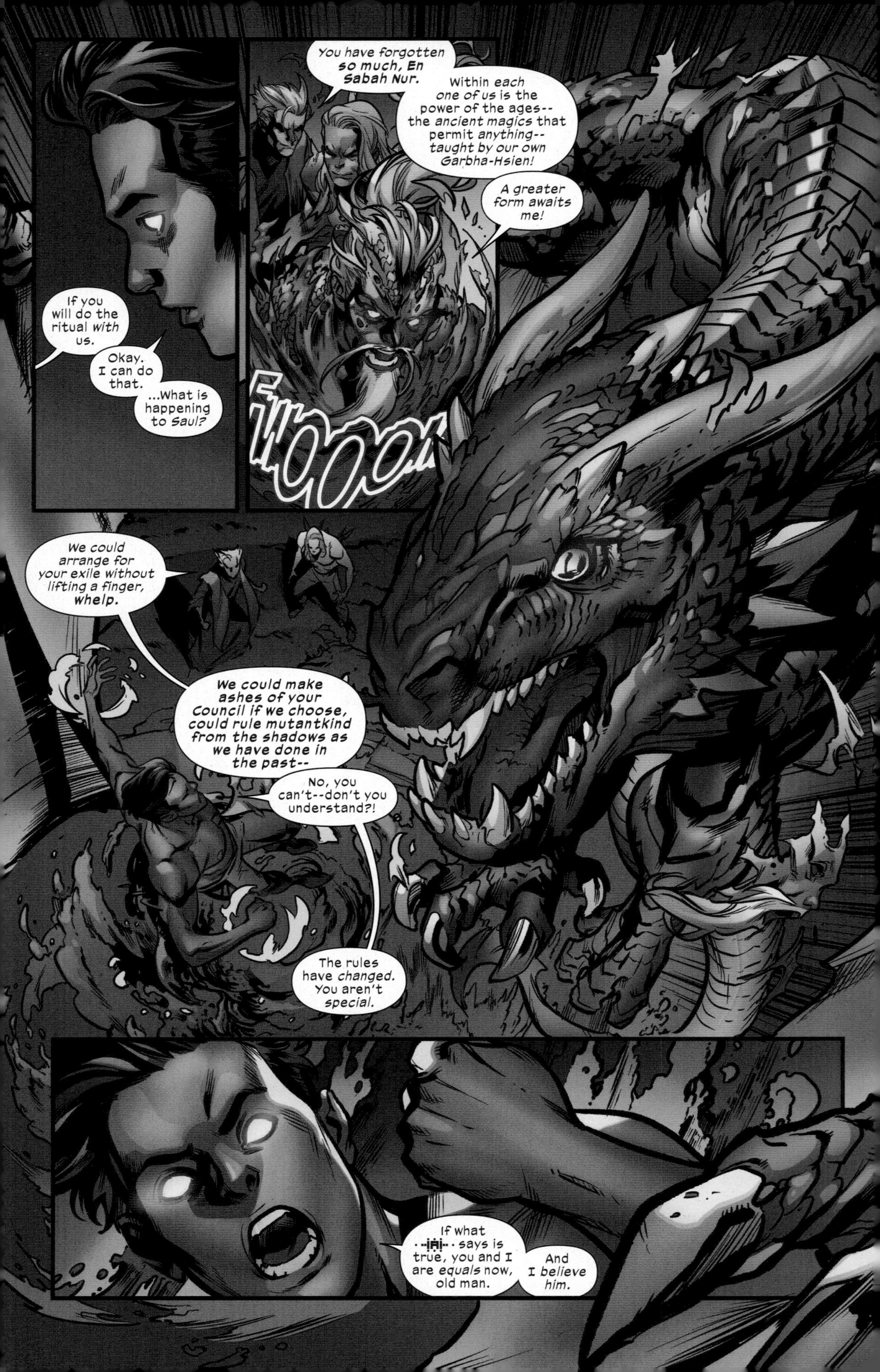
You have forgotten so much, En Sabah Nur.
Within each one of us is the power of the ages-- the ancient magics that permit anything-- taught by our own Garbha-Hsien!
A greater form awaits me!
If you will do the ritual with us.
Okay. I can do that.
...What is happening to Saul?
We could arrange for your exile without lifting a finger, whelp.
We could make ashes of your Council if we choose, could rule mutantkind from the shadows as we have done in the past--
No, you can't--don't you understand?!
The rules have changed. You aren't special.
If what says is true, you and I are equals now, old man.
And I believe him.

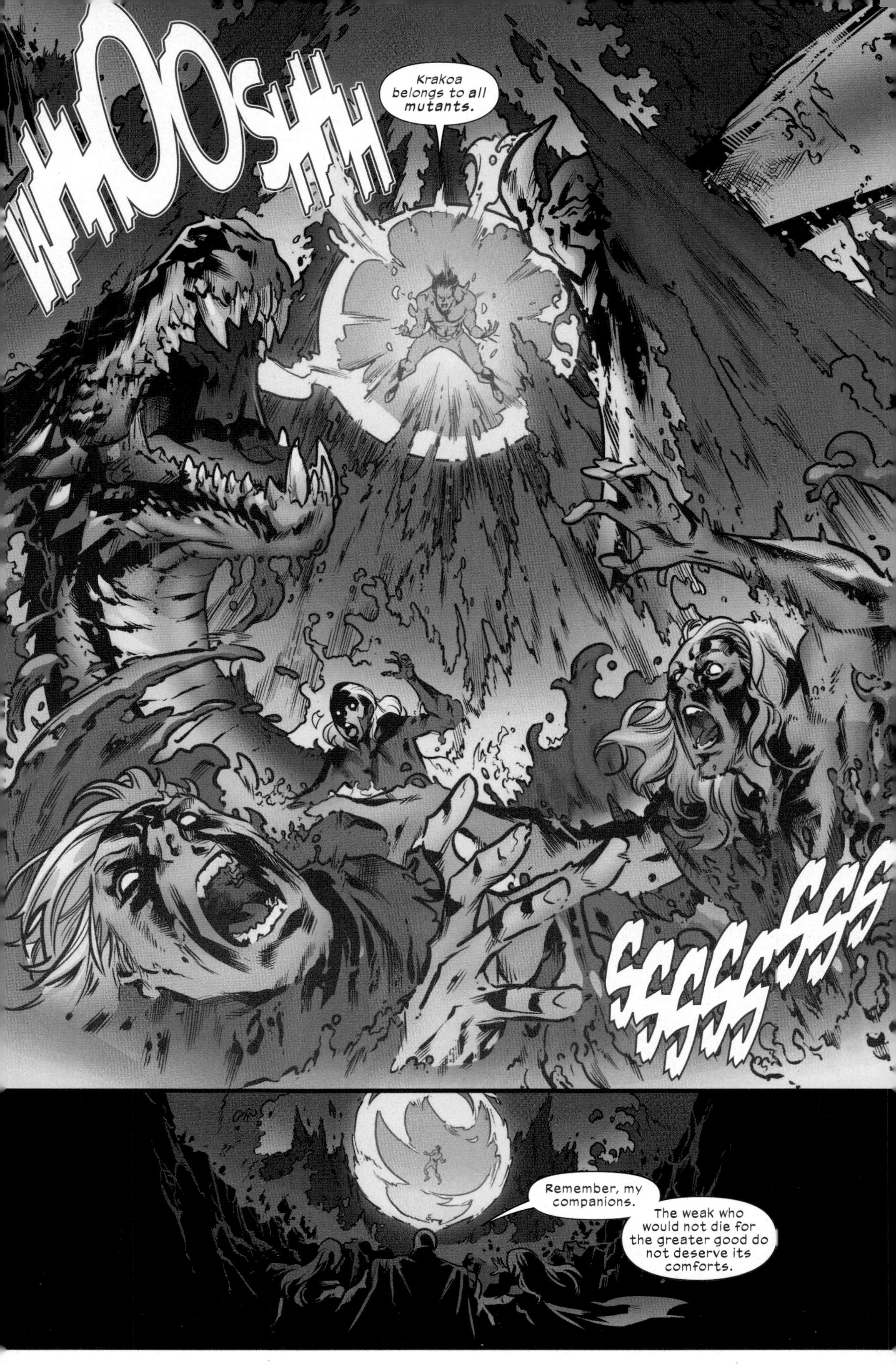
WHOOSHH
Krakoa belongs to all mutants.
SSSSSSSS
Remember, my companions.
The weak who would not die for the greater good do not deserve its comforts.

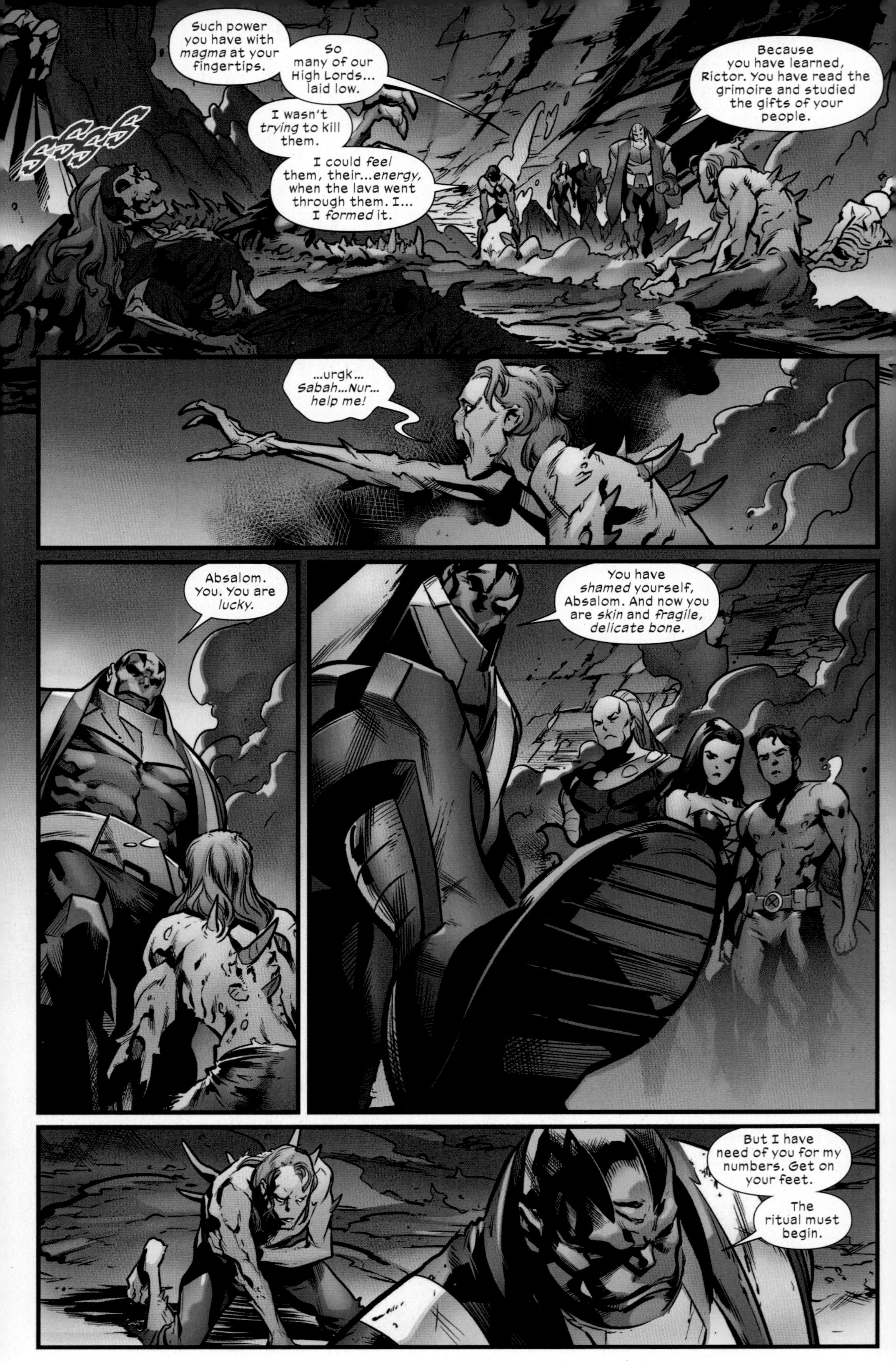
Such power you have with *magma* at your fingertips.
So many of our High Lords... laid low.
SSSSS
I wasn't *trying* to kill them.
I could *feel* them, their...*energy*, when the lava went through them. I... I *formed* it.
Because you have learned, Rictor. You have read the grimoire and studied the gifts of your people.
...urgk... *Sabah...Nur... help me!*
Absalom. You. You are *lucky*.
You have *shamed* yourself, Absalom. And now you are *skin* and *fragile, delicate bone*.
But I have need of you for my numbers. Get on your feet.
The ritual must begin.

FROM THE GRIMOIRE OF

·-·IAI·-·

EX MAGICA: ALMANAC (Fig. 14)

GATE
COMPONENT
COMPONENT
TRANSMUTER
COMPONENT
COMPONENT

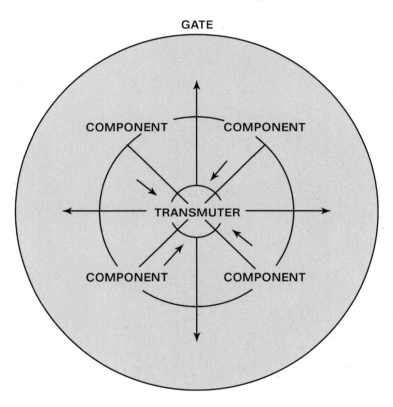

1. :: NEUTRALIZE PHYSICAL COMPONENTS TO FREE UP HIGH LORD LIFE FORCE. ENERGIES WILL TEND TOWARD CENTRAL CONDUIT

2. :: FORCE FLOWS TOWARD SORCERER (EARTH TRANSMUTER)

3. :: SORCERER TRANSMUTES EXTERNAL ENERGIES INTO ROCK CRYSTAL FORMATION (see: *Notes Upon an Ancient Darkness: CANDRA.*)

4. :: ROCK CRYSTAL FORMATION CREATES EMPOWERED EXTERNAL GATE, ALLOWING MASS OTHERWORLD ACCESS AT SPECIFIC DESIRED LOCATION. (For further reading see: EX MAGICA: ALMANAC (fig. 1)

[ava_[0.12]...]
[lon_[0.12]...]

[GRIMOIRE....]

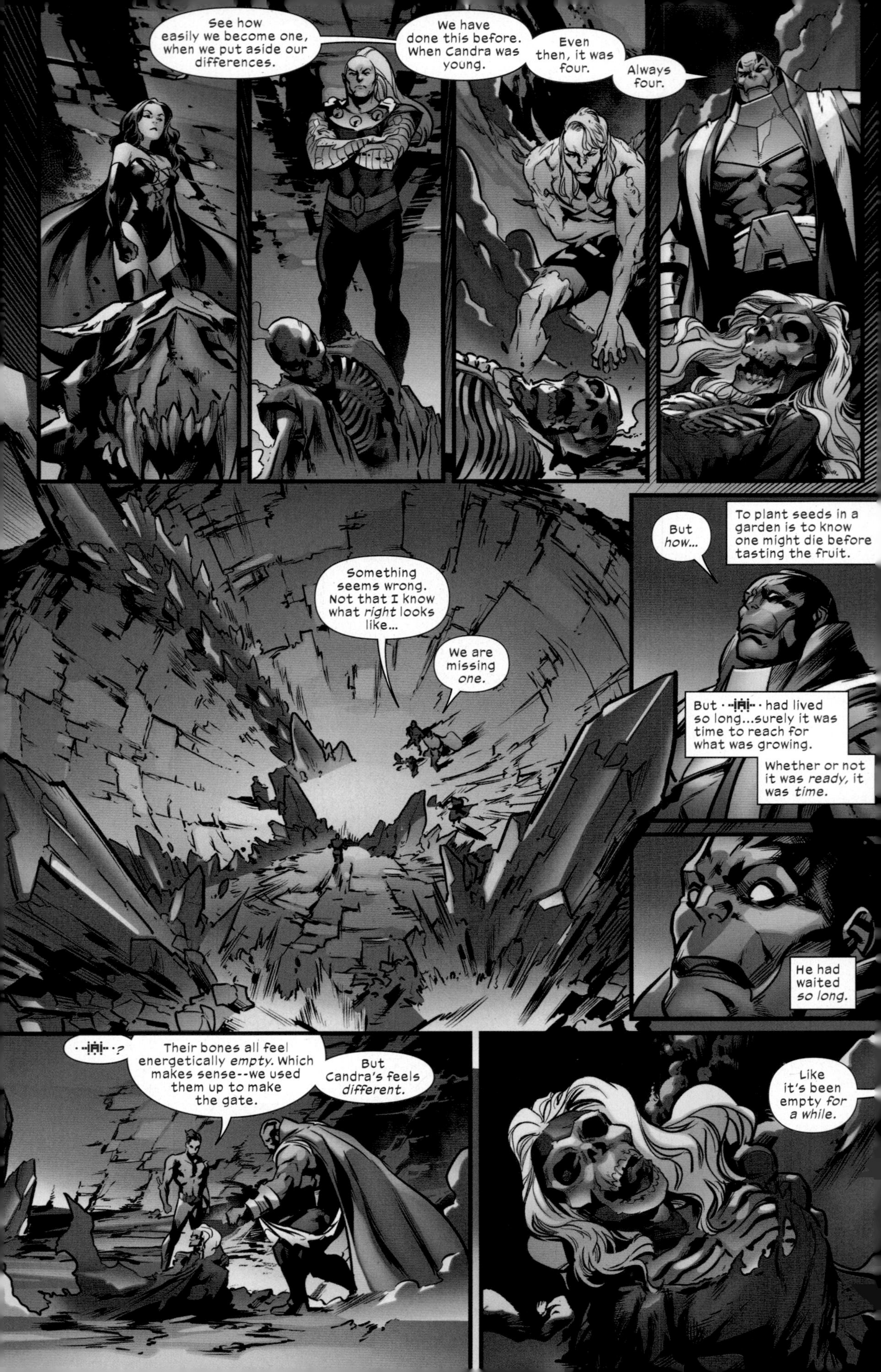

See how easily we become one, when we put aside our differences.
We have done this before. When Candra was young.
Even then, it was four.
Always four.
Something seems wrong. Not that I know what *right* looks like...
We are missing *one*.
But *how*...
To plant seeds in a garden is to know one might die before tasting the fruit.
But ·-ꟾꟾꟾ-· had lived so long...surely it was time to reach for what was growing.
Whether or not it was *ready*, it was *time*.
He had waited *so long*.
·-ꟾꟾꟾ-·?
Their bones all feel energetically *empty*. Which makes sense--we used them up to make the gate.
But Candra's feels *different*.
Like it's been empty *for a while*.

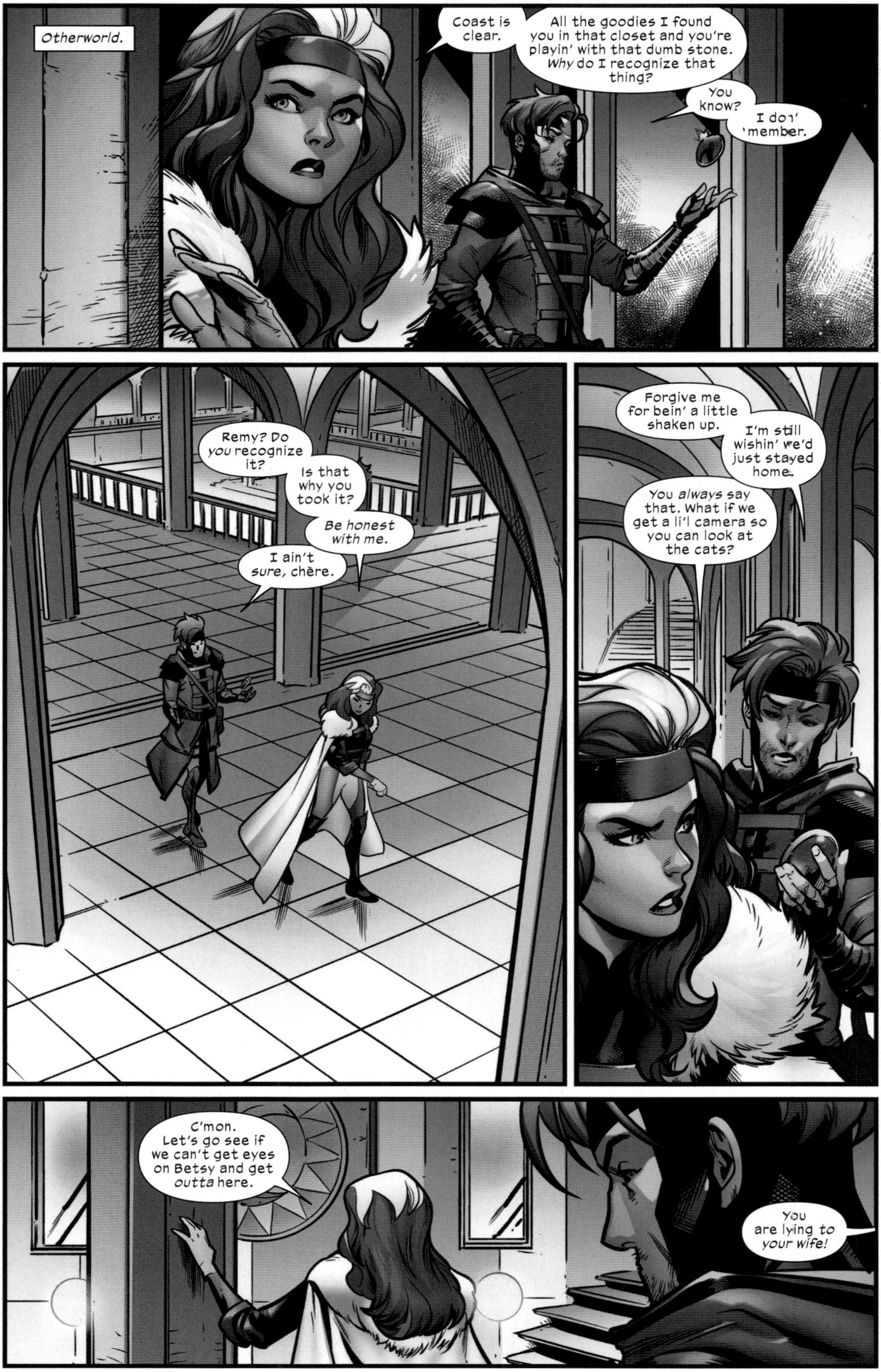
Otherworld.
Coast is clear.
All the goodies I found you in that closet and you're playin' with that dumb stone. Why do I recognize that thing?
You know?
I don' 'member.
Remy? Do you recognize it?
Is that why you took it?
Be honest with me.
I ain't sure, chère.
Forgive me for bein' a little shaken up.
I'm still wishin' we'd just stayed home.
You always say that. What if we get a li'l camera so you can look at the cats?
C'mon. Let's go see if we can't get eyes on Betsy and get outta here.
You are lying to your wife!

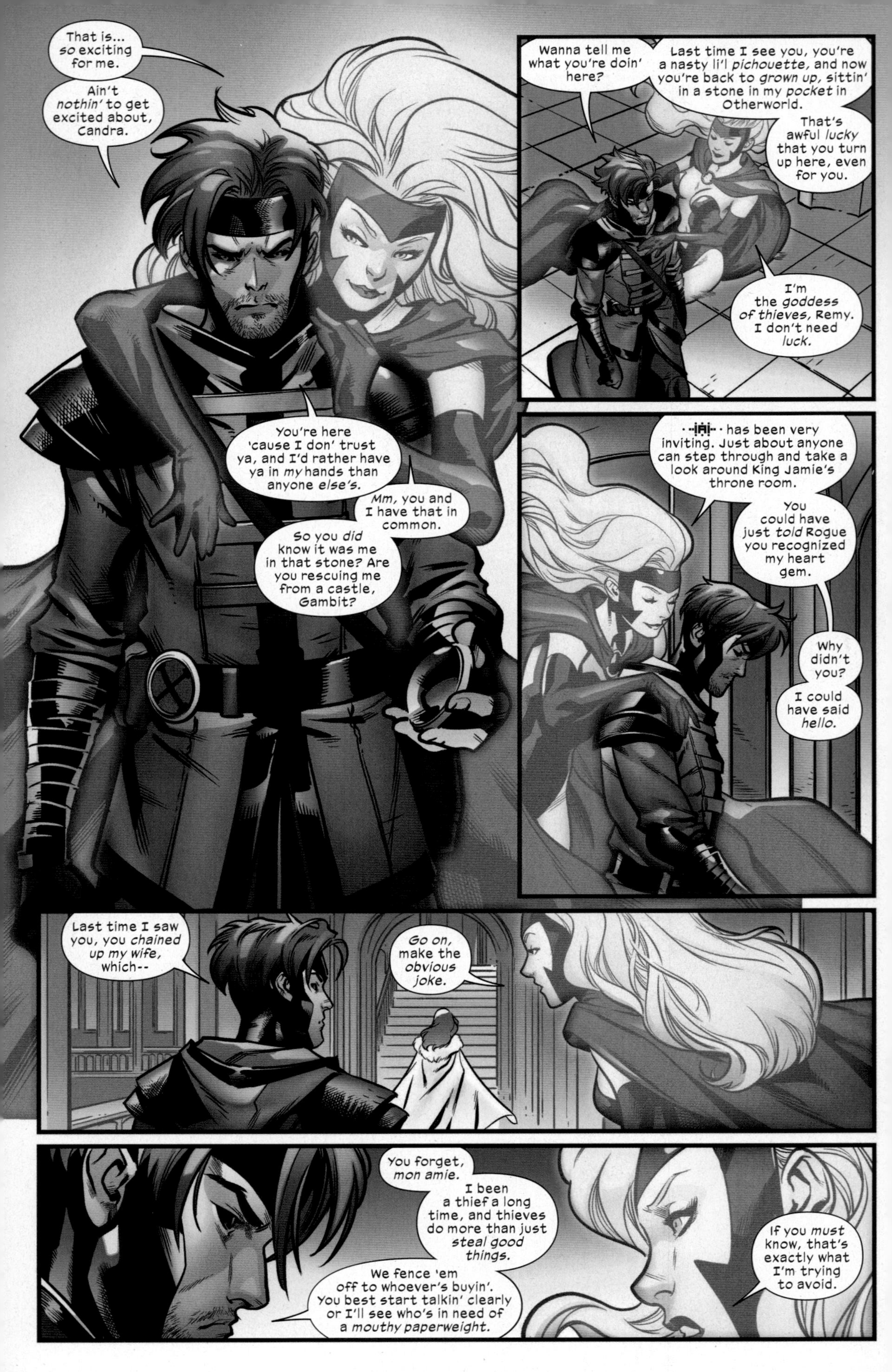
That is... *so* exciting for me.
Ain't *nothin'* to get excited about, Candra.
You're here 'cause I don' trust ya, and I'd rather have ya in *my* hands than anyone *else's.*
Mm, you and I have that in common.
So you *did* know it was me in that stone? Are you rescuing me from a castle, Gambit?
Wanna tell me what you're doin' here?
Last time I see you, you're a nasty li'l *pichouette,* and now you're back to *grown up,* sittin' in a stone in my *pocket* in Otherworld.
That's awful *lucky* that you turn up here, even for you.
I'm the *goddess of thieves,* Remy. I don't need *luck.*
has been very inviting. Just about anyone can step through and take a look around King Jamie's throne room.
You could have just *told* Rogue you recognized my heart gem.
Why didn't you?
I could have said *hello.*
Last time I saw you, you *chained up my wife,* which--
Go on, make the *obvious* joke.
You forget, *mon amie.*
I been a thief a long time, and thieves do more than just *steal good things.*
We fence 'em off to whoever's buyin'. You best start talkin' clearly or I'll see who's in need of a *mouthy paperweight.*
If you *must* know, that's exactly what I'm trying to avoid.

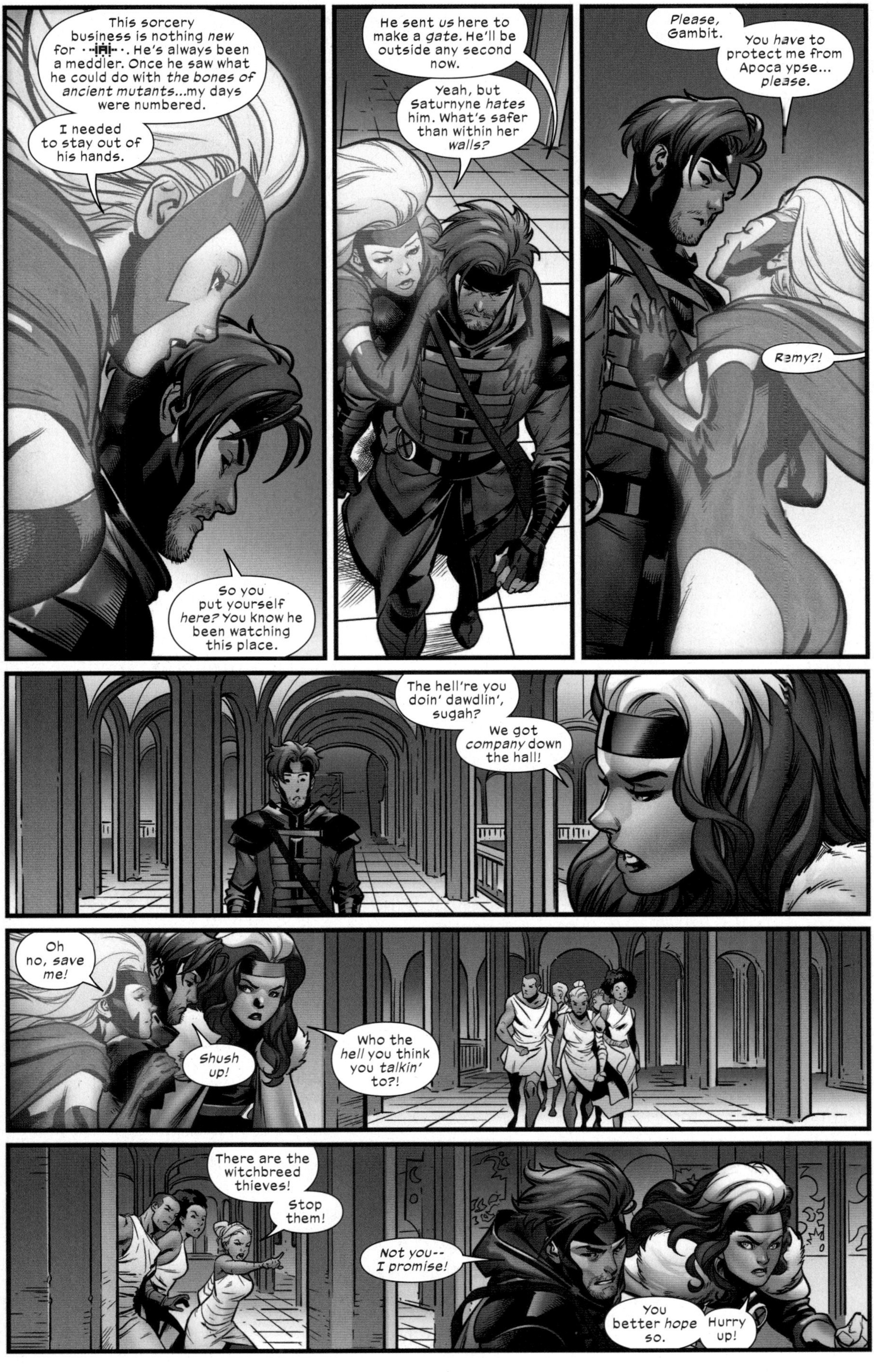
This sorcery business is nothing *new* for . He's always been a meddler. Once he saw what he could do with *the bones of ancient mutants*...my days were numbered.
I needed to stay out of his hands.
So you put yourself *here?* You know he been watching this place.
He sent *us* here to make a *gate*. He'll be outside any second now.
Yeah, but Saturnyne *hates* him. What's safer than within her *walls?*
Please, Gambit.
You *have* to protect me from Apoca ypse... *please.*
Remy?!
The hell're you doin' dawdlin', sugah?
We got *company* down the hall!
Oh no, *save me!*
Shush up!
Who the *hell* you think you *talkin'* to?!
There are the witchbreed thieves!
Stop them!
Not you-- I promise!
You better *hope* so.
Hurry up!

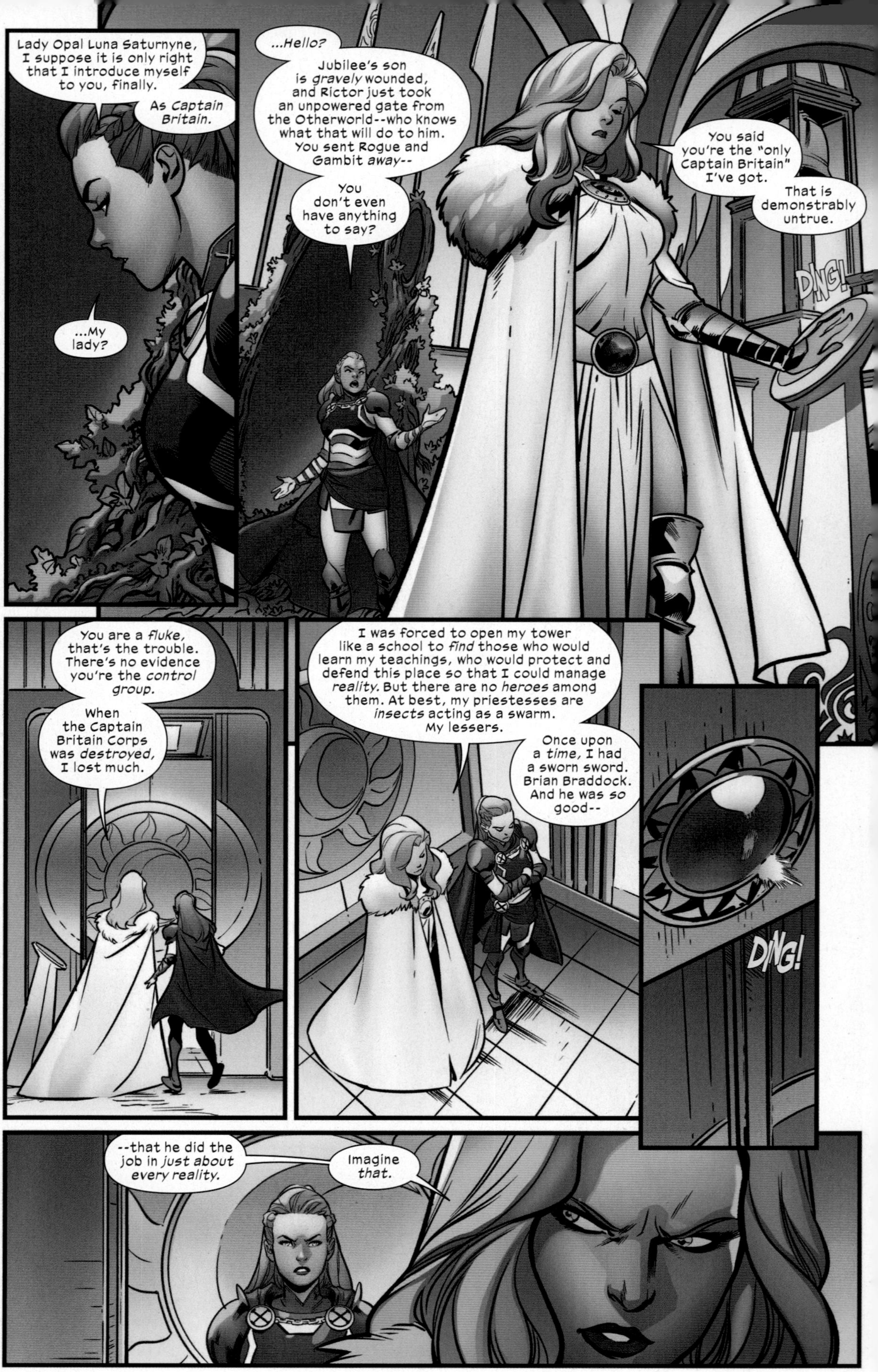
Lady Opal Luna Saturnyne, I suppose it is only right that I introduce myself to you, finally.
As Captain Britain.
...My lady?
...Hello?
Jubilee's son is gravely wounded, and Rictor just took an unpowered gate from the Otherworld--who knows what that will do to him. You sent Rogue and Gambit away--
You don't even have anything to say?
You said you're the "only Captain Britain" I've got.
That is demonstrably untrue.
DING!
You are a fluke, that's the trouble. There's no evidence you're the control group.
When the Captain Britain Corps was destroyed, I lost much.
I was forced to open my tower like a school to find those who would learn my teachings, who would protect and defend this place so that I could manage reality. But there are no heroes among them. At best, my priestesses are insects acting as a swarm. My lessers.
Once upon a time, I had a sworn sword. Brian Braddock. And he was so good--
DING!
--that he did the job in just about every reality.
Imagine that.

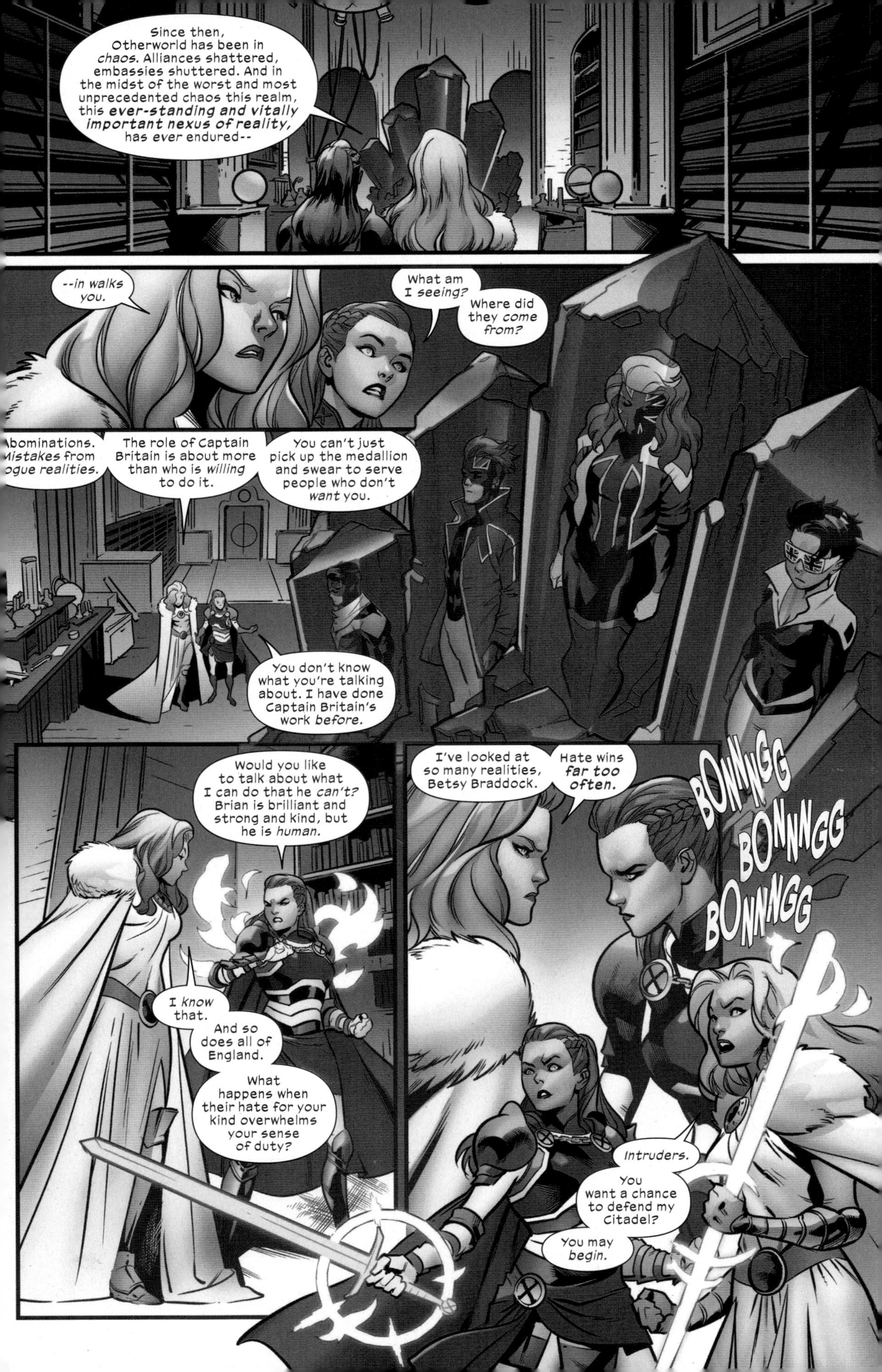

Since then, Otherworld has been in *chaos.* Alliances shattered, embassies shuttered. And in the midst of the worst and most unprecedented chaos this realm, this ***ever-standing and vitally important nexus of reality,*** has *ever* endured--
--*in walks* you.
What am I *seeing?*
Where did they *come from?*
bominations. *Mistakes* from ogue realities.
The role of Captain Britain is about more than who is *willing* to do it.
You can't just pick up the medallion and swear to serve people who don't *want* you.
You don't know what you're talking about. I have done Captain Britain's work *before.*
Would you like to talk about what I can do that he *can't?* Brian is brilliant and strong and kind, but he is *human.*
I *know* that.
And so does all of England.
What happens when their hate for your kind overwhelms your sense of duty?
I've looked at so many realities, Betsy Braddock.
Hate wins ***far too often.***
BONNNGG
BONNNGG
BONNNGG
Intruders.
You want a chance to defend my Citadel?
You may *begin.*

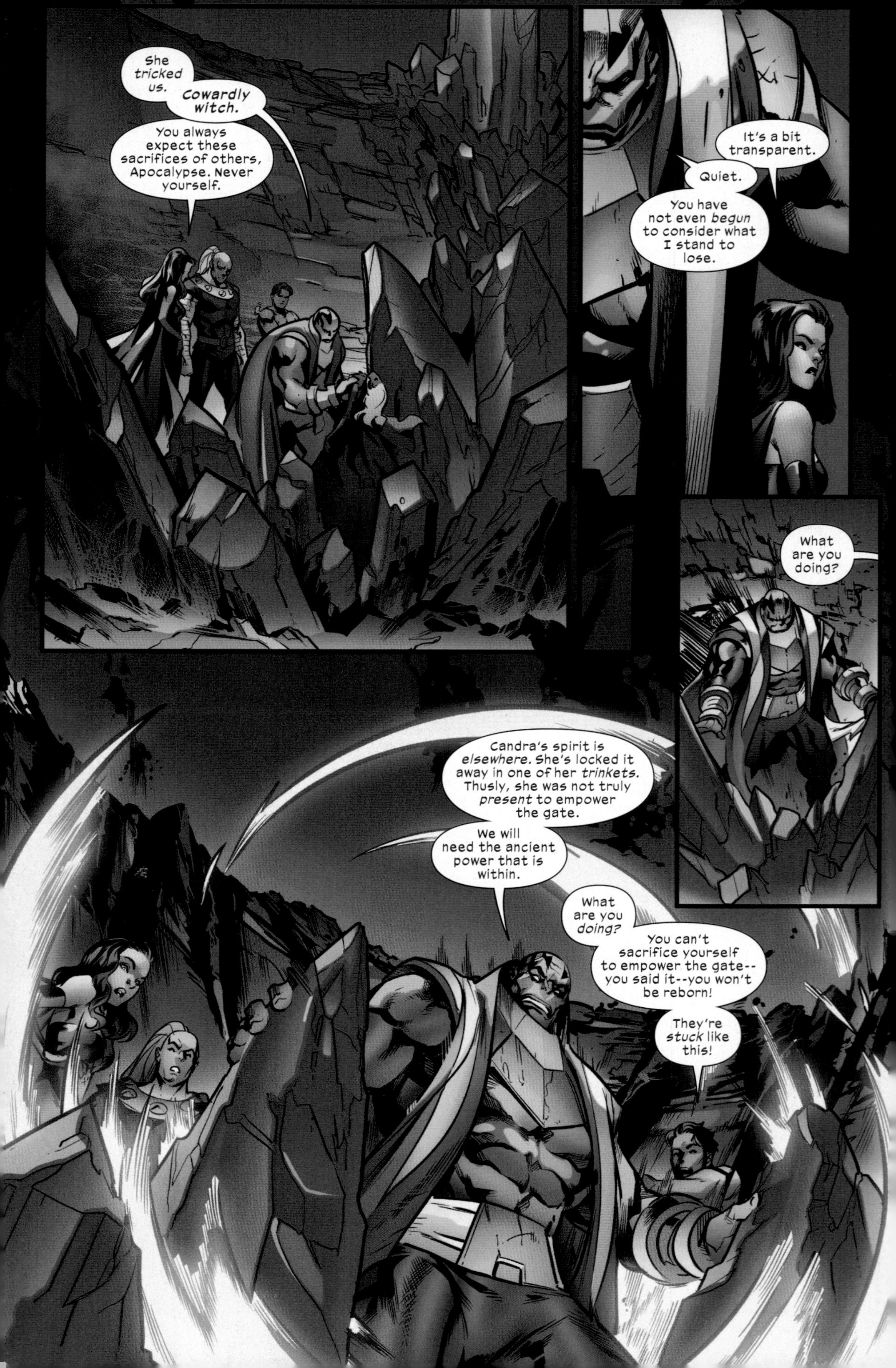

She *tricked* us.
Cowardly witch.
You always expect these sacrifices of others, Apocalypse. Never yourself.
It's a bit transparent.
Quiet.
You have not even *begun* to consider what I stand to lose.
What are you doing?
Candra's spirit is *elsewhere.* She's locked it away in one of her *trinkets.* Thusly, she was not truly *present* to empower the gate.
We will need the ancient power that is within.
What are you *doing?*
You can't sacrifice yourself to empower the gate--you said it--you won't be reborn!
They're *stuck* like this!

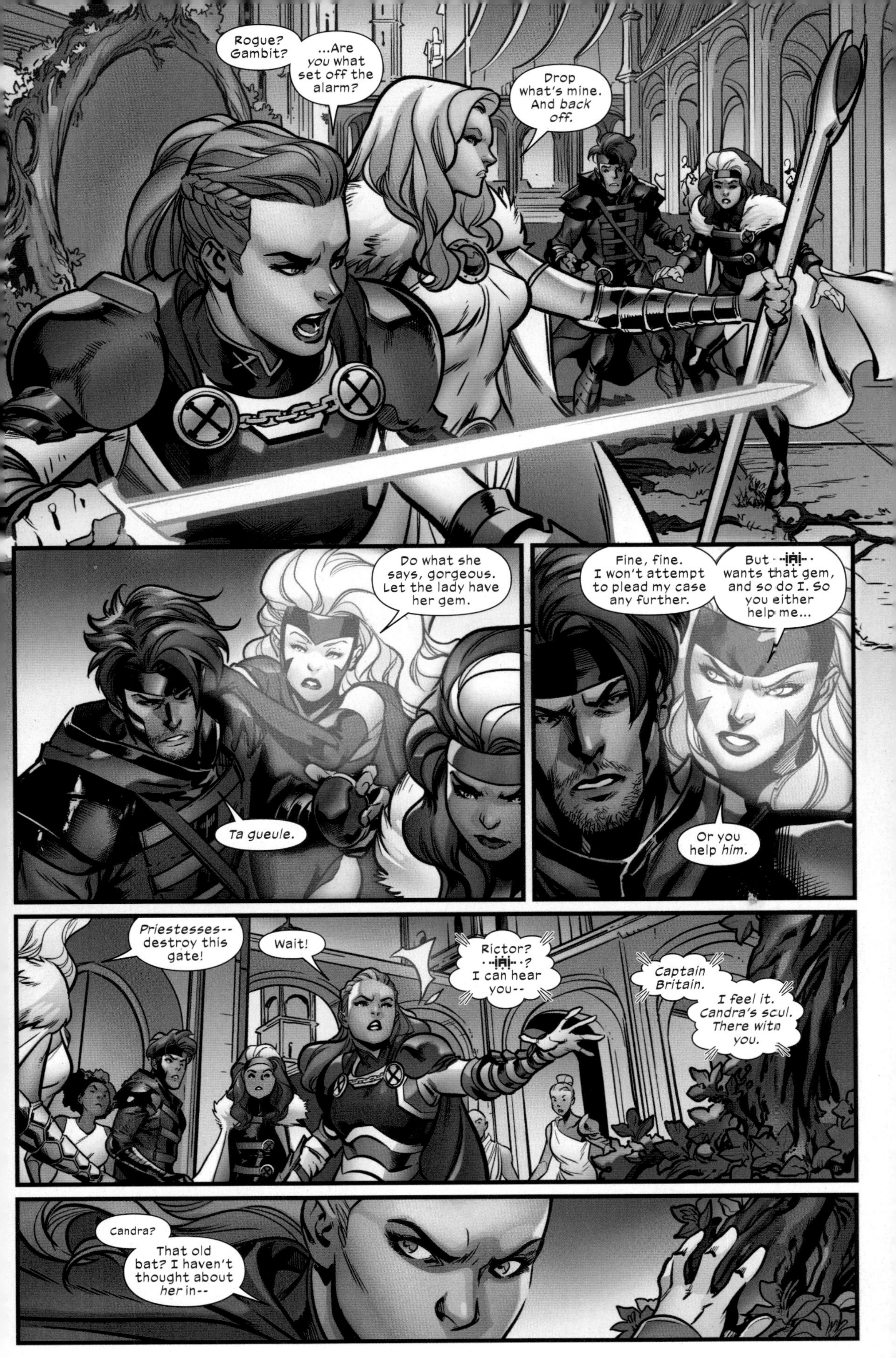
Rogue? Gambit?
...Are you what set off the alarm?
Drop what's mine. And back off.
Do what she says, gorgeous. Let the lady have her gem.
Ta gueule.
Fine, fine. I won't attempt to plead my case any further.
But wants that gem, and so do I. So you either help me...
Or you help him.
Priestesses-- destroy this gate!
Wait!
Rictor? ? I can hear you--
Captain Britain.
I feel it. Candra's soul. There with you.
Candra?
That old bat? I haven't thought about her in--

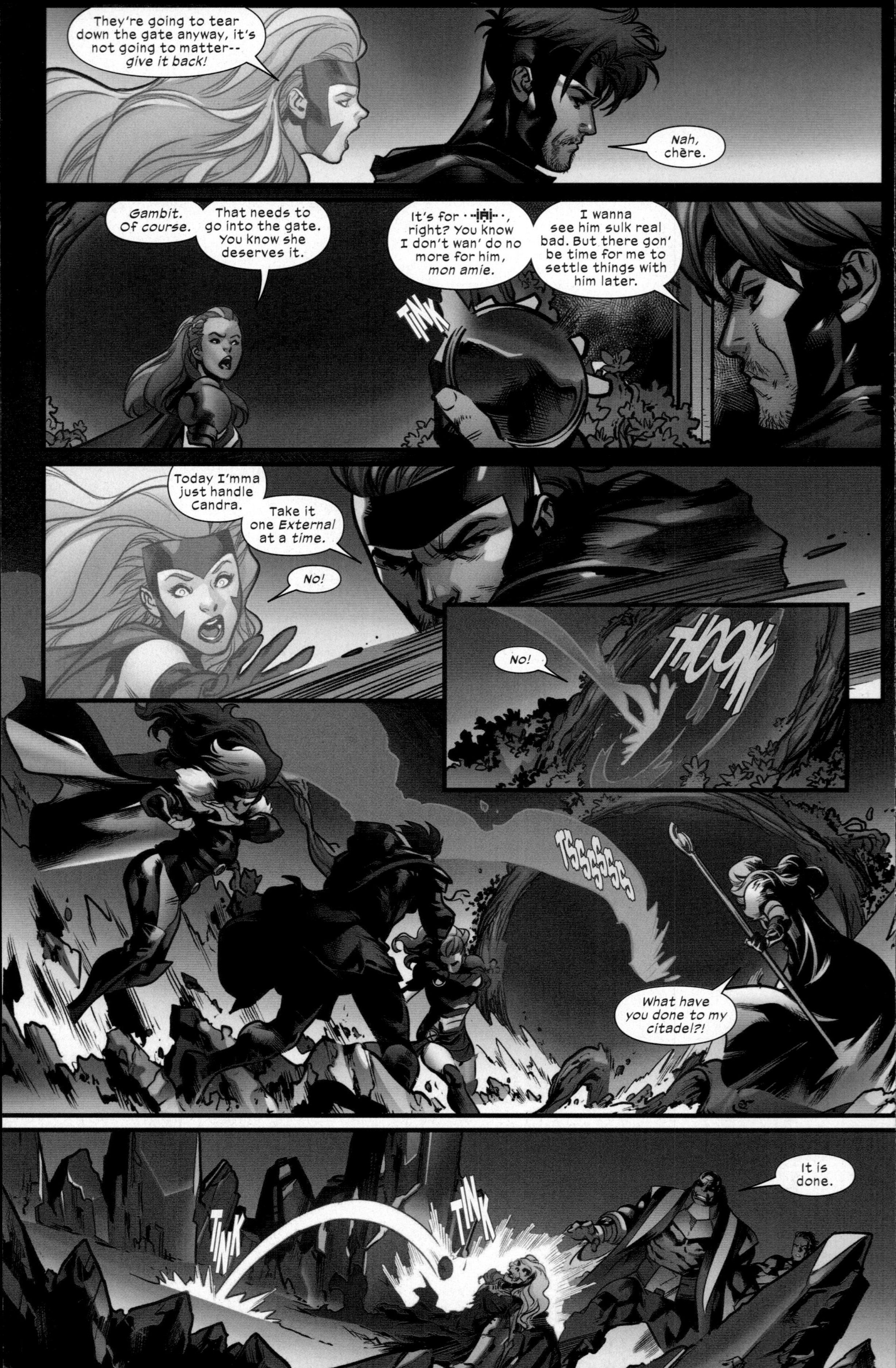
They're going to tear down the gate anyway, it's not going to matter-- *give it back!*
Nah, chère.
Gambit. Of course.
That needs to go into the gate. You know she deserves it.
TINK
It's for ··, right? You know I don't wan' do no more for him, *mon amie.*
I wanna see him sulk real bad. But there gon' be time for me to settle things with him later.
Today I'mma just handle Candra.
Take it one *External* at a *time.*
No!
No!
THOOM
TSSSSSSS
What have you done to my citadel?!
TINK
TINK
It is done.

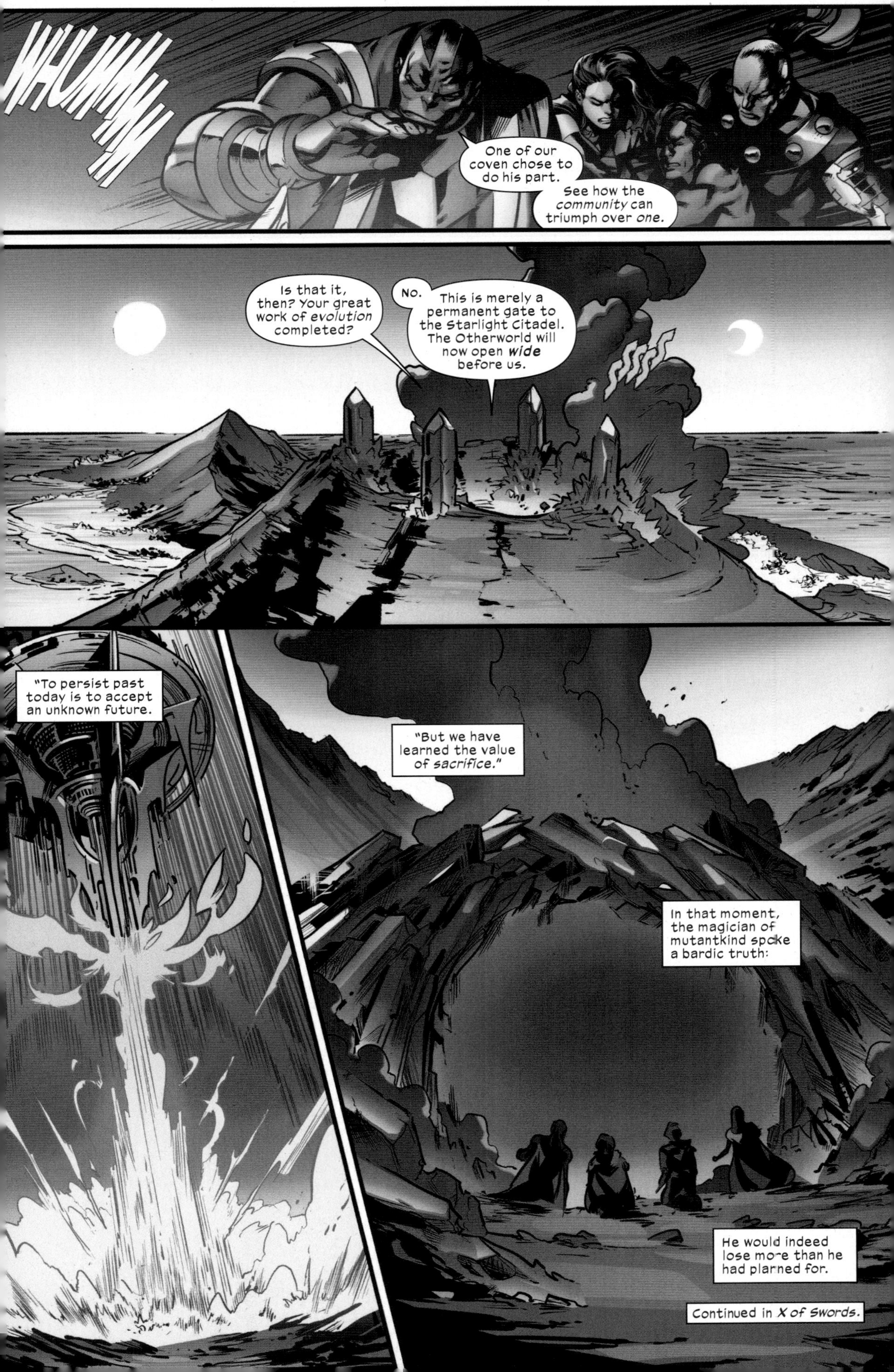
WHUMMMM
One of our coven chose to do his part.
See how the *community* can triumph over *one*.
Is that it, then? Your great work of *evolution* completed?
No.
This is merely a permanent gate to the Starlight Citadel. The Otherworld will now open ***wide*** before us.
"To persist past today is to accept an unknown future.
"But we have learned the value of *sacrifice*."
In that moment, the magician of mutantkind spoke a bardic truth:
He would indeed lose more than he had planned for.
Continued in *X of Swords*.

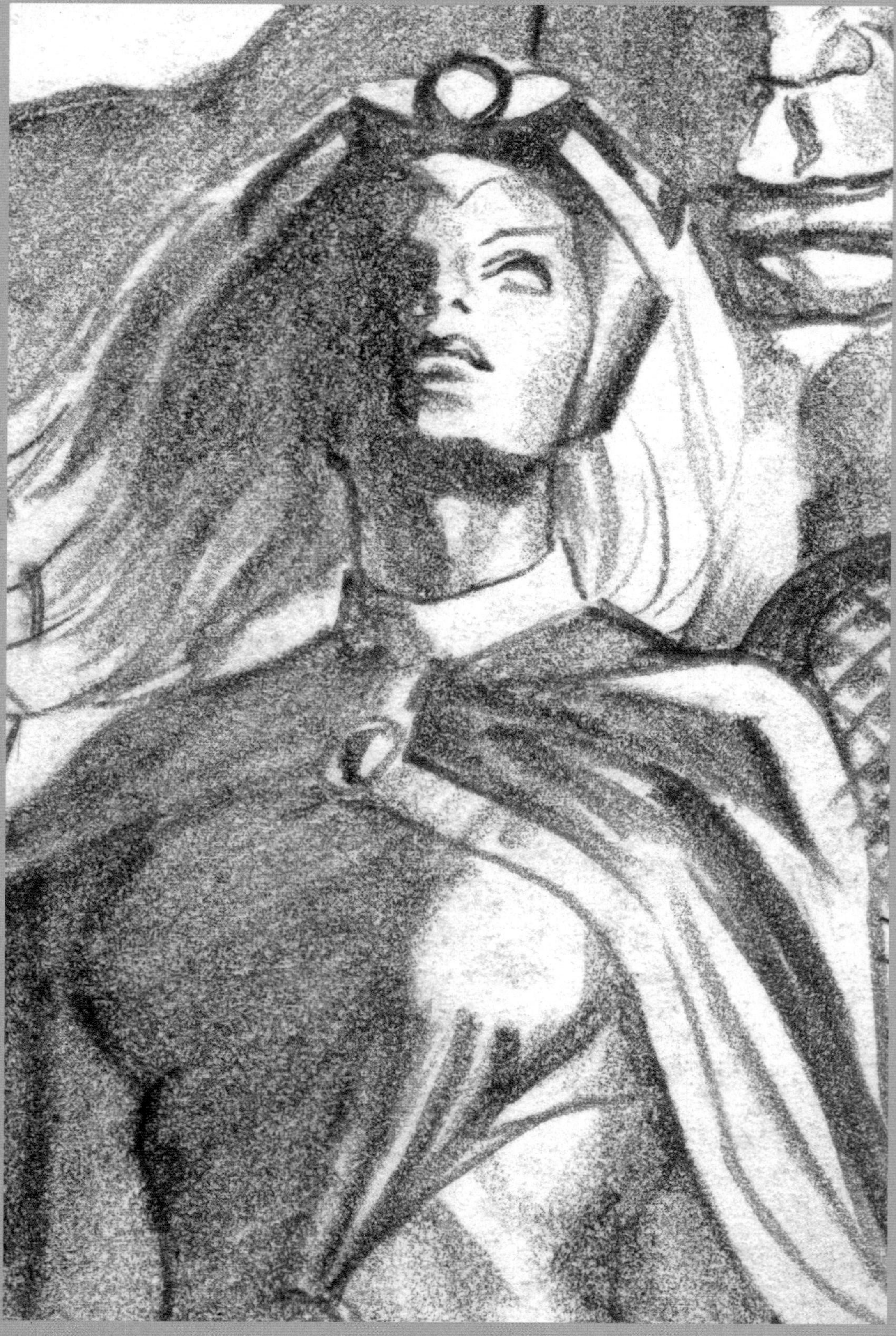

Giant-Size X-Men: Storm #1 Timeless Sketch Variant by Alex Ross

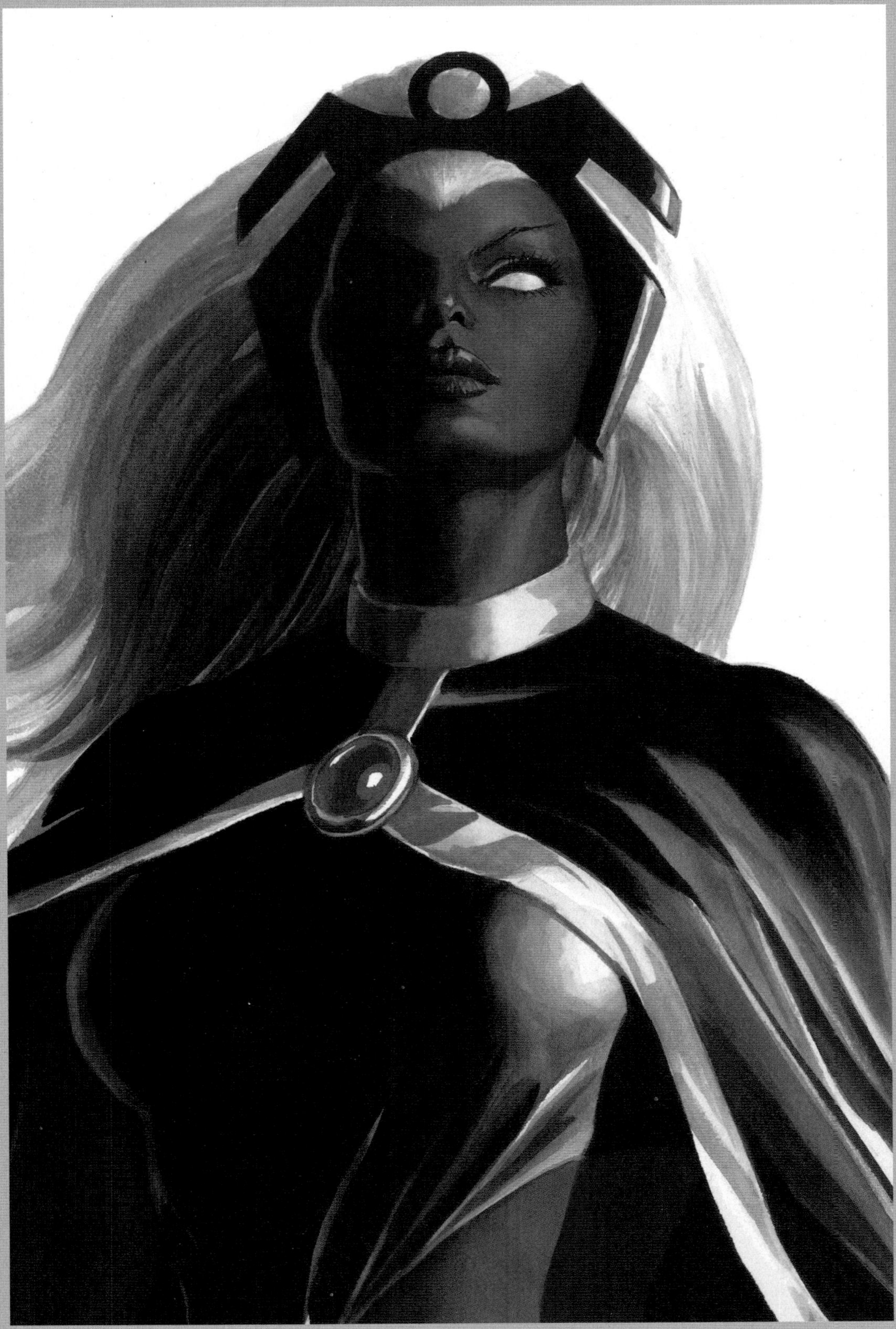

Giant-Size X-Men: Storm #1 Timeless Variant by Alex Ross

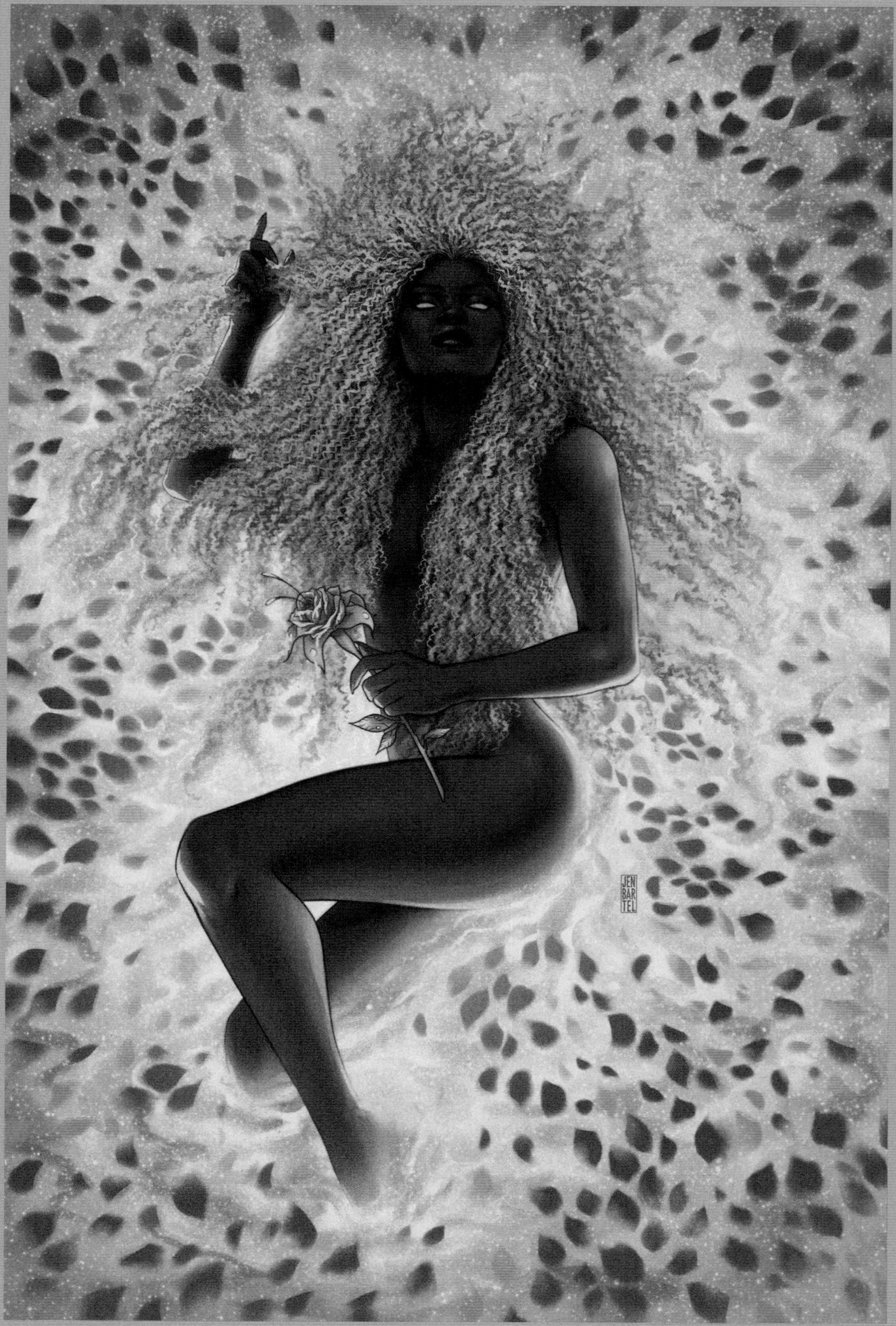
JEN
BAR
TEL

Giant-Size X-Men: Storm #1 Variant by Jen Bartel

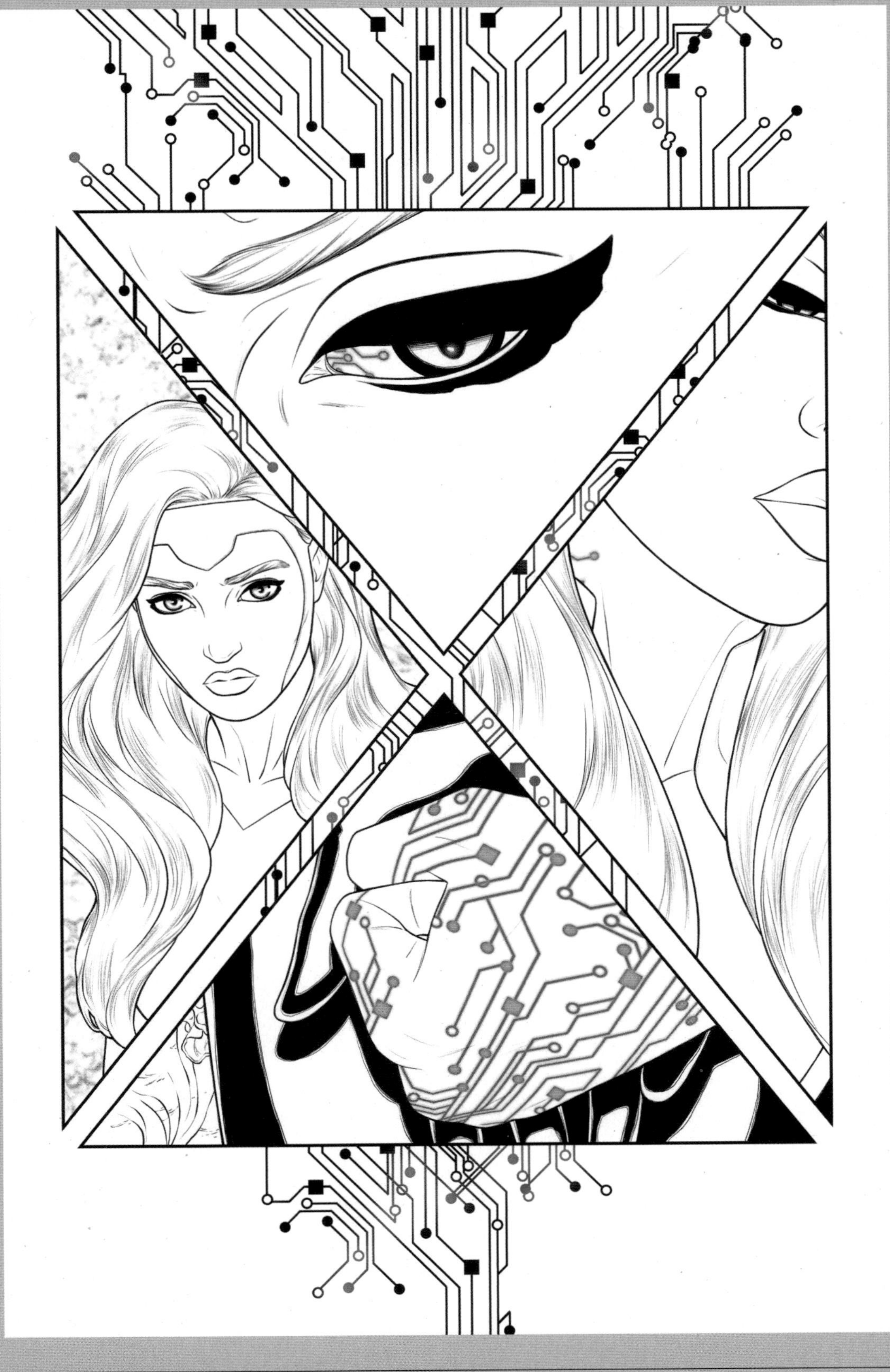

Giant-Size X-Men: Storm #1, Page 1 Art by by Russell Dauterman

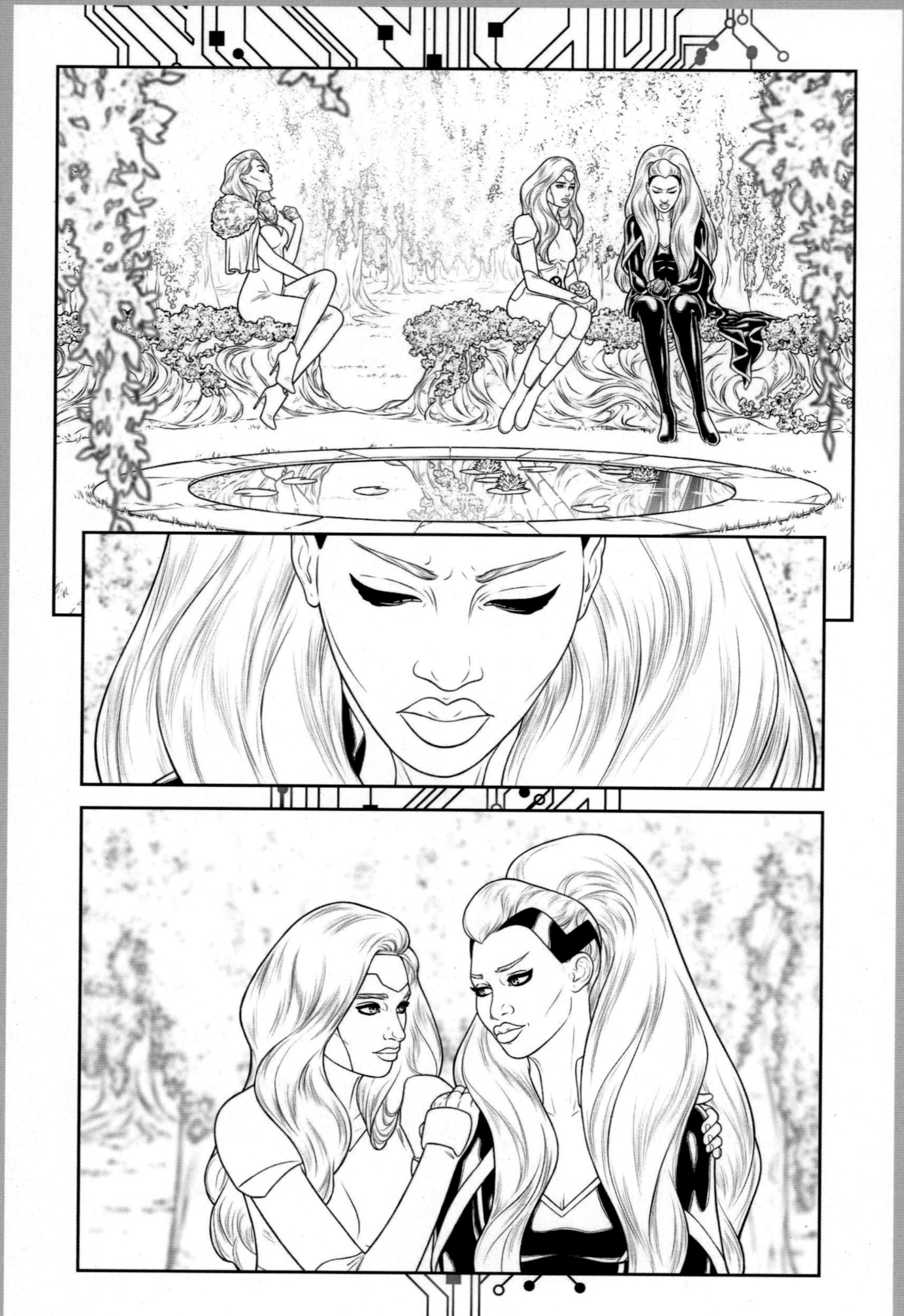

Giant-Size X-Men: Storm #1, Page 2 Art by by Russell Dauterman

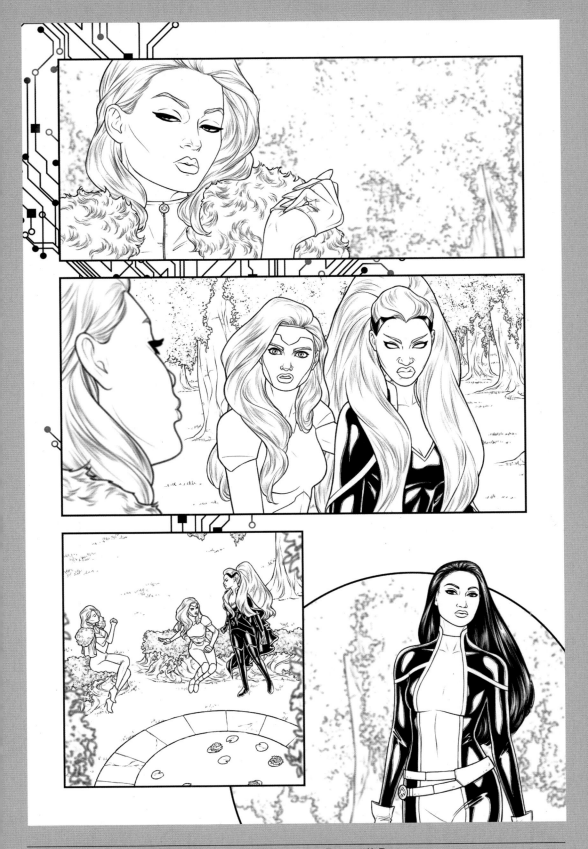

Giant-Size X-Men: Storm #1, Page 3 Art by by Russell Dauterman

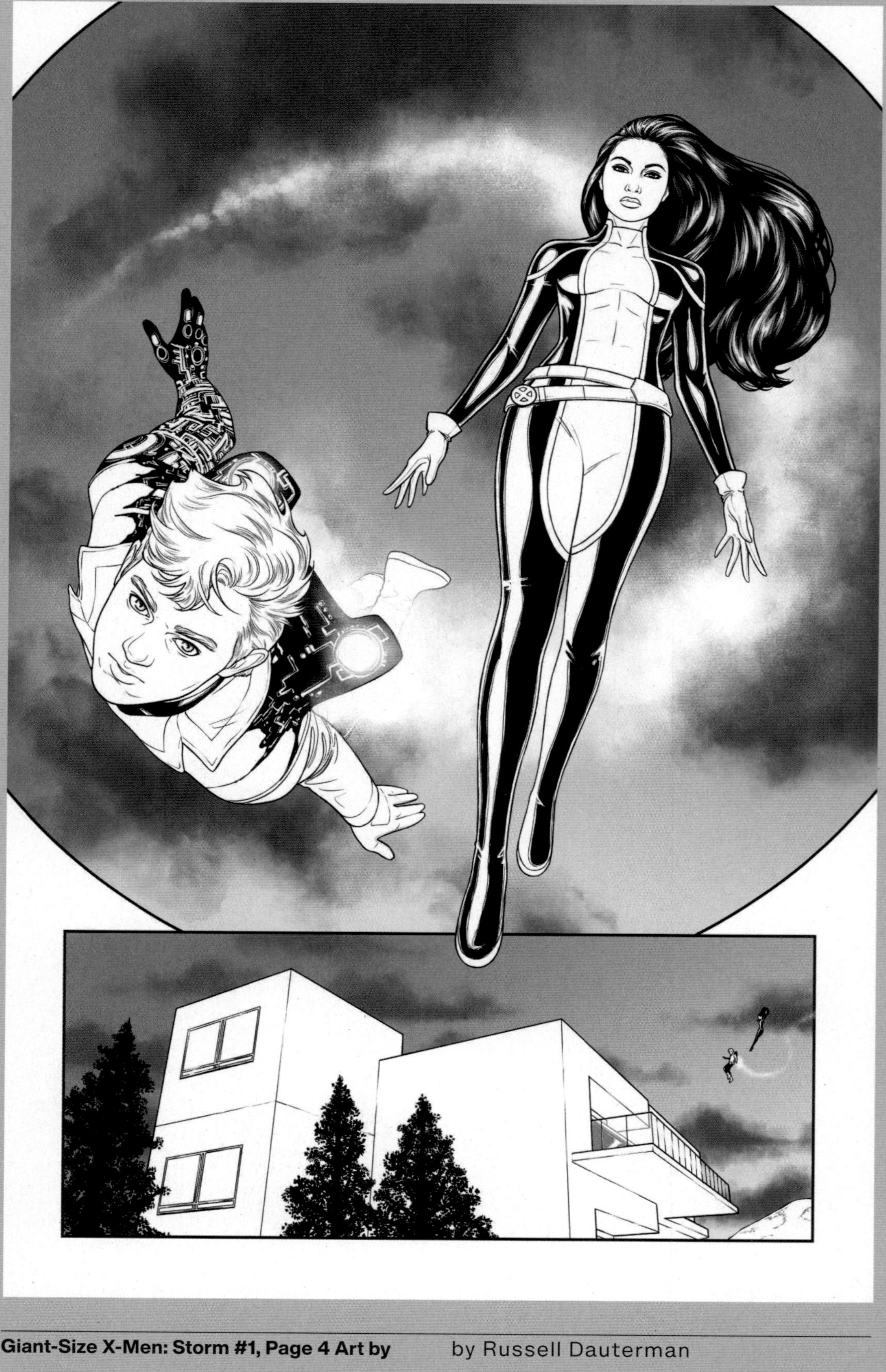

Giant-Size X-Men: Storm #1, Page 4 Art by by Russell Dauterman

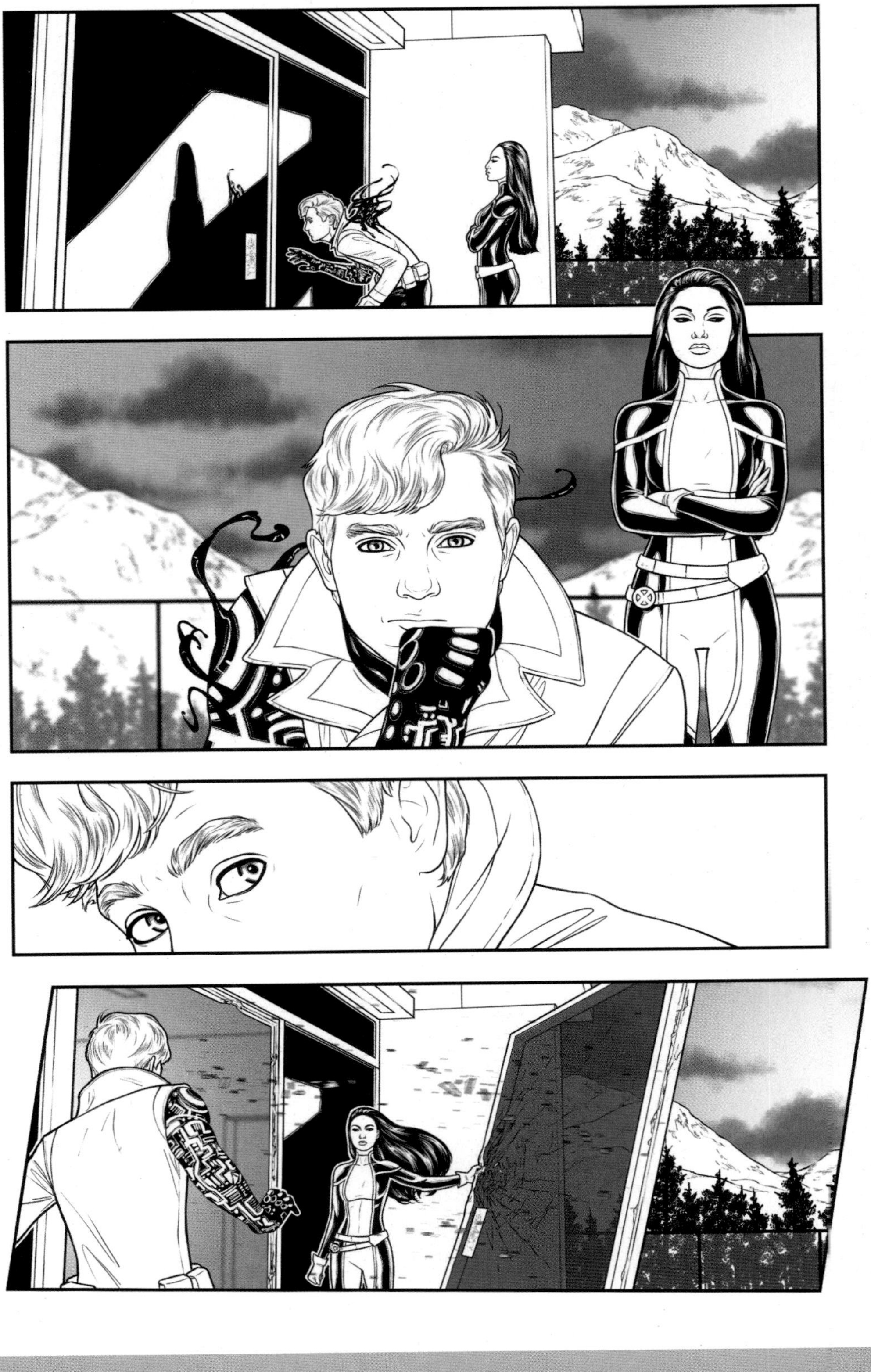

Giant-Size X-Men: Storm #1, Page 5 Art by by Russell Dauterman